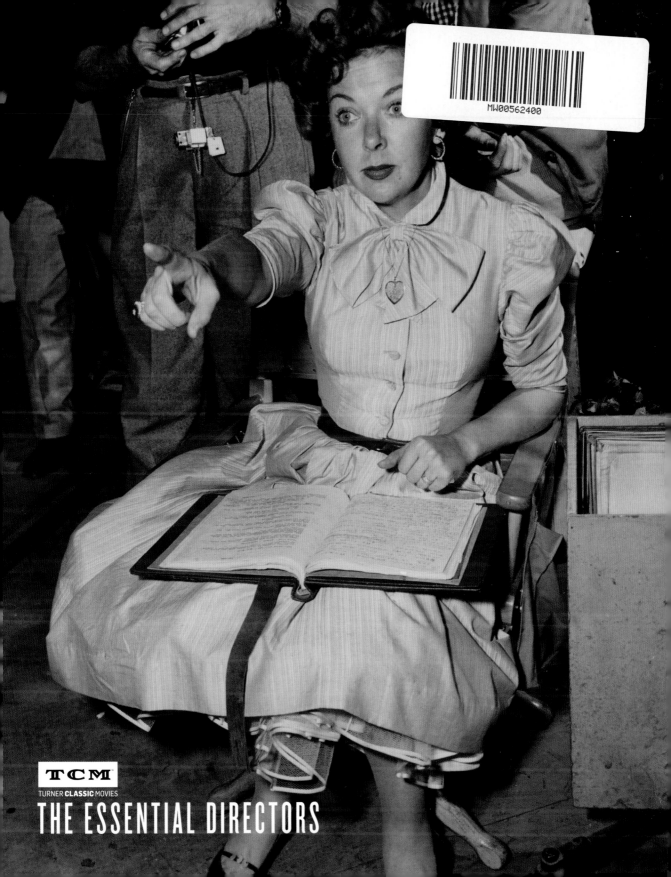

TCM
TURNER CLASSIC MOVIES

THE ESSENTIAL DIRECTORS

TCM
TURNER CLASSIC MOVIES

THE ESSENTIAL DIRECTORS

THE ART AND IMPACT OF CINEMA'S MOST INFLUENTIAL FILMMAKERS

SLOAN De FOREST

forewords by PETER BOGDANOVICH *and* JACQUELINE STEWART
photo editor: MANOAH BOWMAN

RUNNING PRESS
PHILADELPHIA

for my mom,

WHO TOOK ME TO SEE PG-13 MOVIES
LONG BEFORE I TURNED THIRTEEN.

Half-title page: *Ida Lupino directing, 1956*
Title page: *Stanley Kramer directs Sidney Poitier and Katharine Houghton in* Guess Who's Coming to Dinner, *1967.*
Opposite: *Quentin Tarantino visits Martin Scorsese on the set of Scorsese's* Casino, *1995.*

Running Press
Hachette Book Group
1290 Avenue of the Americas, New York, NY 10104
www.runningpress.com @Running_Press

Printed in China

First Edition: October 2021

Published by Running Press, an imprint of Perseus Books, LLC, a subsidiary of Hachette Book Group, Inc. The Running Press name and logo is a trademark of the Hachette Book Group.

The Hachette Speakers Bureau provides a wide range of authors for speaking events. To find out more, go to www.hachettespeakersbureau.com or call (866) 376-6591.

The publisher is not responsible for websites (or their content) that are not owned by the publisher.

Print book cover and interior design by Frances J. Soo Ping Chow

Library of Congress Control Number: 2021937875

ISBNs: 978-0-7624-9893-2 (hardcover),
978-0-7624-9894-9 (ebook)

1010

10 9 8 7 6 5 4 3 2 1

PHOTO CREDITS

All images from Independent Visions Archive, with the exception of:
Pages 32, 57, 67, 114, 127, 131, 169, 184, 235, 292, and 294 courtesy of Turner Classic Movies.
Pages 85 and 250 from the Matt Tunia Collection.
Images from the Independent Visions Archive are exclusively represented by mptv. For more information regarding licensing or purchasing images from mptv, please contact mptvimages at www.mptvimages.com.
The photos and images in this book are for educational purposes, and while every effort has been made to identify the proper photographer and/or copyright holders, some photos had no accreditation. In these cases, if proper credit and/or copyright is discovered, credits will be added in subsequent printings.

CONTENTS

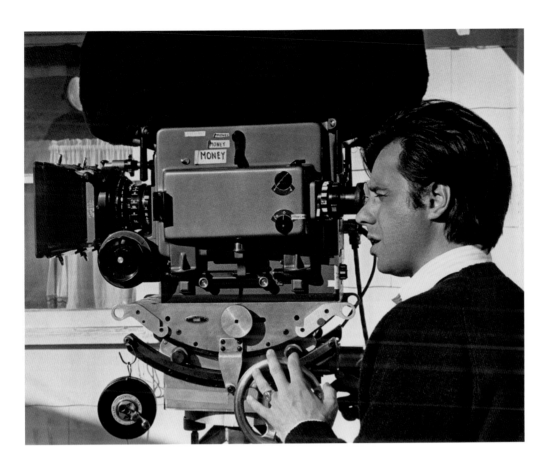

A DIRECTOR'S TAKE
BY PETER BOGDANOVICH

What is an essential director? To a degree, that designation is subjective. Everybody has their own personal favorite directors. When you fall in love with a film, you inevitably start to fall in love with the makers of that film. But history sometimes tells you a filmmaker is not so great, or that a film you love doesn't stand the test of time.

The directors that Sloan De Forest and Turner Classic Movies have chosen as essential may be arguable in some cases; everyone may not agree. But it's a solid place to start. I think the

Peter Bogdanovich directs The Last Picture Show, *1971.*

main factor that determines a great filmmaker is having a compelling sense of personality that comes across in the films. When the work is brilliant and also personal, we as the audience feel connected to the person who made it. There are also plenty of good directors who made brilliant films that are not personal, and personal films that are not so brilliant.

As a director, I was lucky enough to go through the greatest film school imaginable. My teachers were John Ford and Raoul Walsh, Howard Hawks and George Cukor, Orson Welles and Alfred Hitchcock. Even Josef von Sternberg—by then disheartened by the business and possibly the saddest man I ever met—was kind enough to share his perspective and his experience making some of the finest silent and sound pictures of his day. All of these and more are profiled here.

Movies are affected by the time in which they are made, and the time in which they are seen. I grew up watching the Golden-Age classics, so I may be prejudiced, but I believe the silent-reared masters of the black-and-white era are still and will always be great. Their work, at its best, is timeless. It is profoundly influential. It is essential.

John Huston, Orson Welles, and Peter Bogdanovich on the set of The Other Side of the Wind, *1974*

A DIRECTOR'S TAKE BY PETER BOGDANOVICH

FOREWORD
BY JACQUELINE STEWART

When all five TCM hosts were asked, "Who is the first director you were aware of," three of us said that director was Alfred Hitchcock.

Eddie Muller, Alicia Malone, and I all recalled watching Hitchcock films on television when we were kids. Eddie and Alicia said that the landmark interview collection *Hitchcock/Truffaut* was the first film book they ever owned. For me, the experience of seeing Hitch-

cock films was striking because no matter who the stars were—James Stewart in *Rear Window*, or Cary Grant in *North by Northwest*, or Laurence Olivier in *Rebecca*—I was always keenly aware that there was another artistic presence shaping the look and feel of the film. Dave Karger's first director awareness came watching the films of John Hughes. And for Ben Mankiewicz, it was Martin Brest. As different as these directors are in their styles, they inspired the same response from us during our film formative years: a consciousness of the director as the person behind the scenes pulling all of the elements of a film together.

Hitchcock, of course, did show up in cameos in his films. And he cultivated a public persona that made him a household name. A key aspect of his brilliance is the way he kept us aware that we are watching a Hitchcock film while simultaneously immersing us into the worlds he crafted so meticulously on screen. As Sloan De Forest, author of this wide-ranging appreciation of influential directors, points out: "a director's main job is not simply to call 'Action!' but to make us *believe*; to make the audience forget there *is* a director."

Over the years, it has arguably become harder to forget there is a director when we watch a film. More and more directors have achieved celebrity status. And film fans (not just scholars and critics) routinely recognize directors' signatures, from the freeze-frames of Martin Scorsese to the double dolly shots of Spike Lee. What is more, we are learning details about the personal lives and behind-the-camera conduct of current and past directors, including revelations about inappropriate and discriminatory behavior, that can make it difficult to separate artists (including Hitchcock) from their art. And yet, even when we are aware of the director's presence (in positive or negative terms), we rarely appreciate the full range of skills, activities, and responsibilities that film directing entails.

The Essential Directors highlights the many facets of directing. These profiles illustrate how directors actualize their vision on screen. And they trace the influence directors have on their collaborators, on subsequent generations of filmmakers, and on cultural history. Importantly, De Forest shines a light on directors who have been forgotten not just because they created compelling narratives but because they hail from historically marginalized groups. Filmmaking pioneers Lois Weber and Oscar Micheaux get the attention they deserve here, alongside under-recognized studio directors of the classical Hollywood era and many more famous and celebrated auteurs. As we read about their trailblazing careers and visionary films, we are inspired to pay closer attention to the history and craft of directing in all of its diversity and complexity.

INTRODUCTION

We're not selling clothes or cars or wood," writer/director Samuel Fuller once observed of the film business. "We're selling emotions." For well over a century, those who create motion pictures have touched our hearts and souls; they have transported and transformed our minds, intoxicated and entranced our senses.

Billy Wilder directs Marilyn Monroe and Tom Ewell in The Seven Year Itch, *1955.*

When we enjoy a great movie, we willingly suspend our disbelief, allowing ourselves to get swept away by the power of the moving image. This makes it easy to forget that someone painstakingly planned every detail of what we're seeing. That someone is the director. Also crucial to any production are screenwriters, cast, editors, cinematographers, producers, composers, sound engineers; it's a group effort. But the director is the single most important force behind the scenes.

Lois Weber chose to divide the screen into three parts at the climax of *Suspense* (1913), and the split-screen process was born. Michael Curtiz, himself a refugee, insisted on casting actual European refugees as patrons of Rick's Café, lending a vital authenticity to *Casablanca* (1942). William Wyler devotedly guided Audrey Hepburn through every step of *Roman Holiday* (1953), helping her land a Best Actress Oscar for her first Hollywood movie. Martin Scorsese meticulously plotted every shot of the climactic shootout in *Taxi Driver* (1976) with hand-drawn story-

top: *Alfred Hitchcock, circa 1963* opposite: *Brian De Palma directs Al Pacino in* Scarface, *1983.*

boards, down to the last blood spatter. These are among the thousand creative choices a director makes, some more obvious to movie audiences than others.

And not being obvious is precisely the point. A director's main job is not simply to call "Action!" but to make us *believe*; to make the audience forget there *is* a director. Casting such a magic spell requires a lot of work. "A director," Billy Wilder observed, "must be a policeman, a midwife, a psychoanalyst, a sycophant, and a bastard." The demanding temperament sometimes associated with the job is usually due to the pressure a director feels to deliver the film on time and under budget, a delicate balancing act.

The very first movies were hardly directed at all. Early silent filmmakers of the 1890s, such as W. K. L. Dickson and the Lumière Brothers, were more mechanics than directors, operating the equipment and capturing slices of real life on reels of celluloid. Even when the age of narrative filmmaking began and silent cinema exploded in popularity, the director remained a mysterious invisible force, unseen and sometimes even uncredited. Fast-forward to the 1950s and some directors—Alfred Hitchcock, for instance—became just as famous as the stars on the screen. Other black-and-white visionaries were too easily forgotten in the cultural shift of the 1960s and early '70s, when the film school graduates—the brash young auteurs—took over Hollywood.

The theory of film authorship has been hotly debated for decades. For the purposes of this book, I assume that the individual credited as "Director" has the greatest authority over the final movie, regardless of time period. Even when working with a script written by someone else, even when hired by a producer or studio with its own style, a director must say, "These are the tools that I'm asked to use, but I'm going to use my imagination to bring them to you in a different and more spontaneous way that reflects who I am," Jodie Foster has said.

The goal of *The Essential Directors* is make the invisible visible, to illuminate the unseen forces behind some of the greatest screen triumphs in history. With a focus on narrative films (documentaries are considered a separate pursuit) and a concentration on Hollywood, we embark with the most prominent directors of the silent era and journey through each decade, up to the New Hollywood of the 1970s. Since then, trends and technology galore have altered the moviegoing experience. Arguably, though, the fifty-year period between the 1920s and the 1970s contains some of the most innovative, elegant, and unforgettable movies the world has ever seen.

The already difficult task of selecting fifty-six essential directors from hundreds of noteworthy names was compounded by other challenges. Some of history's most successful filmmakers have tarnished reputations, due to controversies in their personal lives or even in their work. Furthermore, in a time, a place, and an industry that lacked diversity, very few people of color or women were given a fair shot at directing. Still, in these pages, I am able to spotlight gifted women and other diverse artists who broke through seemingly impenetrable barriers to make their mark on the art form and the industry. Ultimately, the final list was based on each filmmaker's influence on the medium, cultural impact, and degree of achievement.

Those who are featured are among the most imaginative and accomplished individuals the business produced. As twenty-first-century director Alejandro González Iñárritu put it, "To make a film is easy; to make a good film is war; to make a very good film is a miracle." Having made not merely one, but often several very good films, the men and women profiled here are nothing short of miracle workers. They have entertained and enlightened on a grand scale, often advancing the art form with their vision and abilities. As social mores shift, taken-for-granted talents can rise to posthumous prominence (Douglas Sirk, for one), and once-revered artists can become deplorable (D. W. Griffith, for example). Love them or hate them, the filmmakers who defined—and redefined—the medium have left behind works so essential, so paradigm-shifting, that they generate powerful feelings long after their creators are gone.

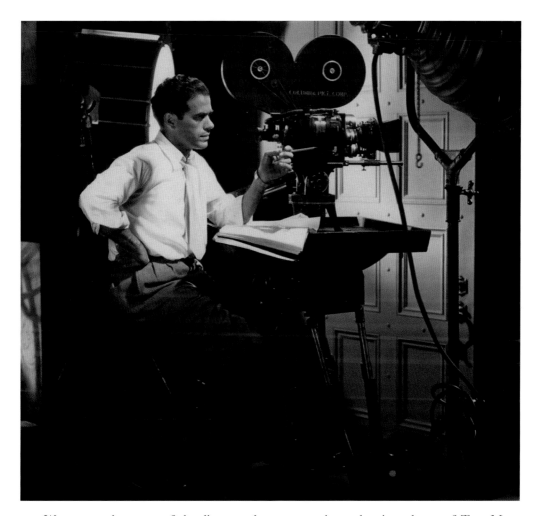

We may not be aware of the director when we experience the visceral rage of Tony Montana, courtesy of Brian De Palma's *Scarface* (1983); or glide across the galaxy to Jupiter, thanks to Stanley Kubrick's *2001: A Space Odyssey* (1968); or feel the delirium of whirlwind romance, conjured by Frank Capra in *It Happened One Night* (1934). But herein, the zoom lens is focused solely on the filmmakers. Turn the page and discover the ideas, the passions, and the dreams that drove the directors of cinema's most indelible films.

Cut. Print. And enjoy.

— Sloan De Forest

Frank Capra at work, 1938

Chapter One

ARTISTS OF SHADOW AND LIGHT

By the 1920s, motion pictures had wildly exceeded expectations. The 1910s was a decade of technical improvements, increasingly sophisticated craftsmanship, and the creative input of a handful of visionaries who laid the groundwork. Thanks to the trial and error of early filmmakers, by the end of World War I, the silent feature film had flourished into not only an immensely popular medium of mass entertainment, but a legitimate form of art.

A new cinematic era dawned with the Jazz Age. With the war and its aftermath halting film production across Europe, the United States dominated the motion picture market. The sunny Los Angeles suburb of Hollywood replaced the East Coast as the hub of a thriving industry, a burgeoning system of ever-more-powerful studios that produced the majority of the world's movies and shipped them to theaters around the globe.

Out of a population of fewer than 125 million, an estimated 80 million Americans went to the movies regularly. Grandiloquent palaces sprang up in cities everywhere to screen this proliferation of silent works; cavernous two-thousand-seat venues were packed nightly with eager patrons enjoying the universal language of pantomime. Live symphonic accompaniment coupled with a lack of speaking voices led to a transcendent audio-visual experience that depended largely on visual artistry. The composition of the shots, the lighting effects, the actors' performances: these were the paints, a director the painter. The silents of the mid- to late 1920s reached a stylistic zenith, though most in the industry were unaware that the end of the parade—the coming of sound—was looming just around the corner.

During this time, stardom soared. The newly popular movie magazines helped bring great fame to the faces in front of the lens. But it was the men and women behind the cameras who were the all-powerful masters of the medium.

Erich von Stroheim and cameramen on the set of Greed, *1924*

CHARLIE CHAPLIN

Years active: 1914–1967

THE WORD *GENIUS* IS OVERUSED IN HOLLYWOOD. Critics have been applying the term to Charlie Chaplin since 1915, when he was still a screen newcomer, his clownish Little Tramp character an instant international sensation. But few realized then that behind the toothbrush mustache and bowler hat was an adroit director. With the exception of his early days in Mack Sennett comedies, every film the Tramp appeared in was written and directed by Chaplin himself. He even composed the musical scores. His bold independence, razor-sharp comedic and dramatic instincts, and storytelling innovations substantiate the claim of genius.

London-born Chaplin was a maverick who had, as biographer David Robinson has written, "a lifelong compulsion to do everything himself," from funding his own productions, to cofounding the independent distribution company United Artists, to casting actors who would faithfully perform their scenes precisely as he instructed. *City Lights* (1931), one of his masterpieces, costars Virginia Cherrill, an untrained actress whose every move was guided off-camera by Chaplin. The first meeting between Cherrill's blind flower girl and the Tramp is one of the most tender, tragicomic sequences in cinema history—and no dialogue is required. The girl mistakes the shabby Tramp for a wealthy man, and he fails to dispel the illusion, creating a multi-layered comic misunderstanding tinged with sorrow. A slapstick gag finishes the scene: the blind girl dumps a pail of water on the Tramp, not realizing he is there. Chaplin spent six weeks shooting and reshooting this sequence, resulting in a world-record 342 takes before he was satisfied. His perfectionism was rewarded with the highest critical acclaim.

Originally a rude bumbler when he debuted in a 1914 Keystone short, the Tramp grew a touch more complex, a trifle more sensitive, with each film. Chaplin even ventured to craft comedies with unhappy endings (as in *The Bank* [1915]), unheard of at the time. "The theme of life is conflict and pain," the auteur wrote in his autobiography. "Instinctively, all my clowning was based on this." His milestone *The Kid* (1921) was not the first feature film to mix comedy and pathos. It was, however, regarded as the most skillful intertwining of laughter and tears yet seen. *Los Angeles Times*

Charlie Chaplin and Jackie Coogan in The Kid

3

> "Chaplin transformed the cinema. Chaplin made the cinema into a world means of artistic communication. And by what he did, he gave a stature to the cinema . . . and a future for the cinema which may not ever have happened if it hadn't been for Chaplin."
>
> —RICHARD ATTENBOROUGH

critic Harry Carr declared it "the best motion-picture comedy yet made. It has more than humor; it has tenderness and literary charm." The winning combination of Chaplin's lonely Tramp and Jackie Coogan's plucky orphan planted the seeds of virtually all subsequent dramedies, Billy Wilder's Oscar-winning *The Apartment* (1960) and James L. Brooks's *As Good As It Gets* (1997) among them.

Because Chaplin's gift for pantomime was the main attraction, his filmmaking style was necessarily static and simple. Some of the most memorable gags in *The Kid* take place in a small room, the stationary, eye-level camera aimed straight at the action as a viewer would watch a play. "My own camera set-up is based on facilitating choreography for the actor's movements," he explained, though he rarely discussed his acting or directing processes in depth. "If people know how it's done," he often said, "all the magic goes."

Soon, Chaplin's finely nuanced performances swept the globe, shifting the direction of screen comedy in general and informing his slightly younger contemporaries, the affable Harold Lloyd

and the deadpan Buster Keaton, two other silent legends who maintained creative control over their own films.

Chaplin managed to surpass *The Kid* with his follow-up, *The Gold Rush* (1925), a longer, more complex comedy set in the snowy Klondike. Three of his most iconic set pieces are seen here: the starving Tramp eats his shoes (made of licorice for the film); he performs a "dance" with bread rolls on forks; he topples from side to side in a cabin precariously perched on the edge of a cliff. Chaplin took great pride in *The Gold Rush*, calling it "the picture that I want to be remembered by." As a writer/director, he will also be remembered for *A Woman of Paris* (1923), a soufflé of subtlety that set the stage for Ernst Lubitsch's refined romantic comedies of the 1920s and '30s.

Only Charlie Chaplin could make a successful silent film nearly a decade into the talkies; the Depression-steeped *Modern Times* (1936) was his final screen appearance as the mute Tramp, though a remarkably similar fellow with a small mustache would appear in Chaplin's first talking picture, *The*

MUST-SEE MOVIES

A DOG'S LIFE (1918)

THE KID (1921)

A WOMAN OF PARIS (1923)

THE GOLD RUSH (1925)

CITY LIGHTS (1931)

MODERN TIMES (1936)

THE GREAT DICTATOR (1940)

LIMELIGHT (1952)

Virginia Cherrill and Charlie Chaplin in City Lights

KEY SCENE TO WATCH

Perhaps no moment in a Chaplin film so effectively tugs at the heartstrings as the finale of *City Lights*, when the blind flower girl, her vision restored, sets eyes on the Tramp, hands him a coin, and recognizes him as the man who made her operation possible. From the surprised Cherrill, Chaplin cuts to a close-up of the Tramp: His finger in his mouth, he smiles self-consciously at being seen for the first time by someone he adores. A gentle cascade of emotions wash across his face; on his timid, hopeful facial expression, the picture fades to black. In 1966, Chaplin recalled the close-up as "a beautiful sensation of not acting, of standing outside of myself. The key was exactly right—slightly embarrassed, delighted about meeting her again—apologetic without getting emotional about it."

Great Dictator (1940). A few years before the full atrocities of the Third Reich were revealed to the world, Chaplin bravely (and mercilessly) satirized Adolf Hitler, making millions laugh at the dictator's absurdity, and yielding the biggest box office hit of his career.

Always striking out against the established order, Chaplin skewered his lovable everyman image in *Monsieur Verdoux* (1947), a savage black comedy about a man who marries wealthy women so he can bump them off and inherit their riches. Despite *Verdoux* being condemned by moral groups and faring poorly at the box office, Chaplin's snappy script was nominated for a Best Original Screenplay Oscar. The silent star, as it turned out, was verbally as well as physically gifted. Although he won only one competitive Oscar (for *Limelight*'s musical score), he was awarded with two special Academy Awards before his death in 1977.

Limelight (1952) emerged as "Chaplin's last great film," author Jeffrey Vance has noted; a swan song that "plays like a self-conscious summing up of his life and career." In the Edwardian music halls where a young Chaplin had learned his craft, his aging entertainer, Calvero, faces depression, irrelevance, and the specter of death with courage and spirit. Although arguably his most poignant and personal movie (and the only screen pairing of Chaplin and Keaton), *Limelight* was not released until 1972 in America, where Chaplin had been labeled an "unsavory character" by the FBI

for his alleged Communist leanings, unpaid taxes, and a dubious history with several very young women. Today—a century past the peak of his popularity—Chaplin's scandals and political views have faded, and he remains one of the most well-known and imitated actor/directors in history, his work still influencing viewers around the world.

Charlie Chaplin choreographs his "roll dance" for The Gold Rush.

CECIL B. DeMILLE

Years active: 1913–1958

W HEN CECIL B. DeMILLE APPEARED AS HIMSELF in Billy Wilder's landmark 1950 noir *Sunset Boulevard*, he had a solid thirty-five years of blockbuster filmmaking under his belt, and he wasn't done yet. The film's famous final stinger (hissed by

Gloria Swanson, a real-life DeMille discovery) "Mr. DeMille, I'm ready for my close-up" carried weight because the public knew DeMille; he required no introduction. Since the late 1910s, his name had been synonymous with Hollywood grandeur, with the larger-than-life movies he orchestrated. "DeMille directed," film historian Kevin Brownlow once noted, "as though chosen by God for this one task."

So iconic was DeMille, in fact, that it can be difficult to see the filmmaker beneath the massive mountain of hype. Peel away the autocratic on-set persona; the riding breeches and leather boots he always sported; the masterful self-promotion; the sonorous, godlike voice that often narrated his own

works; and what emerges is a prolific showman consumed with supervising every detail of the filmmaking process, from storyboards to props to marketing.

Like his predecessor, D. W. Griffith, Cecil Blount DeMille began as an actor. In 1913, following a stint producing stage plays in New York, DeMille partnered with Jesse Lasky to form the Jesse L. Lasky Feature Play Company; it would eventually blossom into Paramount Pictures. Contrary to popular mythology, 1914's *The Squaw Man* was not the very first feature-length film, but it was one of the first made in the up-and-coming film epicenter of Hollywood, California. The modestly budgeted western was a box office smash, and it was DeMille's directorial debut.

7

He honed his craft with more than a dozen subsequent features in two years, but it was *The Cheat* (1915) that earned DeMille recognition as an important director. Though its plot was sheer salacious melodrama, elements in *The Cheat*'s editing and cinematography were years ahead of their time. The courtroom scene, for instance, begins with a high-angle view from the back of the room, and proceeds with an array of unconventional shots, including 180-degree reversals and a slow track across the jury box. Using a special placement of spotlights, DeMille pioneered a high-contrast chiaroscuro style he termed "Rembrandt lighting" (also known as "Lasky lighting"), to drench dramatic moments in atmosphere—such as when the sadistic Tori (Sessue Hayakawa) burns the flesh of his captive (Fannie Ward).

Cecil B. DeMille on location in Egypt for The Ten Commandments, *1954*

"I've learned what to do and what not to do from watching a lot of DeMille's films. There's very naturalistic acting, and then suddenly, out of the blue comes something which is almost preposterous. It's like naturalism and bathos, naturalism and absurdity, it just goes back and forth. And I think he probably knew what he was doing."

—STEVEN SPIELBERG

Taking a cue from Griffith's game-changing 1916 historical epic *Intolerance*, DeMille answered with his own saga that same year, *Joan the Woman*, complete with an early color process to embellish

Joan of Arc's burning at the stake with blazes of orange and gold. Virtually each film he released seemed to top the last, boasting a more impressive effect or larger set piece. DeMille was at the forefront of defining the Roaring Twenties with his sophisticated marital farces, among them *Don't Change Your Husband* (1919) and *Why Change Your Wife?* (1920), both starring Gloria Swanson, who shot to megastardom in these opulently appointed comedies. Making light of love, infidelity, and divorce, these social satires exhibit a wry understanding of women's new roles as equal partners in relationships. DeMille's longtime female collaborators (among them editor Anne Bauchens and screenwriter Jeanie Macpherson) assisted with the feminine viewpoint.

In tackling *The Ten Commandments* (1923), DeMille expanded the definition of epic, constructing towering replicas of ancient Egyptian

Sessue Hayakawa and Fannie Ward in The Cheat, *1915*

monuments, employing 2,500 background extras (not to mention all the camels and goats), and using two-strip Technicolor to enhance major scenes. He also injected sex appeal into the Bible by glorifying sinful scenarios of pagan revelry, only to have Moses condemn them with his tablets of stone. This potent combination of religion and sex would make his talkies just as popular as his silents. The ancient Roman yarn *The Sign of the Cross* (1932) pushed the limit of lasciviousness with a naked Empress Poppaea (Claudette Colbert) frolicking in a bath of asses' milk, a lesbian dance of seduction, and an unbridled pagan orgy.

The post–World War II years found DeMille—then approaching seventy—in greater demand than ever. In 1949, the director delivered a full-scale return to his glory days with *Samson and Delilah*, a Technicolor tale of lust and betrayal snatched from the Old Testament, led by a bejeweled Hedy Lamarr (Delilah) and a bewigged Victor Mature (Samson). The crowds ate it up. *New York Times* reviewer Bosley Crowther offered a tongue-in-cheek checklist comparing *Samson and Delilah* to DeMille's previous epics: "There are more flowing garments in this picture, more chariots, more temples, more peacock plumes, more animals, more pillows, more spear-carriers, more beards, and more sex than ever before." Critics sometimes accused DeMille of bad taste, but no one could deny his

Victor Mature and Hedy Lamarr head a cast of thousands in Samson and Delilah.

dazzling showmanship or his instinct for pleasing the public. The family-friendly circus drama *The Greatest Show on Earth* (1952) ramped up the people-pleasing (and the razzle-dazzle), making it the highest-grossing film of the decade and finally copping the oft-snubbed DeMille an Oscar for Best Picture.

DeMille's grand finale was a mammoth remake of *The Ten Commandments*. No stranger to revamping his own work (he updated *The Squaw Man* twice, in 1918 and 1931), he always defended his remakes with the immodest argument that "You don't throw away a Renoir after you've seen it once. You want to see a masterpiece time and again." For *The Ten Commandments* (1956), he pulled out all the stops. Nearly four hours long and the most expensive picture ever made at the time (at a final cost of over $13 million), the VistaVision spectacle was shot on location in the deserts of Egypt, one-upping the silent version, which had been filmed in central California. DeMille suffered a heart attack while shooting, but returned to the set the next day, and spent two years crafting what would become a timeless biblical classic that's been televised every Easter since 1973.

Although he died in 1959, DeMille's name is still known to millions. His legacy lives on in the Cecil B. DeMille Award, a special Golden Globe given annually to those who have made "outstanding contributions to the world of entertainment." DeMille's influence can be seen in the grand visions of recipients Walt Disney, Steven Spielberg, Martin Scorsese, Oprah Winfrey, and other innovators who think big.

MUST-SEE MOVIES

THE CHEAT (1915)

MALE AND FEMALE (1919)

THE TEN COMMANDMENTS (1923)

THE KING OF KINGS (1927)

CLEOPATRA (1934)

SAMSON AND DELILAH (1949)

THE GREATEST SHOW ON EARTH (1952)

THE TEN COMMANDMENTS (1956)

KEY SCENE TO WATCH

The parting of the Red Sea by Moses had been a technical marvel in the 1923 *The Ten Commandments*, but it paled in comparison to the event as depicted in DeMille's 1956 Technicolor blockbuster. On a rocky cliff overlooking the sea, Moses (Charlton Heston) invokes the power of God as the sea roils and rises up, forming two 50-foot walls of water so that the Hebrews can pass safely through the dry seabed. In the age before digital effects, twenty-four tanks had to dump 360,000 gallons of water into an enormous trough on the Paramount Pictures parking lot; cameras mounted on each side captured the rushing waters to create the spectacle. It earned John P. Fulton the Oscar for Best Special Effects.

D. W. GRIFFITH

Years active: 1908–1931

THE CONTRIBUTIONS OF KENTUCKY-BORN DAVID WARK Griffith to the burgeoning craft of moviemaking can scarcely be over-stated. As reviled today for the overtly racist *The Birth of a Nation* (1915) as he is revered for his groundbreaking artistry, the still controversial "Father

of Film" began his journey as a stage actor. Raised on a farm and forced to drop out of school at fifteen to help his widowed mother, Griffith had nothing in his background to suggest a theatrical career except a poetic streak and a father who used to read Shakespeare aloud. When employed by the Biograph Company as a film performer, he was asked to try directing because no one else wanted the job.

At that time, a director was seen as nothing more than an actor wrangler; fame, wealth, power, creative control—none of these perks was yet associated with the position when Griffith stepped behind the megaphone in 1908. He would soon elevate the role of director to an almost omnipotent status as he established narrative filmmaking as we know it.

Griffith was not the first to employ certain techniques, but he perfected the most ingenious motion picture developments to build the basic conventions of the craft. Cross-cutting two parallel scenes to heighten dramatic tension was a method used by Edwin S. Porter in the seminal *The Great Train Robbery* (1903), but refined by Griffith in his early Biograph shorts, such as *The Lonely Villa* (1909), a tale of a family held hostage by criminals. Close-ups had already been seen here and there, but not in the way that earned Griffith renown: he inserted intimate shots of Mary Pickford's forlorn face at the beginning and end of the romantic melodrama *Friends* (1912) to express the heartbreak of lost love. Griffith's use of the close-up as a subtle way of

revealing thought and emotion (without the interruption of a title card) became one of his signature moves. It was soon adopted by every other director. In short, Griffith taught the world how to tell a story with moving pictures, using edits instead of words.

The term *production value* did not exist in the 1910s, but that's what Griffith and his longtime cinematographer Billy Bitzer brought to the fledgling silents. Exquisite lighting, detailed set design, authentic locations, and actors who exuded emotional realism; these became synonymous with Biograph's output during Griffith's tenure there before he went solo as an independent. Constricted by the one- and two-reel limitations of those early nickelodeon efforts, the director envisioned a more substantial film, one that constituted "a whole evening's entertainment," as he put it. His four-reel *Judith of Bethulia* (1914) proved a successful experiment, but others—including a novice filmmaker

named Cecil B. DeMille—were already producing five- and six-reelers with runtimes of over one hour.

For his first feature-length film (and, at twelve reels, the longest anyone had yet dared), Griffith adapted Thomas Dixon's inflammatory novel *The Clansman* as *The Birth of a Nation*. It was instantly recognized as the most technically advanced motion picture yet made—but also one of the most famously offensive films of all time. The Civil War drama stoked racial tensions by depicting its Black characters as savage criminals and the Ku Klux Klan as heroic saviors. Riots and protests from the NAACP and other groups ensued, but *Nation* still became the most profitable movie of its time. Despite the film's unprecedented success (by 1977, it was estimated that 100 million people had seen it), the vicious, violent racism of *The Birth of a Nation* would outrage audiences for generations

D. W. Griffith directing The Birth of a Nation

> "Whenever I had the chance, I watched while he [Griffith] directed, and tried to remember everything he said and did. Not many people are lucky enough to have a genius for a teacher and the lessons were free. All I needed to do was keep my eyes and ears open."
>
> —RAOUL WALSH

to come. The film introduced many of the negative distortions and stereotypes about Black Americans that became ingrained in popular culture, and even sparked a revival of the KKK and a wave of terrorizing attacks on the Black community. Griffith tried to deflect criticism by claiming, years later, that he had never intended to indict an entire race, reminding detractors that "the leading villain in the story is a white man." But his words only revealed his obliviousness—not only to the damaging iconography he perpetuated, but to *The Birth of a Nation*'s detrimental effect on his legacy and to the contribution to generations of racial oppression.

Griffith's next production was even bigger, and was conceived, in part, to defend *The Birth of a Nation* against censorship. *Intolerance* (1916) was an epic diatribe against oppression and discrimination through the ages, from 539 BC to the present. Vast in its scope and colossal in its ambition, the thirteen-reel saga featured countless innovations, such as the tracking crane shot that establishes an enormous palace courtyard in ancient Babylon (Griffith and Bitzer achieved this effect by constructing a special elevator rigged with two cameras). As the four parallel narratives that compose *Intolerance* reach their denouements, Griffith does not merely cut back and forth between scenes, but leaps across centuries with ever-intensifying speed so that the audience is catapulted from era to era in split seconds.

So convinced was Griffith that his magnum opus would lead to world peace that he largely funded its extravagant production costs, initiating a descent into debt from which he never fully recovered. Yet he had given birth to the Hollywood epic. *Los Angeles Times* headlines heralded "a remarkable feat in photoplay construction" that held "thousands entranced" at its 1916 premiere. It could be said that all subsequent historical spectacles—from *The Ten Commandments* (1923) to *Lawrence of Arabia* (1962) and beyond—owe a debt to *Intolerance*.

Thomas Burke's story of an abused young woman (Lillian Gish) who finds solace in a forbidden interracial relationship with a Chinese man (Richard Barthelmess), 1919's *Broken Blossoms* was sublime screen poetry that reverberated through such later classics as Erich von Stroheim's *Greed*

14

MUST-SEE MOVIES

THE BIRTH OF A NATION
(1915)

INTOLERANCE (1916)

HEARTS OF THE WORLD
(1918)

BROKEN BLOSSOMS (1919)

WAY DOWN EAST (1920)

ORPHANS OF THE STORM
(1921)

ISN'T LIFE WONDERFUL
(1924)

*Lillian Gish on Vermont's White River
for* Way Down East

KEY SCENE TO WATCH

The final climactic sequence of *Way Down East* (1920) follows Lillian Gish's long-suffering heroine, Anna, as she stumbles through a raging blizzard and collapses on a frozen river. The ice breaks, sending her careening dangerously toward the rapids. Griffith shot these scenes during an authentic New England blizzard in White River Junction, Vermont. Gish spent hours in the river wearing only a woolen dress, her hand and hair trailing in the icy water. "After a while, my hair froze, and I felt as if my hand were in a flame," she recalled. This pulse-pounding finale was not in the source material (an 1898 play by Lottie Blair Parker), but was added by Griffith because he felt it would have a powerful impact on viewers.

D. W. GRIFFITH

(1924) and Federico Fellini's *La Strada* (1954). *Blossoms* was Griffith's first film distributed by United Artists, the company he cofounded with Mary Pickford, Douglas Fairbanks, and Charlie Chaplin. By the time the beautiful but highly melodramatic *Orphans of the Storm* was released in 1921, the Jazz Age was in full swing, and Griffith's Victorian values—characterized by virtuous, wide-eyed heroines tormented by villains—were gathering dust. To make matters worse, he lavished so much time and money on his self-produced movies that they were incapable of earning profits.

When talkies took over, Griffith demonstrated a keen understanding of the process with 1930's *Abraham Lincoln* (he had even dabbled in early sound with *Dream Street* in 1921). But it was too late. By then, techniques he pioneered had become commonplace; the cross-cutting, the ratcheted pace,

the impressive locales. D. W. Griffith's vision was now the norm, and he was left behind by the very industry he had shaped. Hollywood had become a factory, cheaply churning out movies with more speed and mass appeal than he possibly could.

Griffith was presented with an honorary Oscar in 1936 for his achievements as a director, and for his "invaluable initiative and lasting contributions to the progress of the motion picture arts." Though honored by the gesture, he was by then derisive about the assembly-line direction the medium had taken. As his relevance waned, Griffith challenged the next generation of filmmakers to "attempt, at least some time in your life, to make pictures, or at least one picture, for posterity, for truth, for beauty, knowing full well it will not be popular."

Ancient Babylon as depicted in Intolerance

FRITZ LANG

Years active: 1918–1960

STARTING IN THE LATE 1910s AND WORKING STEADILY through the 1950s, prolific and ingenious director/screenwriter/producer Fritz Lang was an unstoppable filmmaking force for over forty years. His German Expressionist–rooted sensibility was sometimes diluted by the budgetary

constraints and breakneck pace of the Hollywood studio system, but he never surrendered. While the genres Lang visited appear disparate at first glance (espionage, science fiction, film noir, western), most of his movies concern the criminal underworld, society's underdogs, and the cruelty of fate. He was not especially concerned with exploring criminals, he has said, but "the social evils."

Vienna-born Lang got his start writing screenplays for noted producer Erich Pommer in Berlin. But, almost immediately, Lang sought more control. "I didn't like the way my scripts were developed on film," he recalled, and cut a deal to direct his next script himself: the romantic tragedy *Halbblut* (*Half-breed* [1919]), now lost. In 1922, he intro-

duced archvillain Dr. Mabuse in *Dr. Mabuse the Gambler*, and would revisit the supercriminal in later decades with two sequels.

One of many collaborations with his second wife, novelist/screenwriter Thea von Harbou, *Metropolis* (1927) broke new ground as the world's first science fiction epic, yet was neither a critical nor a box office success in its day. Lang had the last laugh, though, when *Metropolis* was later hailed as "one of the greatest sacred monsters of the cinema," in the words of film historian David Bordwell. The iconography of *Metropolis* is monumental: the oppressed masses who toil underground versus the carefree elite who play in the sunshine, the backdrop of towering skyscrapers and

17

awe-inspiring technical progress. Embodying the ills of technology, the haunting image of Robot Maria (played by Brigitte Helm) later inspired the designs of C-3PO of the Star Wars series and *Robocop* (1987). Seemingly unaware that he had built a massive pop culture quarry to be mined by later filmmakers, Lang simply shrugged off *Metropolis*, dismissing it as "silly" as he forged onward.

A perennial classic and the template for virtually all serial-killer movies to come, 1931's *M* might be Lang's greatest triumph. With his first sound feature, he realized his dream of commercial and critical success by incorporating the best elements of silent cinema into a talking picture. As the vile murderer (Peter Lorre in his first major screen role) stalks children in the city streets, whistling the ominous "In the Hall of the Mountain King," sound effects are employed instead of reams of dialogue, while the camera crawls, explores, and lurks in the shadows. When the killer is caught by a gang of petty criminals, his gut-wrenching plea that he

Fritz Lang sets up a camera angle for Scarlet Street, *starring Edward G. Robinson and Joan Bennett.*

> "There is only one word to describe Lang's style: inexorable. Each shot, each maneuver of the camera, each frame, each movement of an actor is a decision and is inimitable. . . . The man was not only a genius, he was also the most isolated and the least understood of contemporary filmmakers."
> —FRANÇOIS TRUFFAUT

is overpowered by his own compulsions turns the expected vengeance scenario on its head. Ninety years after its release, *M* still shocks and challenges audiences.

Fleeing Nazi Germany shortly after Hitler came to power, Lang arrived in Hollywood in 1934. While not specifically referencing the SS, much of Lang's 1930s output echoes the horrors of Hitler's regime in indirect ways: the creeping hysteria of mob mentality in *Fury* (1936); the sense of ever-encroaching doom as antihero Eddie (Henry Fonda) runs from the law in *You Only Live Once* (1937); the tense concealment of mysterious past sins in *You and Me* (1938). During World War II, the director made a series of openly anti-Nazi statements, starting with *Man Hunt* (1941).

Stylistically, Lang denied any attempts at high art. "I am not an artist," he famously said, "I am a craftsman." The tilted Dutch angle shots, the chiaroscuro lighting that characterized his German work, were merely hinted at in his Hollywood films. Never flashy, Lang's crisp directorial style was the result of intricate planning and purpose. In his *New*

Republic review of *Man Hunt*, Otis Ferguson noted of Lang: "He is a careful and thorough man with detail; and his first concern is with the tightness and immediacy of each fragment as it appears to you, makes its impression, leads you along with each incident of the story, and projects the imagination beyond into things to come." The scene in which Lang seamlessly switches to an aerial view as a cabin boy (Roddy McDowall) attempts to hide the hunted Thorndike (Walter Pidgeon) in an underground cellar is typical of the director's subtle use of unconventional angles.

Lang put his signature on a few popular westerns—*Western Union* (1941) and *Rancho Notorious* (1952) among them—but he found his comfort zone in the bleak, hard-boiled world of crime films, or what would later be called film noir. By the time he made the cynical, salacious *Scarlet Street* (1945), Lang had founded his own production company to gain more autonomy after developing a reputation in the movie colony for being difficult. "I was something that is always hated in Hollywood," he admitted later in life, "a perfectionist."

The typical Lang story tended to spotlight society's sins but not solve them; in a Fritz Lang movie, the fight against evil matters more than the outcome. And the outcome is often grim. Particularly in his '50s noirs, such as his late-career coup, *The Big Heat* (1953), the struggle against sinister forces is all-consuming. Both of their lives shattered by mafia racketeers, ex-cop Dave Bannion (Glenn Ford) and kept woman Debby Marsh (Gloria Grahame) join forces to put the thugs in jail. The underlings, the powerless rising up to fight for decency—these themes connect Lang's later work to such films as *Metropolis* and *M*.

In an almost cinematic twist of irony, the visionary dubbed the "Master of Darkness" by the British Film Institute was virtually blind by the end of his career. Although he stepped away from directing in 1960, Fritz Lang's influence on film is omnipresent today. He shaped the modern suspense thriller with *M*, his noirs raised the bar for pessimistic angst, and the ultramodern *Metropolis* cityscapes informed *Blade Runner* (1982), *The Fifth Element* (1997), and *Dark City* (1998), to name a few.

Peter Lorre in M

MUST-SEE MOVIES

DR. MABUSE THE GAMBLER
(1922)

METROPOLIS (1927)

M (1931)

FURY (1936)

YOU ONLY LIVE ONCE (1937)

SCARLET STREET (1945)

THE BIG HEAT (1953)

WHILE THE CITY SLEEPS
(1956)

Gloria Grahame and Glenn Ford in
The Big Heat

KEY SCENE TO WATCH

The Big Heat is packed with intense scenes, but the most shocking ones happen off camera. Watch the sequence that starts with Debby (Gloria Grahame) fixing her lipstick in the mirror as mob henchman Vince (Lee Marvin) questions her loyalty. Vince brutally wrenches Debby's arm, then, when she refuses to confess, he grabs a pot of boiling coffee and throws it in her face. But the act is implied: we only see the coffeepot being removed from the burner, and hear Debby's screams. Lang preferred not to show explicit violence, relying on the power of imagination. "I force the audience to become a collaborator of mine," he once said.

OSCAR MICHEAUX

Years active: 1919–1948

A S THE INDUSTRY'S FIRST MAJOR FILMMAKER OF color, Oscar Micheaux succeeded at what few others were able to attempt: he wrote, directed, produced, and distributed a steady stream of movies aimed at Black audiences, starring Black performers, from

the end of World War I through World War II. Because Micheaux worked outside the studio system, he was one of only a handful of classic-era directors who could truly claim the title of auteur; those toiling inside the iron gates typically had less control over their finished products.

Race pictures, as they were called in Micheaux's day, were made for Black filmgoers, and screened in roughly one hundred movie theaters that existed across the country after World War I—hardly enough to generate financial returns close to those seen by the big studios. But race pictures represented progress. Before then, Black Americans had largely been depicted on-screen as degrading caricatures. Micheaux and other early Black

filmmakers shifted this narrative to a more progressive, dignified view of the African American experience.

The son of former slaves, Micheaux had departed rural Illinois for Chicago in 1902, using his experience as a train porter and farmer to become a novelist. When the Lincoln Motion Picture Company (the first all-Black film production company) offered to adapt his novel *The Homesteader* for the screen, Micheaux—though he had no experience—opted instead to make it himself, using whatever money he could raise. *The Homesteader* was released in 1919 from the newly formed Micheaux Book and Film Company, later called the Micheaux Film Corporation. The interracial romance was

plagued by low production values, but it established its director as an independent moviemaker with vision and ambition.

Micheaux followed *The Homesteader* with the eight-reel feature *Within Our Gates* (1920). In what may have been Micheaux's response to *The Birth of a Nation*, a virtuous Black schoolteacher (Evelyn Preer), is attacked by a White man who attempts to rape her, only to realize he is her biological father. Without vilifying all Whites, Micheaux presents several scenarios in which Blacks suffer at the hands of a primarily Caucasian establishment. *The Symbol of the Unconquered* (1920) tackled the topic

of mixed-race Blacks passing as White, and their struggles against corrupt Whites and racists, even violent Ku Klux Klan members. A recurrent theme of class distinction between dark-skinned and light-skinned Blacks permeates Micheaux's work.

As his movies were shot on the fly, with bare-bones budgets, makeshift sets, and little time for artistic innovation, his work was often dismissed by critics of the period. It took several decades for Micheaux to be recognized as a seminal figure in movie history. According to biographer Patrick

Oscar Micheaux on set

"He was always trying to uplift the African American experience.... Through his work, Micheaux was able to create these other images, real-life images of the way African Americans tried to conduct their lives."

—DANNY GLOVER

McGilligan, Micheaux was "a Muhammad Ali decades before his time, a bragging Black man running around with a camera and making audacious, artistic films of his own maverick style, at a time when racial inferiority in the United States was custom and law."

Micheaux gave his characters dignity, dressing the men in sharp suits and the women in furs and finery; in contrast, 1920s Hollywood almost always cast Black actors in subservient roles supporting White stars. The Micheaux Film Corporation launched its own galaxy of stars, including the beautiful Ethel Moses (known as "the Black Jean Harlow") and renowned stage-and-screen baritone Paul Robeson, who made his film debut in *Body and Soul* (1925). Micheaux, writes Donald Bogle in his book *Hollywood Black*, "developed strong, independent heroines and noble forthright heroes; and created a star and studio system of his own making just as Hollywood was establishing its star system."

While his self-taught directing style was often hasty and static, Micheaux's films consistently featured arresting and distinctive imagery. In his first talkie, *The Exile* (1931), Micheaux included a siz-

zling jazz dance number by Louise Cook that is arguably as eye-popping as any Beyoncé halftime show. In the second half of the 1932 drama *Ten Minutes to Live*, he moved his camera outside to capture shots of Chicago city life, adding an electric jolt of urban authenticity rarely seen in the heavily staged, backlot-bound realm of studio talkies.

The Betrayal (1948) was a milestone: a major full-length sound feature distributed nationwide with a glamorous Broadway debut. Micheaux had borrowed the plot of *The Betrayal* from *The Homesteader*, updating the tale for a postwar audience. But it failed to find mainstream success. Though noting the slow pace and dialogue-heavy scenes, *Motion Picture Daily* observed "scattered moments of engrossing drama" and supposed that "many a Negro audience may find in the film a reflection of their own problems and thereby be moved." And this was precisely the point: to give Black viewers a healthy alternative to the White Hollywood narrative.

Most of Micheaux's forty-four films, including *The Betrayal*, are long since lost. All that remains are a handful of movies, and his incredible life story. As

MUST-SEE MOVIES

WITHIN OUR GATES (1920)

THE SYMBOL OF THE UNCONQUERED (1920)

BODY AND SOUL (1925)

THE EXILE (1931)

TEN MINUTES TO LIVE (1932)

LYING LIPS (1939)

Evelyn Preer and Jack Chenault in Within Our Gates

KEY SCENE TO WATCH

Among Oscar Micheaux's most effective surviving features is *Within Our Gates*. A series of scenes late in the film juxtapose the gruesome lynching of a Black family with the attempted rape of a mixed-race Black woman by a White man. As Micheaux cuts back to the hanged bodies being burned in a bonfire by a White mob, Gridlestone (Grant Gorman) enters the home of Sylvia (Evelyn Preer), grabs her, chases her, and attempts to force himself upon her as she aggressively fends him off. Finally, as the bonfire flames rage, her dress is removed, revealing a close-up of the scar that identifies Sylvia as Gridlestone's daughter. *Within Our Gates* was once believed lost, but was preserved by the Library of Congress in 1993 from a nitrate print found in Spain.

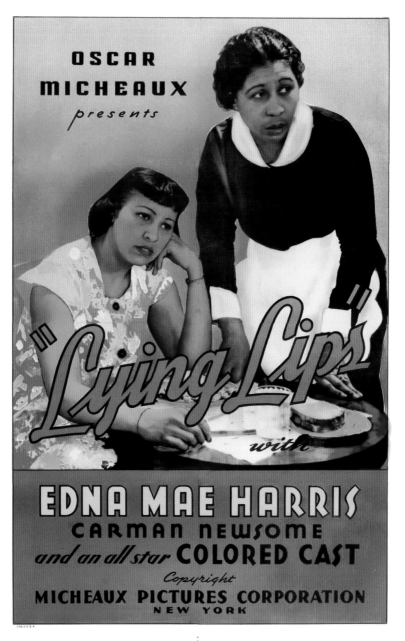

producer Charles Hobson put it, "If there hadn't been an Oscar Micheaux, there wouldn't have been an Oscar Micheaux." Micheaux's existence was statistically against the odds, and yet there he was, making a significant impact on Black lives and popular culture in the 1920s, '30s, and '40s.

Poster art for Lying Lips, *a Micheaux feature that still exists*

KING VIDOR

Years active: 1913–1980

H E AND THE MOVIES WERE BORN RIGHT AROUND the same time. Like his contemporaries, Frank Borzage, John Ford, Tay Garnett, and Josef von Sternberg (all also born in 1894), King Vidor belonged to the first generation to be raised on motion pictures.

When the native Texan relocated to Hollywood in 1916, he dreamed of making movies that spoke to common people. "I have one great principle," he told a reporter in 1921, "to produce pictures that everyone can understand." By the end of the '20s, he was one of the most sought-after filmmakers in the business. And he was just getting warmed up.

Throughout the 1930s, '40s, and '50s, Vidor was able to realize his dream, crafting films that not only illustrated the hopes and struggles of the average American, but have proven just as relatable to later generations. His unforgettable *The Crowd* (1928), described by Vidor (who conceived and wrote the scenario) as "just a succession of the dynamics of life" rather than a convention-ally plotted story, was among the first "culturally, historically, or aesthetically significant" titles added to the National Film Registry in 1989. With an ever-roving camera guided by cinematographer Henry Sharp, *The Crowd* follows John Sims (James Murray) through birth, childhood trauma, love and marriage, and tragedy. By capturing the hardship of working-class city dwellers, *The Crowd* and Vidor's 1931 talkie *Street Scene* helped inspire the Italian neorealism movement of the postwar years.

In some ways, John Sims predicts nonconformist architect Howard Roark (played by Gary Cooper) in *The Fountainhead* (1949), with his desire to rise above the herd, his eternal drive toward individuality—qualities inherent in Vidor himself.

"I'm a firm believer in the fact that you put your individual stamp on your work," he said of directing. "I think the whole job is to show one's individual viewpoint." Because he earned the trust of MGM's production chief, Irving Thalberg, Vidor was granted relative freedom and creative control, whereas other directors often saw their visions suppressed by the studio brass.

Vidor's unique touch permeates 1925's *The Big Parade*. There had never really been a war movie that followed one young man, Jim (John Gilbert), through the experiences of battle, revealing the physical and emotional tolls taken on his life. A certain vitality propels Vidor's work, whether in the

King Vidor on the set of Street Scene, *1931*

"I consider your war film *The Big Parade* the only truly great film ever produced. Over the years I have viewed the film many, many times and with each showing the certainty of its greatness deepens. I have always viewed it with awe and I must tell you that in many abstract ways it has influenced my paintings."

—ARTIST ANDREW WYETH
   IN A LETTER TO KING VIDOR

scene where Jim and his battalion approach the enemy, bayonets drawn, or his French sweetheart Melisande's (Renée Adorée) desperate good-bye as Jim departs for the front, Melisande clinging to Jim's truck and finally kneeling on the road alone in a haunting long shot. *The Big Parade* was Vidor's first smash, playing for two solid years at New York City's Astor Theatre. "As a motion picture, it is something beyond the fondest dreams of most people," raved the *New York Times*. "The scenes are as perfect as human imagination and intelligence could produce them."

The "all talking, all singing" *Hallelujah* (1929) almost didn't get made. As one of the first major Hollywood movies spotlighting Black culture, with an all-Black cast, the project was rejected by MGM until Vidor offered to defer his salary. With its pastoral settings (shot in Tennessee and Arkansas), *Hallelujah* broke the musical free from

Renée Adorée and John Gilbert in The Big Parade

the soundstage yet kept the fluid camera movement of the late silent era—quite a feat, considering the limitations of sound recording technology in 1929. Vidor observes sharecropper-turned-preacher Zeke (Daniel L. Haynes) as he sings gospel and blues-inspired songs, works in cotton fields and sawmills, and is tempted by spitfire Chick (Nina Mae McKinney), all with the intention of realism and honesty. Although *Hallelujah* failed to rise above Black stereotypes, it succeeded in giving its characters their own lives, their own problems, and their own world in which no White people appear to exist.

In *The Champ* (1931), the everyman is past-his-prime heavyweight Andy Purcell (Wallace Beery), a hero to his young son, Dink (Jackie Cooper). Frances Marion's Oscar-winning original script was so good, Vidor "didn't have to concentrate on telling the story," he said, leaving him free to focus on

King Vidor on location for Hallelujah *with cast, including Nina Mae McKinney and Daniel L. Haynes*

MUST-SEE MOVIES

THE BIG PARADE (1925)

THE CROWD (1928)

SHOW PEOPLE (1928)

HALLELUJAH (1929)

THE CHAMP (1931)

STELLA DALLAS (1937)

THE CITADEL (1938)

DUEL IN THE SUN (1946)

James Murray is just one of
The Crowd.

KEY SCENE TO WATCH

One of the most iconic shots in cinema history is the long camera track up the exterior of a Manhattan skyscraper that finds *The Crowd*'s hero, John, seated at one of a seemingly endless number of desks, all neatly spaced in rows. In the days before zoom lenses and camera cranes were commonplace, a scale model was constructed. "We built the building lying down on the stage," Vidor explained, "and then over that, a bridgework affair with the camera could go up the building." The model shot dissolved to a soundstage filled with two hundred men working at two hundred desks, a visual that expresses John's feeling of being engulfed by "the crowd." This sequence was appropriated by Billy Wilder for the introduction of his lead character (Jack Lemmon) in *The Apartment* (1960), and influenced similar shots in Orson Welles's *The Trial* (1962) and the Coen Brothers' *The Hudsucker Proxy* (1994).

KING VIDOR

details, such as the poignant close-up of Cooper's grief-stricken face when his mother (Irene Rich) appears at the very moment he needs her most. A glimmer of hope always saves the day in a King Vidor picture.

The Vidor everyman was not always male. *La Bohème* (1926) gave Lillian Gish (as the poor-but-proud heroine, Mimi) some of her most sublime moments on film. *The Patsy* and *Show People*, his two 1928 silent comedies starring Marion Davies, may be the movies that best showcased the actress's giddy humor. In *Stella Dallas* (1937), Barbara Stan-

wyck whipped up a tour-de-force performance as "a woman so disenfranchised by life that she feels she's not even entitled to her own child," film scholar Jeanine Basinger has observed. The common, crass Stella marries above her station, and ends up forsaking her relationship with her daughter (Anne Shirley) to avoid holding her back in life. The final scene—a heartbreaking yet hopeful tracking shot of Stella striding down the sidewalk—put the finishing touch on Stanwyck's personal favorite role. After directing Judy Garland in her iconic "Over the Rainbow" number in 1939's *The Wizard of Oz* (stepping in, uncredited, for Victor Fleming), Vidor wielded Bette Davis at her baddest in the notorious noir *Beyond the Forest* (1949).

Though he specialized in intimate human stories, Vidor was no stranger to spectacle. In fact, his films grew more expansive as he aged. A highlight of *Duel in the Sun* (1946) is an impressive gathering of hundreds of cowhands on horseback, a culmination of impeccably choreographed scenes from Vidor's past, reminiscent of *The Big Parade*—with the newfangled features of sound, Technicolor, and widescreen. The epics *War and Peace* (1956) and *Solomon and Sheba* (1959) concluded Vidor's feature filmmaking career on a grand scale. After being nominated five times as Best Director, Vidor was finally presented with an honorary Academy Award in 1979.

Barbara Stanwyck in Stella Dallas

ARTISTS OF SHADOW AND LIGHT

ERICH VON STROHEIM

Years active: 1919–1933

ONE OF THE MOST IDIOSYNCRATIC, CONTROVER-
sial figures in silent Hollywood was Erich Stroheim, an Austrian immi-
grant who reinvented himself by claiming to be of noble lineage and
embellishing his name with an impressive-sounding "von." Although

he only directed (or, in some cases, partially
directed) nine films during his brief, volatile career,
he left a giant fingerprint on film history with his
uncompromising devotion to realism and extraor-
dinary attention to detail.

As a character actor in films, von Stroheim
played so many villainous, sadistic World War
I military officers that he became known as "the
man you love to hate." When he began directing,
he cultivated this persona off-camera as well. His
insistence on total artistic autonomy made him an
enemy of the establishment: the movie studios.

Von Stroheim's writing-directing debut, *Blind
Husbands* (1919), was a fairly typical love-triangle
tale of a neglected wife (Francelia Billington) and

the lieutenant (played by von Stroheim, of course)
who seduces her. What made the film exceptional was the director's personally supervised set
design and keen sense of visual storytelling. So
image-driven is its narrative that *Blind Husbands*
was promoted as having "fewer subtitles than any
other feature ever made." With his high standards
and the importance he placed on breathtaking
scenery—such as staging the dramatic climax at
the summit of a Tyrolean mountain (shot at Tah-
quitz Peak in Idyllwild, California)—von Stroheim
lent prestige to the moving pictures, an art form
that was still struggling to be taken seriously.

For *Foolish Wives* (1922), a sizable stretch of
Monte Carlo was accurately reconstructed on the

Universal backlot, drenching the film in Mediterranean glamour. The visual expressiveness was heightened here as well. In one sequence, von Stroheim's rascally Count peers into a pocket mirror to catch the object of his affection (Miss DuPont) undressing in the next room, a typical von Stroheim shot of arresting, if salacious, imagery. Ads touted *Foolish Wives* as "the first million-dollar picture," though studio executives were furious at the amount of footage shot and money spent. Von Stroheim refused to curtail his notorious extravagance on *Merry-Go-Round* (1923), leading Universal's Irving Thalberg and Carl Laemmle to fire the director from his own picture and replace him with Rupert Julian.

But his artistic reputation earned von Stroheim a chance to helm his dream project at Goldwyn Pictures, a faithful adaptation of Frank Norris's epic

Erich von Stroheim, 1930

34

> "An exquisite engraving of human perversity, *Greed* is a monumental fable that will continue to influence cinema for decades to come. As modern and brutal today as it was the day it was released."
>
> —GUILLERMO DEL TORO

novel *McTeague* to be titled *Greed* (1924). "I'm for realism in pictures," von Stroheim told a reporter during this time, "and I get it at any cost." True to his word, the director insisted on extreme authenticity, from renting out an entire San Francisco neighborhood to shooting in 125-degree Death Valley heat until his crew members became physically ill. The result was forty-two reels (nearly ten

Gibson Gowland and Jean Hersholt in Greed

hours) of movie, eventually whittled down by the newly formed Metro-Goldwyn-Mayer to two and a half hours. Devastatingly, the cut footage was destroyed, preventing von Stroheim's original edit from ever being reassembled.

Greed was a critical and commercial flop. The story was too chopped up, the subject matter too grim for 1920s tastes. The Los Angeles Times deemed it "the picture that might have been great," yet, instead, was "one of the very worst that has ever been shown." But the film has aged remarkably well. Though the entirety of von Stroheim's vision is lost, even the shortened version of Greed sets new screen standards in sheer brutality and cynicism—a marked departure from the Hollywood formula of rose-tinted worlds and happy, or at least hopeful, endings—making it something of a holy relic today. The slow, dreary descent of working-class McTeague (Gibson Gowland) and his money-obsessed wife, Trina (ZaSu Pitts), is illustrated down to the tiniest details; the broken dishes in their dirty apartment are given close-ups, as are the hoarded gold coins from Trina's lottery winnings.

Even at its most commercial, von Stroheim's work was routinely described as "sordid" by critics and the public alike. Typical of his style is a scene in The Merry Widow (1925) depicting the young, beautiful heroine, Sally (Mae Murray), shrieking in horror as the elderly Baron (Tully Marshall) suffers a heart attack in their flower-strewn wedding-night bed. The filmmaker defended his penchant for exposing primitive human desires by saying, "I cannot beat around the bush when I make a picture. Human nature is instinctively direct." He was

MUST-SEE MOVIES

BLIND HUSBANDS (1919)

FOOLISH WIVES (1922)

GREED (1924)

THE MERRY WIDOW (1925)

THE WEDDING MARCH (1928)

QUEEN KELLY (1929)

KEY SCENE TO WATCH

Often interpreted as von Stroheim's most romantic movie, The Wedding March features several scenes between Nikki (Erich von Stroheim) and Mitzi (nineteen-year-old Fay Wray in her first leading role) as they stroll through a Viennese wine garden and are showered with white apple blossoms. For this authentic set designed by Richard Day, thousands of imported handmade blossoms were meticulously hung from the trees at a reported expense of $25,000. In the final garden rendezvous, Mitzi sees a ghostly omen of doom and foresees that her relationship with Nikki is destined to fail. The fairy-tale scenario is interrupted as the wind whips up, the blossoms are scattered into the night, and the mood of serenity instantly shifts to one of terror.

up to his old tricks again with *The Wedding March* (1928), re-creating Vienna in lavish detail, racking up thirty or forty takes of a single scene, lagging months behind schedule. The production was another costly catastrophe, though the movie itself was a creative triumph.

The final straw for Hollywood was *Queen Kelly* (1929), a gothic romance that Gloria Swanson

starred in and produced for United Artists. When von Stroheim turned the dance-hall set into a full-blown brothel, Swanson walked off the set and had the director fired. The von Stroheim–directed material is, as usual, visually stunning: an innocent convent girl falls from grace against a backdrop of cavernous palaces, gluttonous banquets, and his signature erotic hedonism—a perfect last hurrah for the silent era.

When silent cinema faded, so did von Stroheim's directing career. He made a few low-budget talkies, returned to acting, and finally moved to France, where he won a key role in Jean Renoir's antiwar drama *The Grand Illusion* (1937). In 1949, he returned to Hollywood to join his former leading lady, Gloria Swanson, as Max the butler in *Sunset Boulevard* (1950), a film that features a clip from the notorious *Queen Kelly*. On the day Billy Wilder met von Stroheim, the younger director told him he was ten years ahead of his time, to which von Stroheim replied "Twenty, Mr. Wilder, twenty." He was right. By the 1940s, audiences had developed a taste for earthier screen fare. Today, when graphic sex and violence are commonplace in entertainment, but the poetry of suggestion has been discarded, Erich von Stroheim is regarded as a heroic visionary.

Mae Murray and Tully Marshall in The Merry Widow

LOIS WEBER

Years active: 1911–1934

LOIS WEBER WAS NOT THE SOLE FEMALE DIRECTOR of silent-era Hollywood. In fact, at the dawn of cinema, motion pictures were so new and the filmmaking business so unstructured, that opportunities for women abounded. Little prevented ladies from picking up a camera and shooting a film—and that's what many of them did. Mabel Normand, Ida May Park, Madeline Brandeis, Dorothy Davenport Reid, and screenwriter/director Frances Marion are among a handful of directors who catered to a filmgoing public that was largely female (according to a 1927 *Moving Picture World* survey, 83 percent of movie audiences were women).

Perhaps the most successful and most inventive of these filmmakers was Weber, a trailblazing auteur who not only wrote, cast, directed, produced, and edited her own movies, but was among the first directors to use the medium as a tool for social justice. Possibly her best-known feature today, *Shoes* (1916) is a searing appeal for a minimum wage for women workers. Shop-girl Eva (Mary MacLaren) is so poor that she must prostitute herself for a decent pair of shoes, a devastating turn of events that Weber builds to with close-ups of Eva's increasingly desperate face and her ragged, threadbare boots. In her *Chicago Herald* review, Louella Parsons called *Shoes* a "masterpiece" that "loosens the heartstrings, stirs the pulse, and makes one choke with emotion." *Shoes* was one of over two hundred films Weber made, most now lost to the ravages of time.

When the former evangelist, singer, actress, and concert pianist made the leap to screenwriting and then directing, Weber worked alongside her husband/producing partner Phillips Smalley,

though she exercised total authority over her pictures. She is believed to be the first woman to direct a feature-length film with her Shakespeare

Weber puts the finishing touches on Bille Dove's costume for The Marriage Clause.

39

"Lois's films tended to be very real. She wanted the characters to be pretty much just how you would experience them if you ran into them in the real world. Some people were still figuring out the impact that film could have on society, but Lois sort of had that figured out."

—ANTONIA CARLOTTA,
GREAT-GREAT NIECE OF CARL LAEMMLE

adaptation *The Merchant of Venice* in 1914. Like her contemporaries D. W. Griffith and Cecil B. DeMille, Weber was instrumental in shaping the art form by crafting lengthier, more complex films early on.

Weber became known for her focus on female characters, and her eye for examining women's social roles. She also had a knack for discovering new talent, as in her casting of Claire Windsor, who became a major star. "I must have players who will let me lead them," Weber once said of her direct, hands-on approach. "I go so fast, they must put their hands in mine and run with me." Billie Dove—a Universal contract actress who rose to stardom in *The Marriage Clause* (1926)—recalled Weber as "the best director I ever had. . . . I had a lot of men directors that I liked too, but she understood women."

Far from being merely a niche filmmaker for female audiences, Weber was a top director (Universal chief Carl Laemmle called her his "best man on the lot") whose movies packed theaters. For a time in 1916, she was the highest-paid filmmaker in Hollywood (netting $5,000 per week), wielding her power to tackle such controversial topics as poverty, drug addiction, and abortion. And she managed to make these weighty issues palatable; *Where Are My Children?* (1916), a plea for birth control, was a box office smash. "We cannot imagine Universal green-lighting a film written and directed by a woman on abortion and birth control today," observed Weber biographer Shelley Stamp in 2019, "and it was their top money-maker over 100 years ago." The fact that it was banned in certain cities only made it more profitable.

Some hallmarks of a Lois Weber film are authentic locations (which she insisted upon whenever possible), the framing of shots from a limited character's point of view (to better reveal their perspectives), and an absence of exaggerated histrionics in favor of naturalism. Weber pioneered the split-screen process when she divided the screen into three sections in the appropriately named *Suspense* (1913), a stroke of brilliance that elevated

MUST-SEE MOVIES

SUSPENSE (1913)

HYPOCRITES (1915)

WHERE ARE MY CHILDREN? (1916)

SHOES (1916)

THE DUMB GIRL OF PORTICI (1916)

THE BLOT (1921)

Mary MacLaren in Shoes

KEY SCENE TO WATCH

Shoes features a shot that is both aesthetically stunning and remarkably simple. When Eva's desperate need for money reaches a critical point, she knows what she must do: she agrees to give herself to a lecherous man (William V. Mong) in exchange for the finer things she can't afford. Wordlessly, listlessly donning her best clothes in preparation to meet him, she pins her hair atop her head and gazes at her reflection in a small, cracked mirror on the wall. Her face divided in two by the mirror's crack, Eva now seems to see herself as an object; she avoids meeting her own eyes, and finally turns away, unable to look at her face. Mary MacLaren was cast in the role of Eva by Weber, who discovered the twenty-year-old aspiring actress on the Universal lot.

ARTISTS OF SHADOW AND LIGHT

tension by depicting the simultaneous action of three different characters unfolding in real time. Based upon D. F. E. Auber's 1829 opera about a mute Italian woman who inspires a revolution, *The Dumb Girl of Portici* (1916) boasts impressive action scenes, proving that Weber could choreograph large crowds, soldiers, and horses with the deftness of DeMille.

Her skills paid off. Before women won the rights to vote or to earn wages comparable to men's, Weber raked in big bucks; in 1919, she closed a five-picture deal with Famous Players-Lasky giving her $50,000 plus one-third of the profits. As her career progressed, the director shifted her focus from ripped-from-the-headlines "social problem films" to lighter domestic fare, her messages becoming subtler. In *The Blot* (1921), her exposé on the secret shame of middle-class poverty, struggling heroine Amelia (Claire Windsor) fares better than Eva in *Shoes*, even managing a happy ending.

Like other ladies in the industry, Weber's status declined with the late-1920s power consolidation of Hollywood studios, when men sought jobs that had become high-paying and women were edged out of powerful positions. Commenting on the situation with characteristic directness, she said in 1928, "Women entering the field now find it practically closed. A male beginning would not be so handicapped." Although practically forgotten by her death in 1939, Weber has been rediscovered and hailed as a masterful filmmaker by twenty-first century audiences.

Left to right: Lois Weber, leading lady Anna Pavlova, and Weber's husband, Phillips Smalley, on the set of The Dumb Girl of Portici

SILENT PIONEERS

East Coast craftsmen **Edwin S. Porter** and **J. Searle Dawley** worked for Thomas Edison, who patented the motion-picture camera in the US in 1891. Porter laid the groundwork for basic editing techniques in his films *The Great Train Robbery* (1903) and the blockbuster feature *Tess of the Storm Country* (1914). Dawley was the first director to bring *Frankenstein* (1910) to the screen. He then made several features for Adolph Zukor at Famous Players before directing early talkies for Lee de Forest, inventor of the first sound-on-film process, Phonofilm.

In France, **Alice Guy-Blaché** and **Georges Méliès** were the premiere experimenters, discovering the movie camera's primary uses as a creative tool. In 1896, Guy-Blaché directed her first effort for Gaumont, the imaginative *La Fée aux Choux* (The Cabbage Fairy), believed to be the world's first narrative film. Former magician Méliès, meanwhile, pioneered special-effects filmmaking with his wildly successful shorts. His inventive and still-popular *A Trip to the Moon* (1902) was the first science fiction film.

Actor, director, and mogul **Thomas Ince** set the template for the Hollywood studio system with "Inceville," his 18,000-acre Southern California lot of studios dedicated to turning out westerns. In 1915, Ince established a filmmaking colony in Culver City when he formed Triangle Pictures with D. W. Griffith and **Mack Sennett**, the influential "King of Comedy" who had founded his own Keystone Studios in 1912. The man behind the Keystone Cops, Sennett also brought slapstick to the screen by casting Charlie Chaplin, Mabel Normand, Harold Lloyd, and W. C. Fields in their first films.

Between 1920 and 1921, explorer **Robert Flaherty** lived among the Inuit people of northern Quebec, capturing their lives in the first major feature-length documentary *Nanook of the North* (1922).

A Mack Sennett Bathing Beauty, circa 1915

Flaherty followed the successful *Nanook* with *Moana* (1926), a semifictionalized documentary of Samoan life. His engaging films broke ground with their respectful depiction of native cultures.

THE GERMAN EXPRESSIONISTS

Taking its cue from the Expressionist art movement of the early 1900s, German Expressionism influenced the art of moviemaking across the world.

Though renowned for his German-made silents, such as the vampire classic *Nosferatu: A Symphony of Horror* (1922) and the innovative *The Last Laugh* (*Der letzte Mann* [1924]), the crown jewel in the legacy of Hollywood success story **F. W. Murnau** is his intimate 1927 drama *Sunrise: A Song of Two Humans*, often considered one of the best silent movies ever made. Murnau and cinematographer Karl Freund's novel "unchained camera" technique freed the movie camera from objectivity, allowing it to roam, search, and soar, much as the human eye does, yielding dynamic and poetic works of art.

Robert Wiene's *The Cabinet of Dr. Caligari* (1920) may be the epitome of Expressionist cinema, with its distorted set design, tilted camera angles, and high-contrast lighting, lending a nightmarish mood to the thriller. Former painter and art

director **Paul Leni** made the fantastical *Waxworks* in 1924, before bringing his Expressionist style to Universal Studios in the atmospheric horror classic *The Cat and the Canary* (1927). The German directors who crafted these stunning, sinister films planted a seed that would later emerge from the shadows as film noir.

Max Schreck as Count Orlok in Nosferatu

Chapter Two

THE STUDIO AS AUTEUR

Sound was not a new concept in motion pictures. Thomas Edison had envisioned sound accompaniment since the inception of his movie camera experiments. But it was Warner Bros. that took the leap, ushering in the talkie revolution with *The Jazz Singer* in 1927. Initially, the sound recording and playback technology was crude, meaning more obstacles, and a greater burden on directors to get creative and deliver quality entertainment for a talkies-crazed and Depression-weary public. By 1930, dozens of silent outfits had gone out of business or were consolidated into what became seven major studios: Paramount, MGM, Warner Bros., Twentieth Century-Fox, Universal, Columbia, and RKO.

Once the switch was made and sound was established as the industry standard, Hollywood entered its Golden Age. Studios became more factory-like than ever, each company a well-oiled machine churning out fifty movies a year like Ford assembly lines churned out hubcaps. And this required a lot of filmmakers. The 1930s saw an explosion of craftsmen: from workmanlike B-movie masters to artistic A-list Oscar-winners and everything in between, scores of directors could be found at any Hollywood studio on any given day.

The bulk of Golden Age directors were employed by studios as long-term salaried workers, and were regularly assigned movies by their bosses. This doesn't mean that studio directors put no creative touches or personal stamps on their films. But ultimately, '30s-era directors answered to the almighty studio, and many were unable to do much except grind out the product. Each studio cultivated its own general style, leaving little room for individual experimentation.

In July 1934, a new gauntlet was thrown down: the strict enforcement of the Hollywood Production Code. Directors had to maneuver more nimbly to avoid direct suggestions of sex, violence, profanity, or interracial relations. Those talented individuals who managed to sculpt a résumé of unique, impactful pictures within the restrictive studio system earned a distinguished place in movie history.

Opposite: *Mervyn LeRoy and Ernst Lubitsch, 1937*

DOROTHY ARZNER

Years active: 1927–1943

FIRST RISING TO PROMINENCE AS AN EDITOR OF SILENTS (*Blood and Sand* [1922]) and emerging as a major director in the 1930s, Dorothy Arzner racked up a small but impressive filmography and cultivated the careers of many a leading lady, from Katharine Hepburn to Lucille Ball.

Although Arzner is often called "the only woman director of the Golden Age," she was, in fact, merely the most prolific. Actress Wanda Tuchock directed a Hollywood film in 1934; Grace Elliott made documentaries in early-1930s Hollywood; Elinor Glyn and Jacqueline Logan directed feature films in England in the same era. Arzner is set apart by her consistent success within the studio system, and her status as the first female member of the Directors Guild of America.

After eight years of ascending the ranks at Paramount (from typist to editor to screenwriter), Arzner aced her first directorial assignment, *Fashions for Women* (1927), a lost comedy described as "a sheer pleasure," "very beautiful," and having "dis-

tinction written all over it" by critic Norbert Lusk. Although she had never picked up a megaphone before, Arzner was a natural. She clicked with "It Girl" Clara Bow (then Paramount's most lucrative star) when they made *Get Your Man* (1927), another coup that earned Arzner the choice job of directing Bow in Paramount's first talking picture, the collegiate romance *The Wild Party* (1929).

Though it suffers from the same woes that plague all early talkies (audible hissing and a slow pace), *The Wild Party* was an effective vehicle for Bow and a solid film. Arzner is often credited with inventing the boom mic when she strung a microphone to a fishing pole to follow the hyperactive Bow as she bounced around the set. This stroke

of ingenuity adds realism to the crowd scenes in the girls' dormitory, classrooms, and a costume ball. Instead of standing in a row speaking into a hidden microphone, Stella (Bow) and her girl-friends move, dance, and chatter naturally. *The Wild Party* was a certified hit, establishing Arzner as an esteemed sound-era expert specializing in female-driven dramas.

Arzner made sixteen features during her Hollywood tenure, and every one focused on a cen-tral woman—always of the spunky, independent variety. Initially, Arzner was averse, she said, to "having any comment made about being a woman director," preferring to let her work speak for itself. But she became increasingly vocal about the dearth of feminine filmmakers, advocating for more women to join the profession. "There should be more of us directing," she told a reporter in 1932. "Try as man may, he will never be able to get the woman's viewpoint in telling certain stories."

One such story was *Christopher Strong* (1933), Katharine Hepburn's first starring role. The script

Dorothy Arzner directs Ruth Chatterton in the 1930 feature Anybody's Woman, *as a sound engineer records the dialogue.*

"Miss Arzner was a very important Hollywood director. . . . She was a wonderful woman, and she was very encouraging to me. I think what meant so much, as I always had self-doubt, was that she would say: you are going to do fine. She was very famous. I just had the good luck that I was her student."

—FRANCIS FORD COPPOLA

by Zoe Akins concerns career-minded aviator Lady Cynthia Darrington (Hepburn) and her love affair with the married Christopher (Colin Clive). Arzner's sensitive direction is evident not only in Hepburn's glowing performance, but in the love scenes. Rather than show Cynthia and Christopher together in the bedroom, the director shows only Hepburn's arm reaching for the alarm clock as the lovers discuss the bracelet on her wrist, a symbol, Cynthia jokes, that she is "shackled" to a man. Arzner had campaigned to have Hepburn cast in *Christopher Strong*; from there, the actress shot to stardom, becoming known for portraying similar types of liberated ladies and eventually earning a record four Best Actress Oscars.

Movies like *Craig's Wife* (1936) were, for many decades, given the dismissive designation of "women's melodramas." But roiling beneath the surface of this polished domestic drama is a sea of rich psychological subtext, and Arzner hits every note on key. Based on George Kelly's Pulitzer Prize–

winning play, *Craig's Wife* gave Rosalind Russell the meaty role of Harriet Craig, an icy antiheroine obsessed with her immaculate home. Arzner and cinematographer Lucien Ballard frame Harriet like an elegant tigress trapped in a cavernous, opulent cage, generating hints of sympathy for this repressed woman who married a wealthy man as "a way toward emancipation," in her own words. When Vincent Sherman remade the film with Joan Crawford in 1950, the woman's perspective seemed to vanish, and Harriet became a full-blown monster.

Although Arzner and Crawford became close working together at MGM (years later, Arzner directed the star in a series of Pepsi-Cola commercials), *The Bride Wore Red* (1937) was a disappointment; Arzner tangled with Louis B. Mayer, who insisted she change the film's ending from poignant to happily-ever-after, and her union with MGM soured. Arzner was used to doing things her way, even editing her films inside the camera as she shot (a method of filming shots with such precision that

MUST-SEE MOVIES

THE WILD PARTY (1929)

MERRILY WE GO TO HELL (1932)

CHRISTOPHER STRONG (1933)

CRAIG'S WIFE (1936)

THE BRIDE WORE RED (1937)

DANCE, GIRL, DANCE (1940)

Lucille Ball in Dance, Girl, Dance

KEY SCENE TO WATCH

A standout scene in *Dance, Girl, Dance* is the climactic moment when Judy stops dancing in the middle of a performance, looks straight into the audience, and gives the men watching a piece of her mind. "What's it for?" she rails. "So you can go home when the show's over and strut before your wives and sweethearts and play at being the stronger sex for a minute? I'm sure they see through you just like we do." Judy's unfiltered tirade suggests Arzner's own strong will and independence. "I never let anyone else tell me how to direct," she recalled later in life. "My philosophy is that to be a director you cannot be subject to anyone, even the head of the studio."

they can't be easily tampered with), to maintain creative control.

In 1940, she fled to RKO to make her chef d'oeuvre, *Dance, Girl, Dance*, the unusual tale of two professional dancers: saucy Bubbles (Lucille Ball in a defining role) and demure Judy (Maureen O'Hara), and their struggles with, as the *New Yorker* put it, "art versus commerce and love versus lust." Though not popular in its day, *Dance, Girl, Dance* has since become a cult favorite (and a National Film Registry selection in 2007) for its subversive feminist tones. Echoing the same theme of female bonding found in *The Wild Party* and Arzner's 1931 comedy-drama *Working Girls*, the earthier *Dance,*

Girl, Dance illustrates the showbiz life from the viewpoint of women who perform for an audience of mostly men.

While still in her prime, Dorothy Arzner left the Hollywood system after being replaced by Charles Vidor when she fell ill with pneumonia while shooting *First Comes Courage* (1943). But she didn't abandon her craft. In World War II, she directed training films for the Women's Army Corps, and later, as a UCLA professor, she passed on her expertise to future filmmakers, among them a young Francis Ford Coppola.

Katharine Hepburn in Christopher Strong

CLARENCE BROWN

Years active: 1920–1952

H E CRAFTED FILMS METICULOUSLY, TAKING NO shortcuts. For his precision and high standards of quality, Clarence Brown was rewarded by becoming—from the late 1920s through the early 1930s—the highest-paid director in the world, pocketing a cool

$6,000 a week. A curiosity about moviemaking led Brown from the automobile business to assisting silent filmmaker Maurice Tourneur (father of 1940s director Jacques Tourneur) for years before wielding the megaphone himself at Metro-Goldwyn-Mayer, starting in 1926.

He had a gift for finessing natural performances from actors (including children and animals), and was a master camera technician with an engineering degree. Although the over-the-shoulder shot may have been used before Brown, he popularized it in such silents as the Greta Garbo–John Gilbert romance *A Woman of Affairs* (1928). As the married Diana (Garbo) leans in toward Neville (Gilbert) for an adulterous kiss, Brown places the

camera over Gilbert's shoulder. We see enough of Gilbert—an ear, his collar, half of the back of his head—to feel we are sharing an intimate moment between them. This technique soon became a staple in movies and, later, television.

Aided by cinematographer William Daniels, Brown had helmed the first screen teaming of legendary lovers Garbo and Gilbert in the stylistically progressive *Flesh and the Devil* (1926). A nod to German Expressionism, the romantic drama looks ultramodern compared to others from its day—especially the innovative dueling scene, done completely in silhouette. The kiss Garbo's Felicitas and Gilbert's Leo share in a moonlit garden is preceded by a stunning shot in which Leo lights a match and

cups his hand around the flame, the fire dancing on their faces. Brown directed Garbo in six more movies, juggling those with his work with Joan Crawford, as both actresses rose to superstardom.

Tasked with making Garbo's first talkie, Brown approached the challenge with characteristic forethought, half of which was having the right material: Eugene O'Neill's Pulitzer Prize–winning play *Anna Christie*. "Talking pictures are great when you have great dialogue, and I have great dialogue because Eugene O'Neill wrote it," Brown declared. His *Anna Christie* (1930) succeeded in the unlikely feat of making the heavily accented Swedish luminary a sound sensation.

Like King Vidor and the trusty Robert Z. Leonard, Brown was a favorite at MGM for his reliability, craftsmanship, and work ethic—and for his sterling output. In 1937, the studio boasted: "Brown is credited with the singular faculty of directing pictures of remarkably artistic quality, but that never fail at the box office." Behind the scenes,

Clarence Brown directs Greta Garbo in her first talking picture, Anna Christie.

> "Clarence Brown is one of the great names of American motion pictures—one of the few whose mastery was undiminished by the arrival of sound. His style is one of deceptive simplicity, but the apparent effortless ease is the result of tremendous care."

—KEVIN BROWNLOW

Brown pushed Metro for the freedom to select his own projects. Moving on from his spate of profitable Garbo and Crawford vehicles, Brown veered toward enriching family fare with *The Human Comedy* (1943), *National Velvet* (1944), and *The Yearling* (1946), all featuring child actors. Brown's affinity for wholesome movies helped to shape MGM's reputation as a studio of high moral principles.

The detail-oriented Brown was known to shoot a scene ten, twenty, thirty times, or more until he had achieved perfection. Gregory Peck recalled one sequence in *The Yearling* requiring a whopping seventy-two takes to get in the can. (The fact that Peck's costar was a fawn undoubtedly added to the difficulty.) By then, Brown had the clout to insist on location shooting, even if that meant spending months hauling enormous three-strip Technicolor cameras through Florida's Ocala National Forest to capture authentic scenery, then looping dialogue in the studio to edit out the noises of nature. But the results were spectacular, earning glowing reviews and an Academy Award for Best Color Cinematography, among others.

The success of *The Yearling*—which garnered young untrained actor Claude Jarman Jr. an Oscar—granted Brown the chance to shoot a pet project. 1949's *Intruder in the Dust* again starred

Gregory Peck and Jane Wyman in The Yearling

Jarman, this time as a southern boy who befriends a wrongly imprisoned Black man (Juano Hernandez). The civil rights movement was simmering on the nation's back burner, and depicting a proud, heroic Black man was problematic for many. As Jarman recalls, "MGM had the guts to let Clarence produce and direct the film, but they faltered on the follow-through. [They] must have gotten nervous about the controversial theme, because they seemed to bury *Intruder in the Dust*." Although promotion was weak, those who did see the film hailed it as a groundbreaker. *New York Times* critic Bosley Crowther called *Intruder in the Dust* "this year's pre-eminent picture and one of the great cinema dramas of our times." William Faulkner, author of the source novel, supervised the production, and later referred to *Intruder* as "one of the best movies I've ever seen."

Clarence Brown earned a record six Academy Award nominations for Best Director without a single win. Whether award-winning or not, Brown's filmography is filled with unforgettable and inspiring works of art, many due to his persistence in battling the studio to get his way. "You had to fight for everything you got onto the screen," he recalled later in life. "That's how things were set up with the old studio system, and it worked out for the best most of the time. But you did have to fight."

John Gilbert and Greta Garbo in Flesh and the Devil

MUST-SEE MOVIES

FLESH AND THE DEVIL (1926)

ANNA CHRISTIE (1930)

A FREE SOUL (1931)

ANNA KARENINA (1935)

NATIONAL VELVET (1944)

THE YEARLING (1946)

INTRUDER IN THE DUST (1949)

Juano Hernandez and Claude Jarman Jr. in Intruder in the Dust

KEY SCENE TO WATCH

The scene in which Chick (Claude Jarman Jr.) visits Lucas (Juano Hernandez) in the jail cell is a highlight of *Intruder in the Dust*. As Lucas asks Chick to help him to clear his name, Brown shows us only Lucas's eye, framed by metal bars, then cuts to Chick's eye, and, finally, to an insert shot of both men's hands on the cell bars. Dappled with shadows, the hands mesh into an interwoven pattern, suggesting harmony between different races. Clarence Brown's intimate knowledge of the moving picture camera, coupled with his fourteen years of experience in the silent medium, informed this stunning black-and-white scene.

CLARENCE BROWN

FRANK CAPRA

Years active: 1921–1964

F RANK CAPRA WAS ALMOST AN ANACHRONISM IN 1930s
Hollywood: a man who insisted on complete creative authority or nothing.
He never believed in assembly-line filmmaking, but in his own vision—the
vision of one single artist. "I knew of no great book or play, no classic paint-

ing or sculpture," he wrote in his 1971 autobiography, *The Name Above the Title*, "that was ever created
by a committee." Wielding his artistic integrity like
a battering ram, writer/director/producer/editor
Capra conquered the industry with a string of classics that espoused faith in traditional American values, and in the goodness of people.

It took only four weeks and $325,000 to make
It Happened One Night (1934), the seminal screen fairy
tale of love transcending social class. Longer than
the average comedy (by about ten minutes), meatier
and more nuanced, the character-driven script by

Clark Gable and Claudette Colbert in It Happened
One Night

Robert Riskin concerned a pampered heiress and a hard-boiled reporter who meet on a bus, hate each other on sight, then slowly fall in love. Its unlikely success is the stuff of legend. No one besides Capra and Riskin—not even Columbia Pictures head Harry Cohn—had faith in the project. Loaned-out stars Clark Gable and Claudette Colbert were loath to appear in it. Critical reception was lukewarm. But then something magical happened: the movie's

Frank Capra and James Stewart on the set of It's a Wonderful Life

"I thought Frank Capra was the cleverest in the business. He was my hero. I literally mean it. I ran everything he made."

—LEO McCAREY

contagious charm, humanity, and heart gradually won over the masses, and it became the first film (and still one of only three) to sweep all "big five" Academy Awards: Best Picture, Best Director, Best Screenplay, Best Actor, and Best Actress. Capra not only made history, he made Gable a megastar, and put Poverty Row outfit Columbia on the map. *It Happened One Night* proved one of the most influential movies of the '30s, popularizing the screwball comedy genre, and spawning a slew of copycats.

As a reward for such unprecedented success, Cohn allowed Capra the honor of his name credited above the title on *Mr. Deeds Goes to Town* (1936), the story of an honest man (Gary Cooper) who inherits millions, but longs for the simplicity of his former life. The comedy-drama reflects an outsider's view of the American Dream, a view held by millions like Capra, whose family had emigrated from Sicily to the US when he was a child. Here, the director began instilling sociological ideas in his films, without losing the humor. *Mr. Deeds* and its follow-up, 1938's *You Can't Take It with You*, resulted in two more Best Director statuettes for Capra, making a grand total of three.

The patriotic *Mr. Smith Goes to Washington* (1939) was an open attack on political corruption; the romantic subplot pairing Capra favorites James Stewart and Jean Arthur took a backseat to the message: a virtuous individual can beat the forces of greed if he tries hard enough. *Film Bulletin* deemed the film "a monument to Democracy," and columnist Hedda Hopper proclaimed, "It makes you think; it makes you prize liberty above everything."

Capra collaborated with the same trusted associates on virtually every film, including screenwriter Robert Riskin and cinematographer Joseph Walker, both of whom were willing to experiment. Capra's methods always went slightly against the grain. As he believed typical Hollywood close-ups of actors (normally taken separately following the master shot) were "absolutely archaic," he filmed with three cameras simultaneously, rather than losing mood and momentum by stopping to shoot an insert. On the big screen, Capra noticed that everything seemed slower than in the cutting room, so he instructed actors to quicken the pace, and the editor to tighten the cuts "to push the audience along," he said.

In the new world of talkies, dialogue was paramount. Riskin, a New York City native with an infallible ear for wisecracks, expertly filled Capra's films with razor-sharp repartee. In *Mr. Deeds*, a newspaper photographer asks, "Say, what's the matter with her?" about the lovesick Babe Bennett (Jean Arthur). "You wouldn't know if I drew you a diagram," snaps Babe's coworker, Mabel (Ruth Donnelly). "Now run along and peddle your little tintypes." On story elements and comedy bits, Riskin worked closely with Capra, who began as a gag writer for Hal Roach's Our Gang shorts.

Soon, the term *Capra-esque* was applied to virtually any film with a happy ending, while his work dripped with such sincerity that naysayers dubbed it "Capra-corn." But Capra delivered so much more than sentimentalism and upbeat finales. The gee-whiz sweetness of his films often belies their acerbic wit, and the dark undercurrents beneath the wholesome optimism. After returning from World

James Stewart in Mr. Smith Goes to Washington

War II, Capra (along with fellow veterans George Stevens and William Wyler) formed the independent Liberty Films to strike out against the system. "The shooting and bombing," of war, Capra recalled, left him "not very happy about the human race." He poured the remnants of his hope, and his newfound cynicism, into *It's a Wonderful Life* (1947), the redemptive tale of an average man (James Stewart) whose life is saved by a guardian angel (Henry Travers) on Christmas Eve. Far from a syrupy celebration, the film is a journey through the depths of despair to reach the light at the end—the life-affirming assistance of friends and family.

Although not the box office smash he envisioned, *It's a Wonderful Life* was the director's personal favorite. "I thought it was the greatest film I ever made," Capra recalled. "Better yet, I thought it was the greatest film anybody ever made. It wasn't made for the oh-so-bored critics or the oh-so-jaded literati. It was my kind of film for my kind of people." For seven decades, all kinds of people have agreed, as the holiday classic has cast its spell over millions.

When Frank Capra died in 1991, the *Los Angeles Times* announced that his passing "rang down the curtain on Hollywood's Golden Age." But Capra's legacy has endured, even descending into subsequent generations of filmmakers. Sylvester Stallone's Oscar-winning underdog tale *Rocky* (1976)—of which Capra was so fond he wrote Stallone a fan letter—along with certain movies by Steven Spielberg, Chris Columbus, and Robert Zemeckis, were deliberately designed to be Capra-esque.

MUST-SEE MOVIES

PLATINUM BLONDE (1931)

LADY FOR A DAY (1933)

IT HAPPENED ONE NIGHT (1934)

MR. DEEDS GOES TO TOWN (1936)

LOST HORIZON (1937)

YOU CAN'T TAKE IT WITH YOU (1938)

MR. SMITH GOES TO WASHINGTON (1939)

IT'S A WONDERFUL LIFE (1947)

STATE OF THE UNION (1948)

KEY SCENE TO WATCH

Near the end of *Mr. Deeds Goes to Town* is a courtroom sequence in which Longfellow Deeds (Gary Cooper) finally breaks his silence and defends himself against trumped-up charges of insanity. With simple homespun common sense, Deeds wins the case, a victory for small-town American values versus big-city corruption—but not before Capra subjects the viewer to a dismal low point, making us certain the hero will be defeated. In this courtroom scene, the words *pixilated* and *doodling* are used. Riskin and Capra concocted these terms that quickly became part of the common vernacular, especially the verb *doodle*, which has been included in every American English dictionary for decades.

VICTOR FLEMING

Years active: 1919–1948

A STUDIO DIRECTOR WITH THE FLEXIBILITY AND flair to tackle any type of film, Victor Fleming is best known today as the man who made *The Wizard of Oz* and *Gone with the Wind*—both released in Golden Age Hollywood's peak year: 1939. A sought-after talent in the industry, a man's man who also had a gift for directing women, Fleming was the hidden wizard behind a wide range of certified classics, from the landmark western *The Virginian* (1929) to the tenderhearted World War II–era romance *A Guy Named Joe* (1943), later remade by Steven Spielberg as *Always* (1989).

As a trained cinematographer, Fleming possessed a knowledge of the movie camera that enabled him to film anything with confidence, from tricky special-effects shots (the Wicked Witch of the West hurling a fireball at the Scarecrow in *The Wizard of Oz*) to sensitive close-ups (Jean Harlow's smoldering glare, her hair billowing in the wind, in *Red Dust*). *Gone with the Wind* producer David O.

Selznick called Fleming "a master of cinematics" because he was technically inventive, and had an unerring eye. After serving an apprenticeship with veteran filmmaker Allan Dwan, Fleming developed a particular way of lighting and framing characters that made them pop off the screen; in this sense, he was an adept star-maker.

With *The Virginian*, the first sound western shot outdoors (in Sonora, California), Fleming molded the strong, silent cowboy image that would follow Gary Cooper through his entire career. He had a way with the ladies too. He not only fell in love with Clara Bow, but he showcased the star at her ebullient best in the silent comedy *Mantrap* (1926), highlighting the sexy-sweet quality that would make her

the iconic "It Girl" in 1927. The handsome director later had relationships with Norma Shearer and Ingrid Bergman, among other actresses. Although they were never romantically involved, Hollywood's hottest platinum blonde, Jean Harlow, placed her faith in Fleming thrice—with *Red Dust* (1932), *Bombshell* (1933), and *Reckless* (1935)—and was rewarded with accolades. The *Los Angeles Times* declared Harlow "brilliant" in the satirical *Bombshell*, and noted "Miss Harlow's increasing skill as an actress."

From Judy Garland to Clark Gable, from Hattie McDaniel to Henry Fonda, performers of all stripes did some of their best work under his intuitive guidance. Fonda always credited Fleming with kick-starting his fame. "I was very fortunate in my director," he said of his screen debut in *The Farmer Takes a Wife* (1935). Fleming made his longtime buddy Gable comfortable enough to

Victor Fleming (seated) shoots a close-up of Jean Harlow in Red Dust *as Clark Gable and Mary Astor look on.*

weep openly in *Test Pilot* (1938), an endearing aviation flick featuring Myrna Loy in her feistiest role since *The Thin Man* (1934), and Spencer Tracy giving a poignant performance as a salt-of-the-earth airplane mechanic. Fleming's strong personal bond with Tracy helped the actor to earn an Oscar for *Captains Courageous* (1937). "He is probably the only guy in the world who really understands me," Fleming once said of Tracy. "We're alike: bursting with emotions we cannot express; depressed all the time because we feel we could have done our work better."

Some have unjustly dismissed Fleming as a middleman who took the reins from the first two directors, Richard Thorpe (who was two weeks into shooting), and George Cukor (only briefly involved) on *The Wizard of Oz*, then was replaced by King Vidor, who helmed most of the Kansas segments. But when Fleming was on a set, he was in charge, lending hands-on devotion to the *Oz* fantasy land—familiar territory for the man behind the beloved

Victor Fleming directs the Munchkin performers and Judy Garland on the set of The Wizard of Oz.

65

VICTOR FLEMING

> *"The Wizard of Oz is a cosmic film and meaningful on many, many different levels, and 'Somewhere Over the Rainbow' is one of the most beautiful songs ever."*
>
> —DAVID LYNCH

1934 version of Robert Louis Stevenson's *Treasure Island*. Fleming's touches are obvious, from the audacious pyrotechnics to the score: he suggested "Follow the Yellow Brick Road" be written, as he felt that Judy Garland's Dorothy needed a big musical send-off from Munchkinland. The *Oz* aesthetics were groundbreaking in their day, leading critic Edwin Schallert to hail the instant classic as "a milestone in fantasy" and "a technical feat." Starting a movie with sepia-toned black-and-white film and then shifting to color had never been done; creating a live-action world of green witches and purple horses was a further challenge, especially since Herbert Kalmus's three-strip Technicolor process was still brand new. Fleming handled the film so well that he vanished beneath the indelible pop culture touchstone *The Wizard of Oz* has become.

After two months of shooting the most anticipated movie of its age, *Gone with the Wind*, Selznick was dissatisfied with the efforts of Cukor, and called in the overworked Fleming to save the day. Sam Wood, William Cameron Menzies, and a couple of other directors worked on the mammoth production—all under the watchful gaze of Selznick—but Fleming's fingerprints are all over the saga. His long history with Gable enriched the star's nuanced portrayal of Rhett Butler, and though Fleming never won over Vivien Leigh (Scarlett O'Hara), who preferred Cukor's direction, Olivia de Havilland credited him with giving her "the key to Melanie's whole character" in just a few simple words of direction. His cinematic expertise served the scenes well, from the field hospital carnage to Scarlett raising her fist against a blazing Georgia sunrise. Fleming garnered a Best Director Academy Award, one of eight Oscars the film won.

Hollywood was shocked when Fleming succumbed to a heart attack upon completing *Joan of Arc* (1948), his forty-fifth feature, one he had planned for years with producer Walter Wanger and star Ingrid Bergman. But his legacy has earned him a posthumous following. Director of the Oscar-winning *The French Connection* (1971) William Friedkin has labeled Fleming "the quintessential film director." Biographer Michael Sragow declared him "not just a great director, but also the real Rhett Butler." Though he had the misfortune to die before movie directors became household names, Victor Fleming is now recognized as classic-era Hollywood's secret weapon.

MUST-SEE MOVIES

THE VIRGINIAN (1929)

RED DUST (1932)

CAPTAINS COURAGEOUS (1937)

THE WIZARD OF OZ (1939)

GONE WITH THE WIND (1939)

DOCTOR JEKYLL AND MR. HYDE (1941)

A GUY NAMED JOE (1943)

Vivien Leigh and Clark Gable in
Gone with the Wind

KEY SCENE TO WATCH

Among *Gone with the Wind*'s many indelible images, Scarlett's search for Dr. Meade (Harry Davenport) stands out. For help with Melanie's childbirth, Scarlett seeks the doctor among thousands of wounded Union and Confederate soldiers just brought in from the battlefield, her horror growing as she witnesses the vast bloodshed of the Atlanta Campaign. Shooting this scene in the way Fleming proposed required the construction of the largest camera crane ever built. Weighing 140 tons, the crane had a reach of 85 feet in every direction and was capable of photographing the 1,500 extras on the 40-acre set. The director knew that a slow zoom out from Vivien Leigh's face to the masses of dead and dying soldiers was the ingredient needed for an epic that would endure through the ages, and for a statement about the cost of war in human suffering.

VICTOR FLEMING

HOWARD HAWKS

Years active: 1926–1970

S CREWBALL COMEDIES. GANGSTER PICTURES. WEST-
erns. Musicals. Historical epics. Film noirs. Science fiction. Howard Win-
chester Hawks could—and did—do it all. During his colossal forty-four-year
run as one of Hollywood's top directors, Hawks demonstrated a breadth

and versatility rarely matched by filmmakers in the Golden Age or today. He also crafted more than a dozen undisputed classics illustrative of the American experience in the twentieth century, from the Great Depression to the Vietnam War era.

Cutting his teeth in silent comedies and closing out his career with the John Wayne western *Rio Lobo* (1970), the movie colony's "Silver Fox" (as Hawks was known, due to his prematurely gray hair) racked up a multifaceted filmography for himself in the decades between, not only crisscrossing into a variety of different genres, but seeming equally at home in all of them. With astonishing agility, Hawks darted from intense dramatic action (*Scarface* [1932]) to his pioneering rapid-fire roman-

tic farces (*Bringing Up Baby* [1938]) to films that combined a little of both, such as the slyly witty noir *To Have and Have Not* (1944), the legendary first pairing of Humphrey Bogart and Lauren Bacall.

Nineteen-year-old Betty Bacall was discovered, renamed, and cast in her inaugural acting part by Hawks and his second wife, Nancy "Slim" Keith (whose nickname was given to Bacall's character). As boat captain Harry and singer "Slim" in *To Have and Have Not*, Bogey and Bacall's sparky rapport illustrates a playful battle-of-the-sexes theme that was woven into many of Hawks's films: an observation of male-female dynamics that calls into question the roles each plays. Just watch the way Slim and Harry take turns one-upping each other

THE STUDIO AS AUTEUR

by lighting the other's cigarette at key moments in their flirtatious yet combative conversations, and the way she—the woman—makes the first move in their blossoming romance. "It's even better when you help," Slim coolly informs him after deciding to plant a kiss.

Harry's fraternal relationship with his first mate, Eddie (Walter Brennan), typifies the male "buddy" motif that appears in most Hawks movies. "What do you take care of him for?" a fisherman asks Harry when he sees that Eddie is a hopeless drunk, to which Harry replies with a smirk, "He thinks he's taking care of *me*." Though their

Carole Lombard and Howard Hawks on the set of Twentieth Century

> ## "One of the things I'll do, if it's appropriate in a movie, is I'll just get the actors together and I show them *His Girl Friday.* Just to show them, not that we have to talk that fast in a movie, but you *can* talk that fast."
>
> —QUENTIN TARANTINO

friendship can be antagonistic, these two drifters are bound together because, as Hawks explained simply, "Those are the relationships that happen between men."

Although he created movies with popular mass appeal, in his own subtle way, Howard Hawks was an iconoclast. In 1951, he founded an independent production company to bring one of the first science fiction–horror hybrids to the screen, *The Thing from Another World*. By the time he made his first color western, the now-iconic *Rio Bravo* (1959), Hawks was producing all of his own directorial efforts as well. A masterpiece of the Old West genre, *Rio Bravo* explores the way in which four disparate men interact with one another, philosophically, morally, and emotionally. Years after the success of *Rio Bravo*, remarkably similar story elements appeared in 1966's *El Dorado*, and yet again in *Rio Lobo*. While Hawks refused to acknowledge any of his films as remakes, he did confess to recycling certain scenes, snatches of dialogue, and plot points, admitting, "I steal from myself all the time."

As a craftsman, Hawks tended to avoid making his presence known with self-conscious camera angles or showy tracking shots. Instead, he kept his camera on the static side, favoring conventional, eye-level medium shots, to give the characters room to breathe and the story a chance to unfold. According to biographer Gerald Mast, like the airplanes and car engines that fascinated him, "Hawks's stories might be seen as complicated webs of causality in which each of the parts functions efficiently and effortlessly in producing the whole." Primarily interested in telling great stories, Hawks labored behind the scenes to present movies that seemed to run on their own like well-oiled machines. Plainly put, he perfected a craftsmanship so polished it reached the level of art.

Although he never forced an obvious style upon his films, there are nevertheless a few unmistakable Hawks trademarks that crop up in his work: the crowding of characters into a single frame, as seen when Sheriff Hartwell (Gene Lockhart) accuses Walter (Cary Grant) and Hildy (Rosalind Russell) of hiding an escaped convict in the newsroom in the delightfully frenetic *His Girl Friday* (1940); his appreciation of teamwork, as in the casual camaraderie the Barranca Airways pilots display in the touching

THE STUDIO AS AUTEUR

MUST-SEE MOVIES

SCARFACE (1932)

BRINGING UP BABY (1938)

HIS GIRL FRIDAY (1940)

SERGEANT YORK (1941)

TO HAVE AND HAVE NOT (1944)

THE BIG SLEEP (1946)

RED RIVER (1948)

GENTLEMEN PREFER BLONDES (1953)

RIO BRAVO (1959)

Rosalind Russell as reporter Hildy Johnson, surrounded by her coworkers in His Girl Friday

KEY SCENE TO WATCH

Perhaps the most famous scene in *His Girl Friday* takes place in the office of newspaper editor Walter Burns, when he and his ex-wife, Hildy, spend nine hilarious minutes reuniting, squabbling, and swapping comic insults with the speed of auctioneers on caffeine. Hawks was determined to break the record for fastest movie dialogue here, instructing Cary Grant and Rosalind Russell to speak at a dizzying rate of 240 words per minute (as opposed to the average rate of 100 to 150). But Hawks doesn't haphazardly rush through the lengthy scene; he has Hildy and Walter slowly build to a fever pitch with an almost musical rhythm, gradually picking up speed (and volume) as their annoyance with each other grows.

Only Angels Have Wings (1939); and the snappy, often overlapping dialogue that was later hailed as novel when appropriated by successors Robert Altman and Woody Allen. Hawks would routinely encourage his actors to speak quickly and "step on" each other's words, as people tend to do in life. (The director's keen ear for dialogue and the importance he placed on writing is apparent in his frequent collaborations with Ernest Hemingway and William Faulkner.) Hawks also favored a brand of female

character that has come to be known in academic discourse as the "Hawksian woman," a tough, sexy dame who can match any man wisecrack for wisecrack. Barbara Stanwyck's slang-slinging showgirl Sugarpuss O'Shea in the jazz-infused comedy *Ball of Fire* (1941) and Jane Russell's sassy Dorothy Shaw in the female-buddy musical *Gentlemen Prefer Blondes* (1953) exemplify the type.

Hawks's one and only Academy Award nomination came in 1941 for *Sergeant York*, but the director would not take home a statuette until he was presented with an honorary award in 1975 for being "a giant of the American cinema." Because he made directing look so easy, Hawks was often overlooked as a creative force in the medium until he had already retired.

Shortly before his death in 1977, Hawks was asked whether he thought modern directors "think about [their work] too much." His caustic reply was: "I don't credit them with thinking," just the kind of barbed, Depression-era retort that might have rolled off the tongues of one of his characters; the egomaniacal Oscar (John Barrymore) in *Twentieth Century* (1934), perhaps. An unfiltered original, Hawks may or may not have been flattered by the latter-day emulators—including Peter Bogdanovich, John Carpenter, Brian De Palma, Quentin Tarantino, and Michael Mann—who have taken inspiration from his films.

Howard Hawks directs Barbara Stanwyck in Ball of Fire.

MERVYN LeROY

Years active: 1927–1968

U PON MERVYN LeROY'S DEATH IN 1987, CRITIC Charles Champlin identified the common thread found in all of the director/producer's films: "They were meant to move audiences strongly—to tears, laughter, pride, fear, satisfaction. And most of them did." A moviemaker with the Midas touch, LeRoy had an uncanny knack for delivering popular entertainment to the masses, always done with a hefty dose of heart.

In studio-era Hollywood, a director was required to handle all types of pictures, and LeRoy had the fluency to master opulent musicals (*Million Dollar Mermaid* [1952]), historical dramas (*Anthony Adverse* [1936]), raucous comedies (*Tugboat Annie* [1933]), and even horror (*The Bad Seed* [1956]). During the 1930s, he made headlines for his ability to turn out hit movies like hotcakes. In 1932, *Photoplay* magazine dubbed him (at age thirty-two) the "youngest director of hits." *Screenland* crowned him "Master of the Hit Formula" and "The King of

the Lot." Although he was producer Jesse Lasky's cousin, nepotism didn't make LeRoy; he started as a costume assistant at Paramount, then transitioned to gag writer at Warner Bros., where he worked his way up to director.

LeRoy first built his reputation by launching the career of Edward G. Robinson with a potent one-two punch: the 1931 gangster classic *Little Caesar* and the tabloid journalism exposé *Five-Star Final* (also from 1931). Another iconic Warner Bros. star, Paul Muni, was launched with *I Am a Fugitive from a Chain Gang* (1932), a memorable drama that pulled no punches in depicting the indignities southern labor camps inflicted on an innocent convict (Muni). The hard-hitting, fact-based social

commentary of *Chain Gang* ended up inspiring prison reforms, though LeRoy denied any attempts at sending a message, saying, "I made it because it was a great story." For him, that was always the best (and often the only) reason necessary.

Like his contemporary, Frank Capra, LeRoy's secret weapons were crisp dialogue and applause-inducing endings. By poking fun at the Great Depression, *Gold Diggers of 1933* (1933) had the public rollicking with laughter, singing along to "We're in the Money," and wiping away a tear at the end. Directorial credit for the song-and-dance spectacles goes to innovative choreographer/director Busby Berkeley, but LeRoy packed the non-musical portions of the film with enough ribald wit to keep audiences charmed all the way through. "Maybe it's the piano remover," broke showgirl Carol (Joan

Natalie Wood, Gypsy Rose Lee, and Mervyn LeRoy on the set of Gypsy

74

Blondell) suggests when she hears a knock at the door. Preparing to audition for a Broadway producer, Fay (Ginger Rogers) muses, "If Barney could see me in clothes . . ." as Trixie (Aline MacMahon) interjects, "he wouldn't recognize you." The vitality and urgency in LeRoy's films helped to define the fast-paced Warner Bros. style of the '30s. "Tempo and speech," he believed, were the most important elements. "Let a scene drag for so much as a fraction of a moment, and you have a failure, a ghastly flop," he noted. "The action, the dialogue—they must *live*!"

Aside from employing the wipes and quick dissolves Warners was known for, LeRoy (who once described his own style as "workmanlike") relied on the filmmaking basics. "Camera angles, subtleties, little tricks of treatment are without importance to him," journalist Margaret Reid once opined. "He takes a story and hurls it, incident by incident, at the spectator." (See the first fifteen minutes of *Three on a Match* [1932] for an example.) His special gifts

Ruby Keeler, Mervyn LeRoy, and Dick Powell consult the script for Gold Diggers of 1933.

> ## "Like most of my generation, I was raised on Mervyn LeRoy's films. . . . Whatever the current style in personal cinema, you'll seek it in vain in his pictures. He makes movies about people you root for—that's all. And that's why audiences have adored his pictures throughout the world."
> —WILLIAM FRIEDKIN

were his storytelling sense and his keen eye for discovering new talent. LeRoy is credited with seeing the star potential in Clark Gable, Ginger Rogers, Loretta Young, Boris Karloff, Jane Wyman, and Robert Mitchum before anyone else, and giving them their big breaks. He also cast unknown high-schooler Lana Turner in her first movie role, as a fifteen-year-old victim of rape and murder in the powerful *They Won't Forget* (1937).

LeRoy left Warners in 1938 to succeed the late Irving Thalberg as MGM's head of production. As a producer, he quickly added more crowd-pleasers to his résumé—including a little thing called *The Wizard of Oz* (1939), which he prompted the studio to make, having been a fan of L. Frank Baum's Oz books since childhood. Wearing his director hat, he continued to turn out winners. *Thirty Seconds Over Tokyo* (1944) detailed the US bombing of Japan in 1942; and a touching trio of tearjerkers starred Greer Garson: Best Picture nominees *Blossoms in the Dust* (1941) and *Random Harvest* (1942), followed by the biographical *Madame Curie* (1943).

His flair for female-driven dramas resumed later in his career with the pensive *Home Before Dark* (1958), featuring Jean Simmons as a woman teetering on the brink of insanity. The film's introspective mood indicated that LeRoy's once-quick pace had matured, making for thought-provoking cinema. More typical for the director was *Gypsy* (1962), a splashy screen adaptation of the Broadway musical about stripper Gypsy Rose Lee. Natalie Wood's vivacious striptease numbers and the flashy "You Gotta Get a Gimmick" number recalled LeRoy's Hollywood heyday of unrelenting glitz, making *Gypsy* one of the biggest hits of 1962.

When tastes changed, and the feel-good idealism of the Golden Age gave way to the raw cynicism of the late 1960s and '70s, Mervyn LeRoy retired, confident that he had given the public enough laughter and tears to last a lifetime. For the hundred-plus classic movies he directed and produced, and his thirty-five years as one of the industry's top talents, LeRoy was honored with the Irving G. Thalberg Memorial Award in 1976.

THE STUDIO AS AUTEUR

Paul Muni in I Am a Fugitive from a Chain Gang

KEY SCENE TO WATCH

The haunting ending of *I Am a Fugitive from a Chain Gang* left 1932 audiences shaken, and still has the power to unnerve. After a brief reunion with his girlfriend, Helen (Helen Vinson), James (Paul Muni) must continue to run for his life. When he refuses her offer of money, Helen asks, "How do you live?" The unkempt James backs into the shadows, enveloped in complete darkness. Only his hoarse whisper is heard: "I steal." The law has made James into a criminal, doomed to eke out an existence lurking in perpetual night. Accounts vary as to whether LeRoy, head of production Darryl Zanuck, or screenwriters Howard J. Green and Brown Holmes were behind this memorable final shot, but LeRoy revealed in 1973 that Robert Burns himself assisted with the script. An actual fugitive who had written the autobiographical source story, Burns was smuggled into the Warner Bros. offices and kept hidden for two weeks while he supervised the adaptation.

ERNST LUBITSCH

Years active: 1914–1948

WHAT WAS THE FAMOUS YET ELUSIVE INGREDIent known as "the Lubitsch touch"? It was a certain effervescent sparkle that the legendary Ernst Lubitsch infused into his films; the tone was witty, mischievous, and sophisticated all at once—think

of Herbert Marshall's suave pickpocket returning the garter he swiped from Miriam Hopkins's leg in *Trouble in Paradise* (1932), or Don Ameche spontaneously sweeping Gene Tierney off her feet and whisking her across the room in *Heaven Can Wait* (1943). Lubitsch had a profound influence on the art of motion pictures, steering the medium away from the obvious and toward the elegant.

The German-born filmmaker's style was fine-tuned in Berlin, where he pioneered the use of minor gestures to encapsulate characters, and devising props as symbols rather than merely décor. Lubitsch cleared away the background clutter, making his sets clean stages for the action to take place. This way, every object held a meaning: in *The*

Marriage Circle (1924), when Charlotte (Florence Vidor) hands a suitor (Monte Blue) his hat, it's a way of wordlessly telling him to leave—she's not interested. In Lubitsch's 1925 screen version of Oscar Wilde's *Lady Windermere's Fan*, he replaced Wilde's verbal quips for what he termed "visual epigrams," such as the shot of dowagers at a racetrack consulting their race cards in unison, a comment on the conformity inherent in high society.

America's Sweetheart herself, Mary Pickford, had brought Lubitsch to America to direct her in *Rosita* (1923), a comedy about a Spanish street singer who charms a king. The turn-of-the-century-set bonbon *The Student Prince in Old Heidelberg* (1927) was a sheer delight, brimming with "brilliant bits

of satire and impressive composition," as the *New York Times* observed. Instead of traditional gags, the humor in *The Student Prince* was embedded in lifelike situations and character reactions, setting it miles ahead of the slapstick-based comedies Hollywood had specialized in since the days of Mack Sennett's Keystone Cops.

His silent films always had a musical quality, so it was unsurprising that Lubitsch leaped at the chance to make an actual musical as soon as technology allowed it. *The Love Parade* (1929) brought together Maurice Chevalier and newcomer Jea-

nette MacDonald for a melodic masterpiece that ushered in a new romanticized style of ordinary people bursting into song, without relying on Broadway backdrops as an excuse.

Lubitsch took to talkies naturally, even hitting his creative stride in the 1930s. The economy of images that defined his pantomime pictures was more effective with sound, as visuals could be wedded to music and sound effects. In the shimmering

Ernst Lubitsch, Gary Cooper, Miriam Hopkins, and Fredric March on the set of Design for Living, *1933*

> *"Trouble in Paradise*—a great Lubitsch movie. I don't know if anybody can make a movie like that anymore—that perfect tone, like a soufflé-type of movie. A confection, I guess."

—WES ANDERSON

Trouble in Paradise, gentrified burglar Gaston (Herbert Marshall) falls for Mariette (Kay Francis), the wealthy widow he's planning to rob, and the two enter his bedroom and shut the door. With the aid of set designer Hans Dreier (and composer W. Franke Harling), Lubitsch focuses on an art deco clock in the hallway, leading the audience to imagine what may be going on behind closed doors. This sense of sly suggestion made *Trouble in Paradise* "the most polished comedy of manners in American movies," according to Lubitsch biographer Scott Eyman, as well as the premiere precursor to the screwball comedy. Like many Lubitsch films, it failed to earn a profit, but it was worth its weight in prestige.

Although the free expression of his sexual innuendo was hampered by strict enforcement of the Production Code in 1934 (he managed to squeeze in the piquant *Design for Living* [1933] just in time), Lubitsch rose to the occasion with increased subtlety and maturity. He delivered a dynamic duo in 1939 and 1940, with *Ninotchka* and *The Shop Around*

MUST-SEE MOVIES

THE STUDENT PRINCE IN OLD HEIDELBERG (1927)

THE LOVE PARADE (1929)

TROUBLE IN PARADISE (1932)

THE MERRY WIDOW (1934)

NINOTCHKA (1939)

THE SHOP AROUND THE CORNER (1940)

TO BE OR NOT TO BE (1942)

HEAVEN CAN WAIT (1943)

KEY SCENE TO WATCH

Lubitsch's renowned touch is on full display in one simple sequence of *The Student Prince in Old Heidelberg*, when Prince Karl Heinrich (Ramon Novarro) makes amorous advances toward Kathi (Norma Shearer), the barmaid who has won his heart. From behind a row of stone columns, the camera follows Karl as he whimsically chases Kathi through a garden, trying to kiss her. With each column, he gets a little closer, until the camera stops, and only a dachshund wanders through the shot. The audience is left to assume that Karl has received his kiss, off-camera. Though *The Student Prince* was Lubitsch's final silent effort before the talkie revolution, he would continue to use such restrained visual devices in his sound films as well.

the Corner, respectively. Coscripted by budding comic genius Billy Wilder, *Ninotchka* was a smart, ethereal slice of elegance that served the dual purpose of poking fun at Communist Russia and unveiling Greta Garbo's giggle. After fifteen years of drama, Garbo reveled in her first comedy—she laughs, she drinks too much Champagne, she even lampoons her famous line "I want to be alone." It was a worldwide success (except in Russia), but Lubitsch deemed *The Shop Around the Corner* "the best picture I ever made in my life," because he felt its characterizations rang the truest. As two rival coworkers who unwittingly fall in love via anonymous letters, James Stewart and Margaret Sullavan unleash a full spectrum of emotions to enact the deft dialogue of screenwriter Samson Raphaelson at his best. In 1998, Nora Ephron remade the comedy as *You've Got Mail*, costarring Tom Hanks and Meg Ryan.

The director always scoffed at the notion of "the Lubitsch touch," revealing to a reporter in 1935 that making a movie entailed "so much pain and so much hardship" that there was hardly a magic formula. His ability to make it seem effortless is what set Lubitsch apart, inciting generations of imitators. Rather than shifting to match the Hollywood trends, "he converted the Hollywood industry to his own way of expression," in the words of French filmmaker Jean Renoir, one of Lubitsch's many admirers. Frank Capra, Orson Welles, William Wyler, Peter Bogdanovich, Cameron Crowe, and Wes Anderson have also cited

him as an inspiration. Protégée Billy Wilder kept a sign over his desk for years that read: HOW WOULD LUBITSCH DO IT?

For his countless contributions to the craft, Lubitsch received an honorary Oscar in 1946, just before his untimely death at age fifty-five. Before Mervyn LeRoy handed him the award, he extolled the virtues of "the master of innuendo": "He had an adult mind and a hatred of saying things the obvious way. Because of these qualities and a God-given genius, he advanced the technique of screen comedy as no one else has ever done."

Greta Garbo and Melvyn Douglas in Ninotchka

ROUBEN MAMOULIAN

Years active: 1926–1959

WHEN TALKING PICTURES ARRIVED, EVERYTHING changed. The magical interplay between light and shadows, the image-driven storytelling, the free camera movement of silent cinema threatened to go extinct, as the noisy movie camera was now enclosed in an unwieldy soundproof box. Among a few other innovators, visual and audio wizard Rouben Mamoulian helped to resurrect the art of silent film in the early sound era. Under his command, the camera once again became an active participant in the telling of a story, making him one of the most in-demand directors during Hollywood's pre-Code years (1930–1934).

For his incredible debut film, *Applause* (1929), Mamoulian drew on his experience directing stage plays in London and New York to tell the seedy yet heartrending tale of an aging burlesque queen (Helen Morgan) and her daughter (Joan Peers). The director's inventive angles—including a pre–Busby Berkeley overhead shot of chorus girls—demonstrate his conviction "that the camera should not be treated as a witness of things happening, but that it should be the main actor in a picture." Vibrant tracking shots of authentic Manhattan locations (the Brooklyn Bridge, Grand Central Station) make *Applause* look arrestingly modern compared to other talkies from 1929.

Mamoulian's use of sound was revolutionary. For one scene in *Applause*, the director insisted on hearing two sounds simultaneously: a mother's lullaby and her daughter's whispered prayer. "It can't be done," he was told by the sound technician. "Why not use two mics and two channels and combine the two tracks in printing?" Mamoulian asked. This audio layering not only worked beautifully,

but soon became standard practice in the industry.

Paramount practically gave Mamoulian carte blanche with *Dr. Jekyll and Mr. Hyde* (1931), allowing him to have thirty-five historically accurate Victorian sets constructed. The result was a truly chilling pre-Code hair-raiser that meshed Gothic atmosphere, ingenious effects, and openly sinful sex appeal in the character of dance-hall damsel Ivy (Miriam Hopkins). Mamoulian's shadows-and-fog lighting scheme and nightmarish imagery (aided by some subjective point-of-view shots in which we

are the tortured hero) rival the artistry of Universal's monster maestros, Tod Browning and James Whale. Fredric March's Jekyll even transforms into Hyde right before our eyes, with no editing (cinematographer Karl Struss used colored filters that revealed hidden layers of makeup on March). In the soundtrack that accompanies this scene, Mamoulian recorded his own heartbeat and overdubbed it

Rouben Mamoulian, Helen Morgan (seated on stage), and supporting cast in Applause

"There's a great Maurice Chevalier movie called *Love Me Tonight*, directed by Rouben Mamoulian. . . . I liked being able to go back to the style in which those things were shot. It isn't hyperkinetic in terms of editing: There is more of a sense of holding things for longer, and that thing that early musicals did, which was make you feel the performance because you're not depending on cuts."

—BILL CONDON ON HIS INSPIRATION
FOR *BEAUTY AND THE BEAST* (2017)

with the sound of a gong played backward. Struss earned an Oscar nomination for his work, and March took home a statuette for Best Actor.

The enchanting *Love Me Tonight* (1932) might be screendom's closest facsimile of "the Lubitsch touch" that didn't involve Lubitsch; it has the Mamoulian touch instead. He crafted the Maurice Chevalier–Jeanette MacDonald musical with whimsy and liberal doses of risqué humor. When Gilbert (Charles Ruggles) asks the boy-crazy Valentine (Myrna Loy), "Can you go for a doctor?" she replies, "Certainly, bring him right in!" Victor Milner's mobile camera work made every scene dance on air. Mamoulian recorded the soundtrack in its entirety before shooting began—the better to synchronize lively action with music, like the melodic Rodgers and Hart hit "Isn't It Romantic?" The public was thoroughly romanced, and critics favorably compared *Love Me Tonight* to René Clair's seminal *Under the Roofs of Paris*

(1930). *The New Movie* judged the film "a model for perfect pictures."

The smashing success of *Love Me Tonight* earned Mamoulian the plum assignment of directing Greta Garbo, the top star at MGM (and possibly the whole world) at the time. Based on the life of a real seventeenth-century Swedish monarch, *Queen Christina* (1933) was a standout role for the actress. The filmmakers faced contention with the Hays Office over the erotic bedroom scene, in which Christina caresses pieces of furniture as though they were alive. Today, the sequence is considered a masterpiece of visual sensuality. *Queen Christina*'s celebrated finale gave Garbo perhaps the most iconic shot in her legendary career. The invention of a new camera lens was required for the stunning tracking shot that zooms in, without interruption, from a wide shot to a close-up of Christina on the prow of a ship, her facial expression inscrutable. "I want your face to

MUST-SEE MOVIES

APPLAUSE (1929)

CITY STREETS (1931)

DR. JEKYLL AND MR. HYDE (1932)

LOVE ME TONIGHT (1932)

QUEEN CHRISTINA (1933)

BECKY SHARP (1935)

GOLDEN BOY (1939)

THE MARK OF ZORRO (1940)

A film frame featuring Miriam Hopkins in the first full-color feature, Becky Sharp

KEY SCENE TO WATCH

A half-hour into *Becky Sharp*, Becky (Miriam Hopkins) and Rawdon (Alan Mowbray) attend a grand society ball near Waterloo, Belgium, in 1815, unaware that Napoleon's army is planning an attack. Mamoulian depicts Napoleon as an ominous silhouette approaching on horseback, then slowly dissolves to an overhead view of formally dressed couples waltzing in circles across a ballroom floor. Every detail was carefully planned by the director to elicit an emotional reaction. "Color," he said, "is symbolic. It is not an accident that traffic stop lights are red, go lights are green. Red means danger, green safety and hope." To hint at impending disaster, Mamoulian started the scene on dancers wearing cool colors, and finished with couples attired in golds and flaming reds.

ROUBEN MAMOULIAN

be a blank sheet of paper," the director told Garbo. "I want the writing to be done by every member of the audience."

As his output was superior, his technical skills beyond reproach, Mamoulian was entrusted with the first full-length, full-color film: *Becky Sharp* (1935). For playing the wily heroine of William Makepeace Thackeray's *Vanity Fair*, Miriam Hopkins received her only Oscar nomination; for his savvy use of Technicolor, Mamoulian was awarded at the Venice Film Festival, though critical reception of *Becky Sharp* was mixed. *High, Wide and Handsome* (1937) was an epic hybrid, a western–musical–period piece pastiche, which Mamoulian described as "a very difficult story to film." The result was sprawling and inconsistent, a costly failure at the box office.

Although he continued to direct on Broadway, Mamoulian and Hollywood grew apart. Like many uncompromising artistic visionaries, he developed a reputation as one of those troublesome non-conformists who struck fear into the hearts of studio moguls. He was replaced by Otto Preminger twice, first on *Laura* in 1944, and again in 1958, when Mamoulian planned to direct the screen version of his 1935 stage success, *Porgy and Bess*.

Rouben Mamoulian retired early from the Hollywood hustle, with only sixteen features to his credit, all of them exceptionally well made. His latter-day contributions include two effective Tyrone Power vehicles for Twentieth Century-Fox, and MGM's *Silk Stockings* (1957), a lilting, song-filled spin on 1939's *Ninotchka*, with Cyd Charisse and Fred Astaire.

Fredric March in his Oscar-winning role as Dr. Jekyll and Mr. Hyde

LEO McCAREY

Years active: 1921–1962

ALTHOUGH HIS NAME MAY BE LESS FAMILIAR TO twenty-first-century ears than Frank Capra or Howard Hawks, Leo McCarey was an esteemed director/producer in the 1930s—he even commanded a name-above-the-title credit like Capra, a filmmaker he idolized. Humor was his stock-in-trade, but his brand of funny often featured poignant undertones. Whether generating laughter (*The Awful Truth* [1937]) or tears (*Make Way for Tomorrow* [1937]), McCarey's movies are informed by a deep understanding of human nature, in all its hilarity and its heartache.

He broke into movies in the days of silent slapstick, after an unfulfilling attempt at practicing law. While working for Hal Roach's studio, McCarey had the brilliant idea to team Stan Laurel with Oliver Hardy, and his guidance helped to define their signature humor: the gags were subtler, the reactions slower than the hyperactivity of other screen comics. McCarey worked with the comedy greats, from W. C. Fields to Mae West, and directed what many consider the Marx Brothers' masterpiece, *Duck Soup* (1933).

McCarey mastered one of the most difficult movie maneuvers: the tonal shift from comedy to drama. In *Ruggles of Red Gap* (1935), Charles Laughton plays a refined British manservant who clashes with the rough-hewn American West, a broadly comic setup that tapers into pointed satire and social commentary. McCarey's immortal *Love Affair* (1939) is a fairy tale of star-crossed lovers: a continental playboy (Charles Boyer) and a spoken-for singer (Irene Dunne) who meet aboard a cruise ship. Again, there is a change in tone: *Love Affair* starts as bubbly romantic comedy, then

THE STUDIO AS AUTEUR

swerves into deep sincerity, then takes a dramatic—even tragic—turn. In the end, the sunny romantic elements shine through once again.

In his seminal screwball gem *The Awful Truth*, McCarey induced Irene Dunne to unleash her inner wackiness as Lucy, a woman who resorts to a ludicrous (but hilarious) false identity to win back her soon-to-be-ex-husband, played by Cary Grant.

The dashing Grant had never sunk his teeth into full-blown comedy, but the seasoned comic mind of McCarey encouraged both stars to loosen up and improvise. During shooting, though, Grant had such doubts about his ability to be funny that he

Leo McCarey, Chico Marx, and Groucho Marx on the set of Duck Soup

THE STUDIO AS AUTEUR

"Leo McCarey is not only a great director, but in my opinion, the greatest comic mind now living."

—CHARLES LAUGHTON

offered Columbia Pictures $5,000 to buy his way out of the movie. Fortunately, he remained, and *The Awful Truth* established the casual wit that made Grant an icon for the ages.

When McCarey won an Academy Award for directing *The Awful Truth*, he felt the wrong movie had been honored, as he believed *Make Way for Tomorrow* to be the superior effort. The topic of old age is typically avoided in cinema, even today, so this touching story of a seventy-something couple (Victor Moore and Beulah Bondi, both aged several years through the magic of makeup) whose grown children are unable to house them, was a rarity. It was virtually ignored by the public. The critics, how-ever, praised its "humanity, honesty, and warmth," and McCarey's "brilliant direction," to quote Frank S. Nugent of the *New York Times*, who placed *Make Way for Tomorrow* in the top ten movies of 1937.

McCarey was injured in a car crash in 1939, but the recovery afforded him time to write and produce another Grant-Dunne comedy, *My Favor-ite Wife* (1940), directed by Garson Kanin. The story is delicately interwoven with wistful moments, such as the scene when long-lost shipwreck victim Dunne reunites with her children, who don't rec-ognize her; it's also packed with outrageous laughs,

such as when the smartly dressed Dunne falls into a pool, and when Grant tries on a lady's hat and frilly dress. Director Peter Bogdanovich remembered the veteran filmmaker as "one of the wittiest men in the picture business. There was a delightfully wry way he had of looking at things."

A devout Catholic, McCarey noticed a lack of movies about priests and nuns, and remedied this by conceiving, producing, and directing *Going My*

Irene Dunne and Cary Grant in The Awful Truth

Way (1944) and its sequel, *The Bells of St. Mary's* (1945). Although he was warned that religious pictures never make money, McCarey followed his instincts—and wound up with the two most lucrative and Oscar-winning films of his career. Featuring Bing Crosby in a defining role as Father O'Malley and Ingrid Bergman as Sister Benedict, these sentimental dramas remain appealing and lighthearted as only Leo McCarey could make them. "I like my characters to walk in clouds, I like a little bit of the fairy tale," he admitted. "As long as I'm there behind the camera lens, I'll let somebody else photograph the ugliness of the world."

Leo McCarey directs Ingrid Bergman and Bing Crosby in The Bells of St. Mary's.

From aging to religion, McCarey had a gift for making difficult subjects entertaining.

An Affair to Remember was McCarey's 1957 update of his 1939 romance, this time boasting DeLuxe color, CinemaScope, and two marquee favorites: Cary Grant and Deborah Kerr. Though the remake was popular, the director later confided that he preferred the first version, and many agreed with him. "A lot of people said it was the best love story they ever saw on the screen," he said in 1969, near the end of his life, "and it's also my favorite love story." Warren Beatty produced and starred in (with his wife, Annette Bening) yet another remake of *Love Affair* in 1994, and it served as writer/director Nora Ephron's inspiration for the nouveau classic *Sleepless in Seattle* (1993).

MUST-SEE MOVIES

DUCK SOUP (1933)

RUGGLES OF RED GAP (1933)

MAKE WAY FOR TOMORROW (1937)

THE AWFUL TRUTH (1937)

LOVE AFFAIR (1939)

MY FAVORITE WIFE (1940)

GOING MY WAY (1944)

AN AFFAIR TO REMEMBER (1957)

KEY SCENE TO WATCH

For a taste of the McCarey charm, see the scene in *Love Affair* between Terry (Irene Dunne) and Michel (Charles Boyer) as they share an intimate talk on the ship's deck during the last night of their voyage. The dialogue is lyrical but real, and undercut with humor. "My father used to say, 'Wishes are the dreams we dream when we're awake,'" Terry tells Michel, adding with a chuckle, "He drank a lot." McCarey specialized in scenes like this that were a little bit funny, a trifle melancholy, and warm without being sugary. These elements converge to make *Love Affair* perhaps the classic screen's definitive shipboard romance.

Irene Dunne and Charles Boyer in Love Affair

W. S. VAN DYKE

Years active: 1917–1942

VERSATILE MGM DIRECTOR W. S. "WOODY" VAN DYKE was a marvel of efficiency, a reliable studio journeyman who managed to inject streaks of creative brilliance into his rapidly shot movies. Although he made over eighty films in twenty-five years, he is perhaps best remem-

bered for *The Thin Man* (1934), an undisputed cinema treasure.

Like many an aspiring filmmaker in the silent era, former child actor Woodbridge Strong Van Dyke II began by assisting D. W. Griffith on his mammoth production of *Intolerance* (1916). From there, he wrangled a herd of quick-and-dirty B-westerns, and when he ascended to A-list status at MGM, continued to work just as quickly, earning him the nickname "One-Take Woody." He never fussed over the design of his sets, never hovered over the editors, and didn't believe in rehearsals. On a W. S. Van Dyke set, a script supervisor once revealed, the first take "*is* the rehearsal." And if there were no technical hiccups, there was no second take.

Typically, in his movies—whether comedy (*Love on the Run* [1936]), drama (*Manhattan Melodrama* [1934]), or adventure (*The Pagan* [1929])—people move; no sitting still for emotional monologues or glacially paced conversations. He favored wide shots filled with activity, intercut with close-ups. Typical is a sequence in the frantic *Love on the Run*, in which Mike (Clark Gable) locks his rival, Barney (Franchot Tone), in the back of a truck, then enjoys a romantic stroll with Sally (Joan Crawford), replete with full-frame shots of the stars' faces. In Hollywood's Golden Age, Van Dyke's name became associated with "fast action, snappy dialogue, clean-cut, unfancy filmmaking," observed critic Richard Schickel. While adhering to a strict schedule, he kept

the atmosphere of his sets loose and jovial, even playing pranks on the cast and crew.

The trusted Van Dyke often inherited assignments that others had abandoned. In 1935, he replaced Robert Z. Leonard after one day of filming on *Naughty Marietta*, the first screen pairing of soprano Jeanette MacDonald and baritone Nelson Eddy. Van Dyke had no say in his material. "I never have the slightest inkling of what my next picture will be until the studio calls me in and hands it over," he said in 1936. And he would travel wherever he was sent. *Trader Horn* (1931) was the first sound feature film ever shot in Africa: a challenging experience that resulted in the death of two crew members and a career-ruining bout of malaria

Left to Right: *Producer Hunt Stromberg, Norma Shearer, and Woody Van Dyke filming* Marie Antoinette

for lead actress Edwina Booth. So, it was back to MGM's Culver City soundstages for *Tarzan the Ape Man* (1932), the now-iconic introduction of Olympic swimming champ Johnny Weissmuller as Tarzan and newcomer Maureen O'Sullivan as Jane. Leftover African footage from *Trader Horn* came in handy to flesh out the scenery.

Woody Van Dyke made only one suggestion to the studio in his entire career—but what a suggestion it was. In 1934, he asked MGM to adapt Dashiell Hammett's lighthearted mystery novel *The Thin Man*, and insisted on casting William Powell and Myrna Loy in the leads. Van Dyke's alacrity worked ideally for *The Thin Man*, which was shot in roughly two weeks. In the hands of a more fastidious filmmaker, the levity might have been suffocated, but he captured a breezy spontaneity between married sleuths Nick (Powell) and Nora Charles (Loy) that remains fresh nearly ninety years later. The often-inebriated Nick calls Nora "Shugah," while she insists on matching him martini for martini as they swap endearing insults. The Charleses made marriage fun, exciting, and just a little naughty.

In addition to making Myrna Loy a major star, *The Thin Man* scored a hefty profit, and snared four Academy Award nominations (including Best

Johnny Weissmuller as Tarzan and Maureen O'Sullivan as Jane in Tarzan the Ape Man

MUST-SEE MOVIES

TRADER HORN (1931)

TARZAN THE APE MAN (1932)

MANHATTAN MELODRAMA (1934)

THE THIN MAN (1934)

NAUGHTY MARIETTA (1935)

SAN FRANCISCO (1936)

AFTER THE THIN MAN (1936)

MARIE ANTOINETTE (1938)

JOURNEY FOR MARGARET (1942)

KEY SCENE TO WATCH

For a glimpse of One-Take Woody's casual comic flair, check out the brief scene in *The Thin Man* when Nick introduces Herbert MacCaulay (Porter Hall) to Nora. When Nick playfully pokes at a hung-over Nora, she retaliates by smacking her husband in the back of the head, to which he responds by jokingly threatening to elbow her in the face. "Oh, excuse us," Nick says when MacCaulay gapes at Mr. and Mrs. Charles. In addition to encouraging such ad-libbing, Van Dyke personally supervised the script by married couple Albert Hackett and Frances Goodrich, who he instructed to place more importance on the relationship between Nick and Nora than on the mystery angle.

William Powell and Myrna Loy in a publicity photo for The Thin Man

"*The Thin Man* is just a sheer delight. I think it has a great rhythm and a great energy about it. . . . W. S. Van Dyke, the director, was notorious for doing very minimal takes, and I have to wonder that it had so much to do with the levity and the lightness in the performances."

—DREW BARRYMORE

Picture and Best Director). Five sequels followed, reinforcing Powell and Loy as one of screendom's great couples. Hammett was even shuttled to Hollywood to keep scribbling original stories for Van Dyke and company to film.

Decades before Universal released the disaster blockbuster *Earthquake* (1974), the director and his crew re-created the great 1906 earthquake in *San Francisco* (1936), a romance set against a backdrop of mass destruction. He earned another Best Director Oscar nomination for his handling of both the love story and the quake, deftly suggested by off-kilter camera angles and crushing piles of debris. *Marie Antoinette* (1938) may be Van Dyke's only stab at "art for art's sake" (MGM's motto), and it was a spectacular achievement. Producer Irving Thalberg's final starring vehicle for his wife, Norma Shearer, the lavish historical saga benefited from Van Dyke's no-nonsense approach (and from the talents of art director Cedric Gibbons). His goal, he told the *New York Times*, was to "make my characters as little like kings and queens and princes and as much like ordinary human beings

as possible." It paid off in glowing reviews and four Oscar nominations.

Van Dyke became ill with cancer while making *Journey for Margaret* (1942), a popular wartime drama that set then-unknown five-year-old Margaret O'Brien on the path to being the biggest child star since Shirley Temple. He died in 1943, at only fifty-three. *The Thin Man* franchise reluctantly rolled on without him, though the final two entries lack his distinctive light touch.

"He's a speed demon and an economist," Clark Gable said at the height of his 1930s fame, "but I'll trust my popularity and my sense of humor in Woody Van Dyke's hands any day of the year." A favorite with not only Gable and the Powell-Loy team he made a sensation, but with Jeanette MacDonald, Nelson Eddy, Joan Crawford, and other stars, Van Dyke was fondly remembered in Hollywood. The secret to his success? He took it all in stride. "The trouble with most movie people is that they take the whole thing too seriously," he once shared. "It's no great matter of life and death."

THE STUDIO AS AUTEUR

JOSEF VON STERNBERG

Years active: 1925–1953

K NOWN PRIMARILY TODAY FOR THE SEVEN FEA-
tures he made starring his muse, Marlene Dietrich, the Vienna-
born, New York City–bred Josef Sternberg had been influenced by
fellow Austrian transplant Erich von Stroheim—even down to add-

ing a "von" to his name. Like his predecessor, von
Sternberg was an uncompromising artist who was
ultimately cast aside by the very industry he helped
to define.

Starting as a film projectionist in Fort Lee, New
Jersey, von Sternberg worked his way up to writing,
producing, and directing the low-budget drama *The
Salvation Hunters* (1925). Once the film hit Hollywood's radar, von Sternberg fielded several offers,
ultimately helming a gem for Paramount: *Underworld* (1927), the groundbreaking crime picture that
kicked off the gangster-movie trend. Other directors' *Little Caesar* (1931), *The Public Enemy* (1931),
and *Scarface* (1932) grew from the seed of *Underworld*, with its "lonely, moon-flooded" city streets (to

quote the title cards), its unvarnished violence, its
tough mugs and dance-hall dames.

His subsequent silent features—and his first
with sound, *Thunderbolt* (1929)—further demonstrated his skill, but failed to generate commercial appeal until he took a fateful trip to Germany
to make *Der blaue Engel* (*The Blue Angel* [1930]). It
was there, in a Berlin theater, that von Sternberg
first spotted stage-and-screen ingénue Dietrich,
and cast her in the lead role of sensuous cabaret
singer Lola Lola. "Never before," the director later
recalled, "had I met so beautiful a woman who had
been so thoroughly discounted and undervalued."
After appearing in nine forgettable German films,
Dietrich would become a Hollywood luminary at

THE STUDIO AS AUTEUR

the hands of von Sternberg, who carefully guided every detail of her look, voice, and performances. He, in turn, would finally experience consistent box office success through their partnership, which was romantic as well as professional.

The Dietrich–von Sternberg brand was cemented with the sultry *Morocco* (1930), a film that helped save the struggling Paramount from bankruptcy. Costarring Gary Cooper as a legionnaire captivated by Dietrich's enigmatic nightclub performer, Amy, *Morocco* was an aesthetically exquisite

smash hit. Layers of latticework, dappled light, and plants fill von Sternberg's smoke-swirled compositions, creating a hazy atmosphere of heightened romanticism, with Dietrich always front and center. Her Amy mesmerizes the nightclub audience in her Travis Banton–designed tuxedo and top hat, flirting with both men and women.

After the success of *Morocco*, which the *Los Angeles Express* proclaimed the "most brilliantly

Josef von Sternberg with his discovery, Marlene Dietrich

"The Scarlet Empress is so singular; there's nothing like it. It's almost like a new cinema is being created; [von Sternberg] is creating a new language for cinema. Not just the way that it looks, but the light, the use of light, and the use of production design becomes, almost, a sensory part of the experience."

—JAMES GRAY, DIRECTOR OF *AD ASTRA* (2019)

acted and directed production of the season and, with one or two exceptions, since the advent of talking pictures," von Sternberg devoted himself exclusively to Dietrich films at Paramount—his sober, faithful adaptation of Theodore Dreiser's *An American Tragedy* (1931) an exception. The sublimely lit and photographed *Shanghai Express* (1932) reveled in pre-Code provocation. By drenching Dietrich in a special chiaroscuro lighting scheme he devised (with cinematographer Lee Garnes, who was awarded an Oscar), von Sternberg compels the audience to root for her Shanghai Lily, a prostitute who literally drives men insane with desire. The pattern was refashioned in *Blonde Venus*, another fallen-woman-with-a-heart-of-gold tale, also from 1932.

The Scarlet Empress (1934) wove the life story of Russia's Catherine the Great into a sumptuous costume drama. Here, von Sternberg outdid himself, filling each frame with baroque beauty and placing his beloved Dietrich on a pedestal for the world

to admire. With this "rich feast of plastic light and shadow in rhythmic movement fused with sound," the *Los Angeles Times* declared, "Josef von Sternberg has made a tremendous contribution to the art of the sound and motion picture."

Although his work was celebrated, the director who had begun as an independent (a rarity in the studio era) found himself under the thumb of the Hollywood system through his lucrative Dietrich vehicles. "I am Dietrich," he once declared, and Marlene never disputed her Svengali's claim. Without him, however, her career thrived, while his declined once they parted ways after their ultra-glamorous swan song *The Devil Is a Woman* in 1935. His union with Columbia was a mismatch, and several other projects were planned but scrapped. Von Sternberg's reputation as a my-way-or-the-highway perfectionist seemed to hinder him at every turn.

Even though RKO head Howard Hughes replaced the reputedly difficult von Sternberg with Nicholas Ray in the midst of production, the mischievous noir *Macao* (1952) still bears some of his signatures: mood-enhancing patterns of light and shadows, and adoring full-frame shots of a woman, this time the earthy Jane Russell. His penchant for the exotic led the director to Japan for his final feature, the erotically charged *Anatahan* (1953). Aiming to please neither critics nor public, von Sternberg wielded total control over the picture, just as he had on *The Salvation Hunters* nearly two decades before.

From his earliest days, von Sternberg was an artist who leaned toward the avant-garde. "I tried to widen the doors of the film, and to see whether other ideas, literature and art, could not be brought into the films," he remarked later in life. "And it's probably a mistake because my career has not been successful." Those who appreciate the significant impact von Sternberg's movies have had on filmmaking and popular culture would disagree. When he died in 1969, he bequeathed to us a legacy of twenty-four movies that are among the most atmospheric and beautifully crafted of the twentieth century.

Von Sternberg set the standard for the violent gangster movie in 1927's Underworld.

MUST-SEE MOVIES

UNDERWORLD (1927)

THE LAST COMMAND (1928)

THE BLUE ANGEL (1930)

MOROCCO (1930)

SHANGHAI EXPRESS (1932)

BLONDE VENUS (1932)

THE SCARLET EMPRESS (1934)

THE SHANGHAI GESTURE (1941)

Marlene Dietrich in Shanghai Express

KEY SCENE TO WATCH

When Dietrich's Lily and Clive Brook's "Doc" encounter each other on the train in *Shanghai Express*, notice the way the two are framed, both in their own windows with a bar between them, ex-lovers separated by five years apart. Lily is a woman with a reputation, a gloved, veiled enigma dwelling in shadows. A close-up reveals hints of sadness and world-weariness in her eyes. When Doc asks whether she is married, she delivers the now-famous line, "It took more than one man to change my name to Shanghai Lily." Von Sternberg carefully builds intrigue by keeping Dietrich at a distance, cloaked and obscured, until he unleashes a painterly shot of her expressive face at just the proper moment.

JOSEF VON STERNBERG

STUDIO SYSTEM STALWARTS

Golden Age Hollywood produced a plethora of skilled directors, some better known today than others. Warner Bros. linchpin **Lloyd Bacon** made more than one hundred movies between 1920 and 1955, specializing in the snappy musicals and dramas the studio was known for. 1933's *42nd Street* and *Footlight Parade* put him on the map, while the Ronald Reagan–starring *Knute Rockne, All American* (1940) remains a favorite.

An accomplished actor, director, and producer, **Jack Conway** helmed some of MGM's biggest hits between 1925 and 1948. Conway aced the transition from silent to sound, making Lon Chaney's first and only talkie, *The Unholy Three* (1930); a notable Jean Harlow pre-Code, *Red-Headed Woman* (1932); and the screwball classic and Best Picture Oscar nominee *Libeled Lady* (1936).

One of many German artists who fled the country in the early 1930s, actor/director **William Dieterle** joined Warner Bros. in 1931. His fanciful big-screen take on Shakespeare's *A Midsummer Night's Dream* (1935) distinguished Dieterle, but it was his two illustrious biopics starring Paul Muni that won him prestige: *The Story of Louis Pasteur* (1936) and *The Life of Emile Zola* (1937), an Oscar recipient for Best Picture.

In his native England, **Edmund Goulding** jumped from actor to playwright; in Hollywood, he leaped from screenwriter to director—and from studio to studio, making the Best Picture–winner *Grand Hotel* (1932) at MGM, the Bette Davis heartbreaker *Dark Victory* (1939) at Warner Bros., and, at Fox, *The Razor's Edge*, one of the top-grossing films of 1947.

By the time sound arrived, former actor **Henry King** had already directed over sixty silent pictures and cofounded the Academy of Motion Picture Arts and Sciences in 1927, and had yet to hit his stride. Of his many films, seven were nominated for Best Picture, including *The Song of Bernadette* (1943), and the gripping war drama *Twelve O'Clock High* (1949).

Raoul Walsh established himself in silents, piloting the Douglas Fairbanks swashbuckler *The Thief of Baghdad* in 1924. He practiced the art of sound pictures at Fox, then Paramount, and finally Warner Bros., where he made his mark with such classic noirs as the intense *High Sierra* (1941) and the electrifying *White Heat* (1949), starring James Cagney.

Edmund Goulding directs Bette Davis in Dark Victory, *1938.*

Chapter Three

A THREAT TO THE SYSTEM

I f a starry-eyed hopeful journeyed to Hollywood to make movies circa 1940, he or she would have been confronted with a harsh reality: the studio was the boss, and the director took orders. A few were dissatisfied with this hierarchy and sought to take creative power into their own hands, often with disastrous results. At RKO, new kid in town Orson Welles fought for complete artistic control, while next door at Paramount, Preston Sturges pulled strings to be among the first writer/director/producers of his time. Both had meteoric but short-lived periods of success.

As World War II raged in Europe, America delivered comforting screen fare, optimistic and escapist treats—many in the newly perfected Technicolor process—to ease the hardship. In stark contrast, a more cynical genre bubbled up from the depths, a dark vein of crime films with moody lighting brought to the US by European refugees, most of whom fled the continent when the Nazis rose to power. Unnamed at the time, the style that would come to be known as film noir would later be seen as the defining movement of 1940s Hollywood.

In 1948, the dissolution of the studios' theater-chain monopoly hit the industry hard. Fissures were forming, cracks that would eventually grow large enough to topple the entire studio system. But in wartime and postwar America, movies were still the national pastime, manufactured in assembly-line fashion to please the crowds. On the sunlit surface of Hollywood, California, everything appeared to be business as usual.

Henry Fonda, Preston Sturges, and Barbara Stanwyck on the set of The Lady Eve, *1941*

GEORGE CUKOR

Years active: 1930–1981

FROM THE STAR-STUDDED, SPRAWLING *DINNER AT EIGHT* (1933) to the intimate *Camille* (1936), the psychological chills of *Gaslight* (1944) to the comic brilliance of *Born Yesterday* (1950), George Cukor was the artist behind dozens of certified classics. A gentleman of exquisite taste, Cukor crafted classy, smart pictures that represent studio-era filmmaking at its best. Succinctly summarizing the director's stellar fifty-year output, journalist Kenneth Tynan concluded in 1961 that Cukor's films "epitomize Hollywood at its most stylish."

From his earliest efforts, Cukor had a special rapport with actresses, particularly Katharine Hepburn and Judy Holliday, both of whom earned Oscars under his direction. Cukor discovered the neophyte Hepburn in a screen test for *A Bill of Divorcement* (1932) and thought, "There was something about her; no one like her had been seen before." The two united on ten films, *Little Women* (1933), *Holiday* (1938), and *Adam's Rib* (1949) among them. Cukor's 1940 cinematic rendering of Philip Barry's play *The Philadelphia Story* (written specifically for Hepburn) is an outstanding testament to their professional kinship. Hepburn was rarely more glamorous or charismatic on-screen than as strong-willed society bride Tracy Lord, and Cukor showcases the actress with luminous close-ups and first-class supporting talent, namely Cary Grant and James Stewart ("only God can make a trio like that," the publicists claimed). A funny, touching love triangle that won Stewart his one and only Oscar, *The Philadelphia Story* vaulted Hepburn back to A-list status after a string of box office flops.

Cukor—who began as a New York theater director—would order as many takes as necessary from his cast until he got a credible performance

in the can. "To me, Cukor can do no wrong. He makes you have a sense of humor about yourself," observed Joan Crawford, who was at the top of her game as an embittered burn victim in *A Woman's Face* (1941). If an actor hit a false note, Cukor might roar (with good humor), "That was terrible! Why in the hell can't you do it better?" He insisted on utter emotional realism.

The tag "woman's director" followed Cukor throughout his life, but he bristled under the label, especially since he launched the careers of comic legend Jack Lemmon (in *It Should Happen to You*

[1954]) and '50s staple Aldo Ray (in *The Marrying Kind* [1952]), and his understated 1947 noir *A Double Life* won Ronald Colman his sole Academy Award. Cukor took his camera to the real streets of New York (rarely done in the studio era) for *A Double Life*, and judiciously used dramatic camera angles and movements when needed, such as the slightly askew framing during the mental

George Cukor directs an all-female cast (including Paulette Goddard, Joan Crawford, Rosalind Russell, Norma Shearer, and Mary Boland) in The Women.

> "The filmmaking in *A Double Life* is some of the most beautiful and purely visual—almost impressionistic—passages to emerge from the Hollywood system."
>
> —MARTIN SCORSESE

breakdowns of Colman's Tony. Cukor always kept distracting camerawork to a minimum.

If there is a motif that runs through his work, it's an exploration of who people really are, as opposed to the personas they adopt. *What Price Hollywood?* (1932) and its descendant, the tuneful Judy Garland tour-de-force *A Star Is Born* (1954), concern talented but vulnerable women who achieve fame by projecting images that contrast with reality. A major theme of the witty and wise *The Women*

Robert Taylor and Greta Garbo in Camille

MUST-SEE MOVIES

DINNER AT EIGHT (1933)

CAMILLE (1936)

THE PHILADELPHIA STORY (1940)

GASLIGHT (1944)

A DOUBLE LIFE (1947)

ADAM'S RIB (1949)

BORN YESTERDAY (1950)

A STAR IS BORN (1954)

MY FAIR LADY (1964)

Katharine Hepburn and James Stewart in
The Philadelphia Story

KEY SCENE TO WATCH

On the eve of her wedding to another man, Tracy (Katharine Hepburn) shares a moonlight dance and swim with writer Mike Conner (James Stewart) in *The Philadelphia Story*, their inhibitions loosened by Champagne. As this seven-minute scene ebbs and flows between comedy, drama, and romance, Cukor demonstrates not only his gift for finessing the finest from actors, but his flawless timing and rhythm, and his understanding of how to translate a stage play into a motion picture. The director was assisted by a team that included producer Joseph L. Mankiewicz, screenwriter Donald Ogden Stewart, and art director Cedric Gibbons, resulting in grade A moviemaking from the glamour factory at its zenith.

GEORGE CUKOR

(1939) is the appearance of happy marriages versus the relationship flaws the ladies keep hidden. *A Double Life* also deals with theatrical pretense, as does his grandiose last hurrah for studio-system musicals, *My Fair Lady* (1964).

Cukor was a gifted filmmaker of the old school: the Hollywood factory. Never one to write or produce his own projects, his career declined with the collapse of the studio system in the 1960s. Later in life, he yearned for the heyday of the moguls, like his longtime boss at MGM, Louis B. Mayer. "The man who had the power to say, 'Yes, we will go forward with it and we will spend this much money'—

it was a comfort to know that there was such a man who was the boss and who did make decisions and who stood by them," he noted.

The Oscars nominated George Cukor for Best Director five times, and for directing the Best Picture seven times, though he didn't win until 1965 for *My Fair Lady*. It may have been a case of making it look too easy. His movies exude such an air of graceful perfection, they almost seem to direct themselves.

Audrey Hepburn, Rex Harrison, Wilfrid Hyde-White, and Jeremy Brett at the Ascot Racecourse in My Fair Lady

MICHAEL CURTIZ

Years active: 1912–1961

MOVIEGOERS IN THE 1940s KNEW THAT JOHN FORD made aesthetically lush westerns and Alfred Hitchcock made sophisticated thrillers. But Michael Curtiz somehow missed becoming a big-name sensation. If he is mentioned today, it's usually as the

force behind one of the most cherished movies from Golden Age Hollywood, Best Picture–winner *Casablanca* (1942), for which Curtiz received his only Academy Award for Best Director.

A native of Hungary, Mihály Kertész had nearly seventy films to his credit by the time he hit Hollywood in 1926, Americanized his name, and secured a contract with Warner Bros. Although the style of Curtiz was never as distinctive as a Josef von Sternberg ("He didn't stamp his pictures at all," said contemporary Howard Hawks of Curtiz), his use of shadows was something of a personal trademark. Curtiz movies commonly feature a shot that's either entirely or partly done in silhouette— picture the prison guards approaching in *20,000*

Years in Sing Sing (1932); Peter Blood tending a wounded soldier in *Captain Blood* (1935); or Rick opening the café safe in *Casablanca*. There is usually fast-paced action and memorable visuals aplenty, such as the arresting camera angles in his two eerie experiments with pre-Code color horror, *Doctor X* (1932) and *Mystery of the Wax Museum* (1933).

After a quarter-century of filmmaking and a decade in Hollywood, the box office smash *The Adventures of Robin Hood* (1938)—featuring Errol Flynn and Olivia de Havilland in glorious Technicolor—was the movie that finally separated Curtiz from the pack. He had first paired Flynn and de Havilland in *Captain Blood*, and both shot to stardom. John Garfield was another Curtiz

discovery, debuting in *Four Daughters* (1938); he also introduced the world to Doris Day in the genial musical *Romance on the High Seas* (1948).

He was an ideal studio journeyman, leaping with gusto from one genre to another. *Yankee Doodle Dandy* (1942) exemplifies Curtiz in his prime. It's a mixed bag: biopic, show-stopping musical, family drama, period piece, and a dash of romantic comedy, all of which the director nails. Many consider James Cagney's Oscar-winning performance as songwriter George M. Cohan the crowning achievement of the actor's illustrious career. As soon as Curtiz completed *Yankee Doodle Dandy*, he started working on another masterpiece, *Casablanca*.

Warner Bros. had purchased the unproduced play *Everybody Comes to Rick's* because of its exotic locale and its topical World War II theme, but the story—even after being revised for the screen with stellar dialogue—was a melodramatic mish-mash of romance and adventure tropes. Along with producer Hal B. Wallis, Curtiz was responsible for cutting through the clichés by making us truly care about the characters: Humphrey Bogart's wounded, cynical Rick; Ingrid Bergman's passionate, conflicted Ilsa; and an ensemble led by Paul Henreid, Claude Rains, Dooley Wilson,

Humphrey Bogart, Ingrid Bergman, and Michael Curtiz on the set of Casablanca

112

and Conrad Veidt. With his dynamic dollies and pans, his shadows and swirling fog, Curtiz made us believe that, somehow, French Morocco could be found on the Warner Bros. backlot. Every element (including Arthur Edeson's Oscar-nominated cinematography) combined to make an instant classic. Before the late-night-television revivals, the oft-repeated dialogue, and the Marx Brothers' spoof *A Night in Casablanca* (1946), the *New York Times* in 1942 praised the picture as "a highly entertaining and even inspiring film that makes the spine tingle and the heart take a leap," and gave Curtiz a special nod for his suspenseful direction. *Casablanca*'s overwhelming success made him Warners' most prized filmmaker.

His speed, excellence, and habit of working eighteen-hour days meant Curtiz was entrusted with the studio's precious projects, such as Joan Crawford's much-anticipated comeback film, the landmark noir *Mildred Pierce* (1945). Curtiz was initially opposed to Crawford in the title role, believing her too polished to play James M. Cain's middle-class waitress. When it was over, each had won the other's respect, Joan won an Oscar, and Cain himself praised the picture. Curtiz and Crawford reunited four years later for another slick, soapy noir, *Flamingo Road* (1949). As his enduring legacy of cinema touchstones suggests, there was more to

Dooley Wilson and Humphrey Bogart in Casablanca

MUST-SEE MOVIES

ANGELS WITH DIRTY FACES (1938)

THE ADVENTURES OF ROBIN HOOD (1938)

THE PRIVATE LIVES OF ELIZABETH AND ESSEX (1939)

THE SEA WOLF (1941)

YANKEE DOODLE DANDY (1942)

CASABLANCA (1943)

MILDRED PIERCE (1945)

LIFE WITH FATHER (1947)

WHITE CHRISTMAS (1954)

Olivia de Havilland and Errol Flynn in
The Adventures of Robin Hood

KEY SCENE TO WATCH

Although Michael Curtiz shares directorial credit with William Keighley on *The Adventures of Robin Hood*, Curtiz shot more than half of the colorful classic. Emblematic of the director's style is the final duel between Robin (Errol Flynn) and Sir Guy (Basil Rathbone) in Nottingham Castle. Flickering candle flames cast enormous shadows of Robin (in green) and Sir Guy (in red and gold) against a stone pillar as they fence, the array of shots and quicksilver editing matching their speedy swordplay. While most 1930s and early '40s movies were in black and white, Curtiz had serious Technicolor know-how: in addition to his pre-Code horror films, he had shot *Under a Texas Moon* (1930) and *Bright Lights* (1930) in a primitive dual-color process.

A THREAT TO THE SYSTEM

> "Michael Curtiz made over 160 films. His films are so good, so well-made, that you forget there's a director. The thing that he did so beautifully was the way he was able to light and set a mood, the feel for visual; that comes from Curtiz, because it's in all of his films."
>
> —WILLIAM FRIEDKIN

Curtiz than skill and hard work. "I put," he once revealed, "all the art into my pictures I think the audience can stand."

For a man who created movies with sensitivity and passion, Curtiz was known as a bully on-set, sometimes assaulting cast or crew with a pack of profanities for making a mistake. "You had to be very strong with him," Bette Davis once said. "He could humiliate people, but never me." Davis refused to be intimidated by Curtiz, and the two made some winners together, the breezy *Front Page Woman* (1935) and the majestic *The Private Lives of Elizabeth and Essex* (1939) among them.

Parting ways with Warner Bros. after nearly thirty years allowed Curtiz to direct Fox's mega-budget epic *The Egyptian* (1954) and Paramount's VistaVision musical *White Christmas* (1954). His greatest period of success, however, came through his union with the brothers Warner. Of their eighty-six features together, the director's pride and joy was *This Is the Army* (1943). It earned a profit of over $9 million, all of which was donated to the

Army Emergency Relief Fund to aid soldiers fighting in World War II and their families.

Joan Crawford and Curtiz on the set of Mildred Pierce

JOHN FORD

Years active: 1917–1970

JOHN FORD WAS ONE OF THE WORLD'S FOREMOST filmmakers for nearly half a century. From the late 1910s through the 1960s, he racked up close to 150 features, made John Wayne a celebrated screen presence, and elevated the movie western, causing the Old West genre to

surge in popularity. Most associated with westerns, Ford, in fact, made various types of movies, and few made them better. Nearly fifty years after his death, he holds the record for most Best Director Academy Awards (four).

"I'm a journeyman director," he used to say, "a traffic cop in front of the camera." He rejected the notion of movies as art—but his straightforward, unpretentious manner belies the undeniable beauty of his films, his painterly compositions and framing. Watch the coach arriving at Dry Fork in *Stagecoach* (1939), or Martha (Dorothy Jordan) opening the front door in *The Searchers* (1956) to see a Ford trademark: the shot from inside a dark doorway, providing a frame for sun-drenched objects on the

other side. "The only thing I always had was an eye for composition," he admitted. "I don't know where I got it."

Like many superb visual directors, he started in silent film. With *The Iron Horse* (1924), Ford took the true story of migrant workers building America's first transcontinental railroad and turned it into an epic with a multicultural cast numbering in the thousands. Thus was introduced another Ford motif: massive throngs of people, such as the Welsh miners flooding the hillside in *How Green Was My Valley* (1941). Pictorial landscapes were the stars of his movies as much as actors— yet he never lost focus on the individual. Character traits are revealed in his tight shots of faces, the

open earnestness of *Valley*'s young Huw (Roddy McDowall), for instance.

With *Stagecoach*, Ford delivered a genuine American masterpiece. Orson Welles watched it forty times in preparation for his directorial debut, another masterpiece titled *Citizen Kane* (1941). And it's clear to see why. *Stagecoach* is a crash course in camera movement, in swift pace and fluid editing, in pitch-perfect acting from all the players, including a young John Wayne in his first starring role for Ford

(the legendary duo would make thirteen more films together). Much of the action takes place inside a cramped stagecoach, but the director counterbalances that with a boundless landscape: the majestic sandstone buttes of Ford's favorite backdrop, Monument Valley, on the Utah-Arizona border. *Stagecoach* restored Hollywood's faith in the western.

John Ford and Victor McLaglen on the set of
The Informer, *1935*

117

Until *Stagecoach*, Ford had practically abandoned the unfashionable western. 1935's *The Whole Town's Talking* was a clever gangster spoof featuring the versatile Edward G. Robinson playing both a cold-blooded killer and a meek file clerk. Also from 1935 was *The Informer*, a passion project Ford got green-lit by taking a percentage of the profits in lieu of a salary. This adaptation of Liam O'Flaherty's tragic novel began his long association with screenwriter Dudley Nichols. Ford boldly tackled Technicolor in 1939's *Drums Along the Mohawk*, a tense frontier drama based on real events in New York during the American Revolution. Color brought the period piece to life, but the director preferred

Natalie Wood and John Wayne in The Searchers

"I like the old masters . . . by which I mean John Ford, John Ford, and John Ford. With Ford at his best, you get a sense of what the earth is made of."

—ORSON WELLES

the rich texture of black and white, such as his cinematic watershed *The Grapes of Wrath* (1940). Under the auspices of Twentieth Century-Fox chief Darryl F. Zanuck, Ford and cameraman Gregg Toland wrangled John Steinbeck's epic novel into a powerful drama featuring Henry Fonda as the downtrodden yet righteous ex-convict Tom Joad.

After some thirty years at Fox, Ford embarked on an independent partnership with *King Kong* (1933) producer Merian C. Cooper to form Argosy Pictures. No longer bound to a long-term studio contract, Ford bounced between Republic, Columbia, and MGM. Republic's *The Quiet Man* (1952) was Ford at his most sentimental, a pastoral love sonnet to Ireland, his ancestral home. Whether nurturing, maternal Maureen O'Hara in *The Quiet Man* or energetic ingénue Vera Miles in *The Searchers*, the women in Ford's films were hardy pioneer types, and often spitfires. Ford cast the same stock company of character actors regularly, including Harry Carey (both Senior and Junior), Ward Bond, and Barry Fitzgerald.

The alcoholic Ford had an irascible temperament, and was known to be verbally—even physically, on occasion—abusive to some of his cast and crew. One senses that the cruel facade, the dark glasses he wore, the handkerchief he chewed on, were to cover the profound sensitivity that shines through in his movies. "He's a poet with a camera," Wayne said of his mentor. "He can be as mean as hell at times, though."

"Duke" and "Pappy" worked together for decades, Wayne's characters growing more complex as the actor and director aged. In *Stagecoach*, he was the Ringo Kid, all chivalry and gun-slinging action. Over the course of *Fort Apache* (1948), *She Wore a Yellow Ribbon* (1949), and *Rio Grande* (1950), known as Ford's "Cavalry trilogy," Wayne gained the self-possession of a married family man. By *The Searchers*, Wayne's Ethan is older, filled with cynical rage, a xenophobe with a special hatred of Native Americans. No longer the good guy, Wayne is closer to antihero or villain as he counters every threat with "That'll be the day," a catchphrase that inspired the Buddy Holly hit.

One of Ford's greatest achievements, *The Searchers* is a mythic, larger-than-life saga that follows its horse-riding search party across the continent, from the dusty Texas plains to the icy Yukon. Packed with action, suspense, and comedy, the epic was rated the Greatest Western of All Time by the American Film Institute in 2008. *The Searchers* influence can be seen in the work of David Lean (*Lawrence of Arabia* [1962]) and Steven Spielberg (*Close Encounters of the Third Kind* [1977]).

In Ford's last feature, *7 Women* (1966), he finally placed a female in the heroic leading role usually reserved for a man. As a tough, independent doctor, Anne Bancroft reacts courageously to dire circumstances in rural 1930s China, leading to a stunning conclusion. "The ending of the film," wrote Richard Brody of the *New Yorker*, "a single shot of slender action and enormous drama, is one of the very noblest in all cinema."

Before and after his death in 1973, Ford amassed countless accolades, including a Lifetime Achievement Award from the Directors Guild of America in 1954, and the Medal of Freedom from President Nixon. Perhaps the most fitting tribute is John Ford Point, a scenic lookout in his beloved Monument Valley.

John Ford with Anne Bancroft on the set of his final film, 7 Women

MUST-SEE MOVIES

STAGECOACH (1939)

THE GRAPES OF WRATH (1940)

HOW GREEN WAS MY VALLEY (1941)

THE QUIET MAN (1952)

MISTER ROBERTS (1955)

THE SEARCHERS (1956)

THE MAN WHO SHOT LIBERTY VALANCE (1962)

HOW THE WEST WAS WON (1962)

7 WOMEN (1966)

KEY SCENE TO WATCH

After committing manslaughter in *The Grapes of Wrath*, Tom Joad must hide from the law, so he plans a life of enforcing justice for those unable to protect themselves. "I'll be everywhere," Tom tells his mother. "Wherever there's a fight so hungry people can eat, I'll be there. Wherever there's a cop beating up a guy, I'll be there." During this scene, Henry Fonda never blinks his eyes, and his gaze stays steadily focused in the distance, some time and place in the far-off future. "The main thing about directing is: photograph the people's eyes," Ford used to say. In his close-up of Fonda, the eyes are truly a window to his character's soul.

Henry Fonda as Tom Joad in The Grapes of Wrath

JOHN HUSTON

Years active: 1941–1987

I N THE GOLDEN DAYS OF HOLLYWOOD, SCREENWRITERS
rarely made the leap to directing, John Farrow being a notable exception. In
Farrow's footsteps came John Huston, gifted son of actor Walter Huston, and
an enterprising filmmaker who began as a staff writer for Warner Bros., thanks

to his friendship with mentor William Wyler. After coauthoring scripts for Oscar-winner *Sergeant York* (1941) and the successful Raoul Walsh picture *High Sierra* (1941), Huston was given the chance to direct his own feature. He chose to adapt Dashiell Hammett's 1930 novel *The Maltese Falcon*. The rest is Hollywood history.

"I do not think any filmmaker should—though many do—consciously strive to maintain a permanent style in his films," Huston once said. It was likely this lack of a conscious insignia, this aversion to repeating himself, that gave Huston's oeuvre such variety and longevity. Scattered over five decades, his films are wildly diverse in genre and tone. But there are certain themes Huston was fond of:

underdogs and misfits, the quest for the elusive, and the insidious effects of greed on the human soul. Lust for "the stuff that dreams are made of" is what drives the eclectic assemblage of characters in *The Maltese Falcon* (1941), Huston's astounding debut.

Falcon had been brought to the screen twice before, in a 1931 pre-Code, and a 1936 comic misfire, *Satan Met a Lady*. Huston saw the flaws in both versions: they strayed too far from the spirit of Hammett's prose. He constructed a classic by staying faithful to the hard-boiled, darkly funny detective tale, the result being a jump start to the 1940s film noir trend and a star-making role for Humphrey Bogart as the slick Sam Spade, the prototype for all morally ambivalent gum-

shoes to follow. The sharp photography and high-contrast lighting were not incidental; Huston saw them as reflections of Hammett's piercing, taut writing style.

Huston loved to film in remote locations partly to escape from studio control, partly to quench his

John Huston in the mouth of Moby Dick, 1955

123

> "*The Treasure of the Sierra Madre* is economical and lean in the way it cuts from one thing to the next, but within that it's such a beautiful mess with stuff everywhere: cigarette smoke wafting into the frame, extras in the background, overhead fans turning. Everything is so alive. . . . In the end, we've been taken for a ride just as we should be, just in the way John Huston is encouraging us to look at life."

—PAUL THOMAS ANDERSON

thirst for travel, heading to Paris for *Moulin Rouge* (1952), Italy for *Beat the Devil* (1953), and Mexico for *The Treasure of the Sierra Madre* (1948). His colorful supporting characters were often natives of the area, such as Mexican American actor Alfonso Bedoya, *Treasure*'s lead bandito. Bedoya's line, "I don't have to show you any stinking badges," was later parodied to perfection in Mel Brooks's outlandish western *Blazing Saddles* (1974). The much-imitated *Treasure of the Sierra Madre* remains a textbook look at avarice south of the border, the ultimate gold-digging adventure, featuring Huston's dad, Walter, in an Oscar-winning character role as a wise old prospector. The film was a family triumph, winning John awards for Best Director and Best Screenplay too.

Huston went straight from *Treasure* to *Key Largo* (1948), the swan song for Bogie and Bacall, the couple's last movie together. Set inside a stifling Florida hotel, the superlative crime drama benefits from cinematographer Karl Freund's roaming camera that follows the characters up and down stairs, outside to the boathouse, and aboard the *Santana* for the final shootout. With *The Asphalt Jungle* (1950), Huston gave Marilyn Monroe her first major role—and, ironically, her last, in *The Misfits* (1961), a cowboy tale with Monroe's sad divorcée Roslyn in a love triangle with Clark Gable and Montgomery Clift. Also the final screen performance for Gable, *The Misfits* stands as a melancholy ode to glory days gone by.

Filming the romantic adventure *The African Queen* (1951) in color meant director and crew spent nine weeks in the Belgian Congo, lugging heavy Technicolor cameras through the jungle. The result was well worth the effort. Huston made the simple story of two people in a boat (Bogart and Katharine Hepburn), falling in love while fighting Germans in World War I, completely absorbing. "It is a picture with unassuming warmth and naturalness," *Variety* cheered. "A worthwhile piece of screen entertainment that will be thoroughly enjoyed by most any adult." As the *African Queen*'s gin-soaked boat captain Charlie Allnut, Bogart snared his only Oscar.

Huston was never intimidated by literary adaptations, whether Stephen Crane's *The Red Badge of Courage* (1951) or *The Bible* itself, which he brought to the screen in 1966. Herman Melville's *Moby Dick* (1956) may have been his most ambitious and effective stab at literature. After relocating to Ireland, Huston spent three years shooting Captain Ahab (Gregory Peck) and his great white whale in County Cork and off the coast of England, resulting in a rousing big-screen event the *New York Times* declared "one of the great motion pictures of our times." *Heaven Knows, Mr. Allison* (1957), based on a Charles Shaw novel, took the restless filmmaker to the island of Trinidad, and he jetted to Puerto Vallarta for *The Night of the Iguana* (1964), sourced from a Tennessee Williams play.

Humphrey Bogart and Walter Huston in The Treasure of the Sierra Madre

Ever the iconoclast, Huston spent his later career exploring the unexpected. He ventured into sports drama with the boxing picture *Fat City* (1972), turned in a powerful acting performance as the ruthless Noah Cross in Roman Polanski's *Chinatown* (1974), did justice to a Rudyard Kipling classic in *The Man Who Would Be King* (1975), took a gamble on the beloved Broadway heartwarmer *Annie* (1982), and directed daughter Angelica Huston to an Oscar in *Prizzi's Honor* (1985). Huston kept working right up until his death. "There's a mystique about film itself," he once said. "That shadow on the screen can be more than the man in the flesh ever was." The films he left behind form a rich tapestry that remains fresh, insightful, and relevant.

Katharine Hepburn and Humphrey Bogart on location in the Belgian Congo for The African Queen

MUST-SEE MOVIES

THE MALTESE FALCON (1941)

THE TREASURE OF THE SIERRA MADRE (1948)

KEY LARGO (1948)

THE ASPHALT JUNGLE (1950)

THE AFRICAN QUEEN (1951)

MOBY DICK (1956)

THE MISFITS (1961)

THE NIGHT OF THE IGUANA (1964)

THE MAN WHO WOULD BE KING (1975)

Huston sets up a shot featuring Jean Hagen and Sterling Hayden in The Asphalt Jungle.

KEY SCENE TO WATCH

After being shot, bank-robber Dix (Sterling Hayden) in *The Asphalt Jungle* escapes to his family's horse farm in Kentucky. "Everything's gonna be okay," he assures Doll (Jean Hagen) as they race down country roads, finally arriving at the serene pasture, only for Dix to fall to the ground. This ironic finale echoes similar scenes in *The Maltese Falcon* and *The Treasure of the Sierra Madre*, in which characters cope with the shattering loss of everything they dreamed of just as they attain it. Now considered a prototypical heist movie, *The Asphalt Jungle* turned only a meager profit at the box office in 1950. MGM head Louis B. Mayer disliked the film, saying: "That 'Asphalt Pavement' thing is full of nasty, ugly people doing nasty things. I wouldn't walk across the room to see a thing like that."

VINCENTE MINNELLI

Years active: 1943–1976

A VISUAL POET FOR THE SOUND ERA, VINCENTE Minnelli expertly directed straight drama and comedy, but is primarily renowned for his revolutionary musicals, in which human action, set decor, camera movement, music, and lighting were synchronized into a

unified whole, the likes of which hadn't quite been seen before. His color musicals often feel like classical paintings brought to life.

Minnelli had been born into a theatrical family, and gained varied experience as an actor, set painter, and costume designer on Broadway. In 1940, he joined MGM under Arthur Freed's musical unit, where, after two years of apprenticeship, "they let me tackle a whole picture by myself," he recalled. *Cabin in the Sky* (1943) was a landmark all-Black musical starring Ethel Waters and, in her sizzling screen debut, twenty-five-year-old singer/actress Lena Horne. Minnelli's flair raises *Cabin* above its low budget and its racially stereotypical characters (a fault of the script that Minnelli fought

against): his fluid camerawork and pioneering use of song and dance to advance the story made for an impressive debut film.

Like *Cabin in the Sky*, 1944's *Meet Me in St. Louis* stands as an indelible slice of Americana, filled with humanity and whimsy. As Esther (Judy Garland) sings of first love in "The Trolley Song," the car shakes just enough to mimic the pounding of her heart. When Esther and her sister Rose (Lucille Bremer) sing the title song, their faces are echoed in a bust of two girls that sits on the piano. Minnelli's finely detailed sets evoke dreamlike nostalgia for the turn of the century, yet appear real enough to reach out and touch. "His genius was to take fixed sets and turn them into a kind of living organism,

through a play of color and constant variations in texture," observed *Cahiers du Cinéma* critic (and filmmaker) Jean Douchet. Minnelli's movies were often theatrical, but never stagey.

Adding to the popularity of *Meet Me in St. Louis* was the much-publicized on-set romance between Minnelli and Garland, and their marriage the following year. The birth of their daughter, Liza, gave Minnelli a family, though he and Garland divorced in 1951. Family is a crucial component in his work, whether the close-knit Smith clan of St. Louis, Stanley and Kay's (Spencer Tracy and Elizabeth Taylor) father-daughter connection in *Father of the Bride* (1950), or the dysfunctional Hirsch brothers

(Frank Sinatra and Arthur Kennedy) in *Some Came Running* (1958).

It was primarily with *The Clock* (1945) and *The Bad and the Beautiful* (1952) that Minnelli proved himself adept at non-musicals. Before there was Peter Tewksbury's *Sunday in New York* (1963) or Woody Allen's *Manhattan* (1979), there was *The Clock*, a Big Apple love story that streaks like a subway train from a couple's (Garland and Robert Walker) chance meeting to their wedding, all in a mere two days. *The Bad and the Beautiful* was a brutally

Vincente Minnelli directs Judy Garland in Meet Me in St. Louis.

129

honest glimpse inside Hollywood, but with a palpable compassion for every character, even Kirk Douglas's cruel movie producer, Jonathan Shields.

"Musicals or straight dramas and comedies—I don't see much difference," Minnelli told a reporter in 1952. "There are passages in *The Bad and the Beautiful* that are almost like a musical. And conversely, when I direct a musical, I try to make the people as real as they are in comedy or drama." And that's one element that made *An American in Paris* (1951) stand out: the poignant relationship between American painter Jerry (Gene Kelly) and French mystery girl Lise (Leslie Caron). A frenzy of adulation met *An American in Paris*; it took home six Oscars including Best Picture, and remains one of the greatest musicals to emerge from Hollywood.

The twenty-year partnership of Freed and Minnelli yielded a spate of increasingly sophisticated musicals that made postwar MGM the leading studio in song-and-dance spectaculars. In the buoyant backstage comedy *The Band Wagon* (1953), Minnelli splashes the screen with fire-engine reds, ultraviolet purples, and vivid sky blues. The film's most inventive number is a movie within a movie, the "Girl Hunt Ballet," a clever, sultry send-up of film noir before the term existed, featuring Fred Astaire and Cyd Charisse as a dancing duo of detective and femme fatale.

During his twenty-five years at MGM, there was one film that Minnelli suggested and convinced the studio to make: *Lust for Life* (1956), a biographical drama about Vincent Van Gogh. Both lead actor Kirk Douglas and director threw themselves

Lena Horne and Eddie "Rochester" Anderson in Cabin in the Sky

MUST-SEE MOVIES

CABIN IN THE SKY (1943)

MEET ME IN ST. LOUIS (1944)

THE CLOCK (1945)

FATHER OF THE BRIDE (1950)

AN AMERICAN IN PARIS (1951)

THE BAD AND THE BEAUTIFUL (1952)

THE BAND WAGON (1953)

LUST FOR LIFE (1956)

GIGI (1958)

Gene Kelly in the dream ballet sequence of An American in Paris

KEY SCENE TO WATCH

Near the end of *An American in Paris*, artist Jerry has lost his true love, Lise, and is standing alone in the Paris night, his pencil sketch of La Place de l'Étoile torn in two. As the camera zooms in for a close-up of his face, we enter Jerry's fantasy world, his sketch brought to life in raging colors. No dialogue is spoken in the seventeen-minute ballet that follows; Jerry's hopes and fears are played out in dance. "The ballet doesn't reflect what's happened in the picture so far," Minnelli wrote of his intentions with this sequence. "It shows instead the conflict within the hero." A nod to Michael Powell and Emeric Pressburger's groundbreaking *The Red Shoes* (1948), yet a wholly original statement choreographed by Minnelli and star Gene Kelly, the "dream ballet," as it is often called, broadened the boundaries of Hollywood musicals by expressing internal feelings via music and dance.

VINCENTE MINNELLI

"Vincente Minnelli's *Meet Me in St. Louis* was a milestone. First of all, the story didn't have a Broadway setting. . . . Its protagonists were the members of a middle-class household. They did not need to be professional performers; anyone could sing and dance if they felt like it. Singing and dancing became as natural as breathing or talking."

—MARTIN SCORSESE

fully into the project, Minnelli insisting on shooting in the obsolete Ansco Color process, one that "more accurately represented those of the canvases," of the postimpressionist painter, he stated. As he had for *The Bad and the Beautiful*, Douglas earned an Oscar nomination. Minnelli finally received his own statuette for *Gigi* (1958), a belle epoque musical

written especially for the screen by Alan Jay Lerner and Frederick Loewe, based on the story by Colette. Although the age of studio musicals was waning, Minnelli's success continued into the 1960s with *Bells Are Ringing* (1960) and *On a Clear Day You Can See Forever* (1970), among others.

Without Vincente Minnelli's influence, there might have been no vibrant 1960s musicals by Jacques Demy, no Damien Chazelle's Oscar-winning *La La Land* (2016). In 1945, *Los Angeles Times* critic Philip K. Scheuer sized up the talents of the then-novice director: "In his attention to background business, Minnelli is like Alfred Hitchcock. In his applied knowledge of sets and décor, he is like Mitchell Leisen. In his use of long, flowing dolly and crane shots, he is like Edmund Goulding. But in the 'feel' he imparts to his scenes, which have the polish and the know-how of the New York stage's best . . . he resembles no one so much as himself."

Kirk Douglas and Lana Turner in The Bad and the Beautiful

A THREAT TO THE SYSTEM

GEORGE STEVENS

Years active: 1930–1970

I N 1965, ACTOR/DIRECTOR/PRODUCER SIDNEY POITIER portrayed Simon of Cyrene in George Stevens's biblical epic *The Greatest Story Ever Told* (1965), and met the director whose movies he had long admired. "I saw his strength and artistry," Poitier remembered, years later. "I saw his integrity reflected in his films." *Strength*, *artistry*, and *integrity* are words that encapsulate Stevens—both the man and his screen style. Whether he focused his lens on comedy or drama, the cameraman-turned-director had unwavering faith in his vision, from the meticulous mirth of *Woman of the Year* (1942) to the rugged dignity of *Shane* (1953).

After he learned that "comedy could be graceful and human," he later said, by shooting thirty-five Laurel and Hardy shorts, RKO tasked him with helming a big-budget feature for Katharine Hepburn. The now-famous dinner scene in *Alice Adams* (1935) intertwines heartbreak and hilarity, as a poor girl's attempts to impress a wealthy suitor (Fred MacMurray) fail miserably. Stevens and Hepburn struck comedy gold again with *Woman of the Year*, the first teaming of Hepburn and Spencer Tracy.

The director spent the 1930s making a string of hits at RKO, many under producer Pandro S. Berman, who described Stevens as "polite and soft-spoken and stubborn as a mule." Self-reliant, with total conviction in his directorial instincts, Stevens proved himself master of various genres: the western-biopic with *Annie Oakley* (1935); the musical, with the graceful Astaire-Rogers outing *Swing Time* (1936); and action-meets-comedy with the smash *Gunga Din* (1939).

New York Film Critics Circle Award–winner *The More the Merrier* (1943) brought together Jean

Arthur (as facts-and-figures expert Connie) and Joel McCrea (as her handsome roomer Joe Carter) for an intimate yet comical tête-à-tête on the front steps of their building, a sequence that Frank Capra called "the sexiest and the funniest scene I've ever seen in any picture." It was Stevens's last comedy. "He came back from the war a different person," his son, George Stevens Jr., said of his father's participation in World War II. "Still with his great sense of comedy, but his senses became deeper."

A Place in the Sun (1951) was Stevens's romanticized update of Theodore Dreiser's *An American Tragedy*, first filmed by Josef von Sternberg in 1931.

As director and producer, Stevens modernized the 1920s tale for a postwar audience, saying, "It's a story, fundamentally, of the behavior of people in our society as it exists today." As poor-relation George Eastman, Montgomery Clift embodied the quintessential ambitious outsider, never quite belonging to the leisure class, while her role as the privileged Angela launched Elizabeth Taylor as the ideal of 1950s glamour. Stevens crafted a sensuous melodrama by transitioning scenes with slow, lingering lap dissolves, and shooting Clift and Taylor

George Stevens and Alan Ladd on the set of Shane

A THREAT TO THE SYSTEM

in ultra-close-ups, cutting off the tops and bottoms of their faces. *A Place in the Sun* nabbed six Oscars, including Best Director, and remains a potent parable of social status in midcentury America.

The fairly standard western tale of a Wyoming range war was given mythic grandeur by Stevens in the widescreen, Technicolor *Shane*. The title role gave Alan Ladd, who had been typecast as a taciturn tough-guy in such films as *This Gun for Hire* (1942), a chance to display more dimension as a drifter who rides into a homesteading community and changes the lives of a farm family. Cinematographer Loyal Griggs frames the simple story as an epic, while Stevens accentuates every gunshot in the film, making each bullet symbolize something significant: the violent destruction of human life. *Shane* had a profound influence on actor/director

Warren Beatty, who consulted with Stevens before he branched out into producing with 1967's *Bonnie and Clyde*.

Heading to Warner Bros. for *Giant* (1956), Stevens continued to weave western tropes into a larger tapestry as he breathed life into Edna Ferber's novel. The sweeping saga of a rancher (Rock Hudson), his wife (Elizabeth Taylor), and their resentful ranch hand who strikes oil (James Dean in his final role) required Stevens to spend five months shooting and a solid year in the editing room. The director declined to film *Giant* in CinemaScope, though Jack Warner urged him use the new process. But for the Benedicts' Victorian mansion perched on a desolate plain and the towering oil derricks of West Texas, he wanted the height of standard proportions, not widescreen. "When you

MUST-SEE MOVIES

SWING TIME (1936)

GUNGA DIN (1939)

WOMAN OF THE YEAR (1942)

THE MORE THE MERRIER (1943)

I REMEMBER MAMA (1948)

A PLACE IN THE SUN (1951)

SHANE (1953)

GIANT (1956)

THE GREATEST STORY EVER TOLD (1965)

KEY SCENE TO WATCH

After killing the bad guy (Jack Palance) and being wounded during the shootout, Shane says goodbye to the Starrett family farm in the now-legendary ending of *Shane*. "There's no living with a killing," Shane tells Joey (Brandon deWilde). "There's no going back." Forced to use violence to fight violence, Shane seems to know he must leave town to stop the cycle of killing. Stevens (along with screenwriters A. B. Guthrie Jr. and Jack Sher, who based their script on Jack Schaefer's novel) subtly conveys a pacifist message in this final scene, without preaching. As the lone gunslinger rides off into the sunset, the Grand Tetons looming in the background, Joey calls to his idol, "Shane, come back!"

"I like what *A Place in the Sun* is about and how beautifully directed it is, and the mood of the piece and how he shot it. I think George Stevens was a great director—a great American director."

—DIANE KEATON

see *Giant*, those figures are bigger than life. There is a nobility, there's strength, there's power in them," observed director Rouben Mamoulian. *Giant* was massive at the box office and earned Stevens a second Best Director Oscar.

The seasoned director tailored *The Diary of Anne Frank* (1959) to be a historical document, as factual and true as he could make it. As the head of President Eisenhower's Special Coverage Unit overseas, Stevens had witnessed firsthand the horrors of the Nazi concentration camp at Dachau. He used this experience to inform Anne's world: a cramped, dimly lit attic that housed the young Jewish girl (Millie Perkins) and her family for over two years. Through Stevens's eye, noted *Los Angeles Times* critic Kevin Thomas, "We experience both the claustrophobia of those in hiding and the soaring of Anne's poetic imagination, which knew no walls."

In the 1930s, '40s, and '50s, the thoughtful, stylish films of George Stevens both reflected his era and defined it. The problem with American moviemaking, he once said, was that it was "almost entirely a dollar-and-cents conjecture." He firmly believed that "there's more to a motion picture than its commerce." Rather than profitability,

Stevens focused on the honest humanity that could be expressed through the medium of moving pictures. Because of this, his movies will live forever.

Montgomery Clift and Elizabeth Taylor in A Place in the Sun

A THREAT TO THE SYSTEM

PRESTON STURGES

Years active: 1940–1955

THE BRILLIANT ONE-MAN BAND BEHIND THE ENDEARing classics *The Lady Eve* and *Sullivan's Travels* (both from 1941), Preston Sturges blazed a path as essentially the first writer/director/producer to conquer the studio system. Charlie Chaplin had done it, but he was

a major movie star. Preston Sturges was a former playwright with no filmmaking experience. Once he succeeded with a streak of rollicking comedies in the early 1940s, his triple-threat talent reminded Hollywood that a great film need not be patched together by a committee, but could be the sole creation of one gifted individual.

Sturges earned some screenwriting success in the 1930s, but had his sights set on directing. So, he sold his political satire *The Great McGinty* (1940) to Paramount for $10—with the stipulation that he would direct it. A precedent was set. Within five years, John Huston, Billy Wilder, Delmer Daves, and Joseph L. Mankiewicz were piloting their own scripts too.

After *McGinty* received the inaugural Academy Award for Best Original Screenplay (a new category created to distinguish adaptations from scripts penned especially for the screen), Sturges rapidly wrote, produced, and directed six more comedy hits in a row for Paramount. *Christmas in July* (1940) was a brisk sixty-seven-minute roller coaster of laughter and tears, the yarn of a young man (Dick Powell) who wins a slogan-writing contest for Maxford House Coffee. Depression-era slang inspired the wordplay of the catchphrase: "If you don't sleep at night, it isn't the coffee, it's the bunk." Sturges had a genius for weaving words together to form laugh-out-loud lines. "If you waited for a man to propose to you from natural causes, you'd die of

old-maidenhood," Jean (Barbara Stanwyck) informs Charles (Henry Fonda) in *The Lady Eve*. His films sprinted along with a madcap urgency, yet every moment was controlled like a fine symphony, his screenplays "constructed like perfect-fitting mosaics," his wife, Louise, observed in 1946.

While concocting the cockeyed romantic farce *The Lady Eve*, Sturges envisioned Barbara Stanwyck as sexy card sharp Jean and Henry Fonda as

wide-eyed ophiologist Charles, and he got them both. Stanwyck's rapid-fire comic timing set the pace for the film, and Fonda was her perfect foil—in romance, repartee, and slapstick. "My dearest friends and severest critics constantly urged me to cut the pratfalls down from five to three," Sturges

Betty Hutton and Preston Sturges on the set of The Miracle of Morgan's Creek

A THREAT TO THE SYSTEM

"There hasn't been a better piece of Americana than Preston Sturges's *The Miracle of Morgan's Creek*. It had no pretensions, yet despite the fact that people went around kicking each other's posteriors, it was truer artistically than most pictures made in America."

—ERNST LUBITSCH

recalled, but he took a risk, having Fonda trip over sofas, fall into curtains, and knock over trays of food repeatedly. And it paid off. "Audiences, including the critics," he recalled, "surrendered to the fun." *The Lady Eve* was a sensation, one of the most praised and profitable pictures of 1941. Notoriously hard-to-please Bosley Crowther of the *New York Times* stated emphatically, "Now there's no question about it: Preston Sturges is definitely and distinctly the most refreshing new force to hit the American motion pictures in the last five years. A more charming or distinguished gem of nonsense has not occurred since *It Happened One Night*."

Sturges was often compared to Frank Capra and Ernst Lubitsch. Sturges gave Lubitsch a nod in *Sullivan's Travels*, when Veronica Lake's aspiring actress asks Joel McCrea's director, John L. Sullivan, for "a letter of introduction to Lubitsch." The fondness was mutual: Lubitsch admired the work of Sturges as well. Compared to Lubitsch's cinematic universe, though, life in Sturgesville was less an elegant fairy tale, more rooted in solid American practicality; blunt instead of ethereal. When Sulli-

van is caught driving without a license, he cracks to the cop, "Isn't that terrible? I suppose that calls for a dollar fine and ten minutes in jail."

A paean to the power of laughter, *Sullivan's Travels* follows a big-shot Hollywood director who gets more trouble than he bargains for when he seeks a hardscrabble experience to inform his dramatic films. In the end, he learns that comedy trumps tragedy. Sturges smoothly navigates the tricky terrain of the tonal shift: the movie's first hour is practically pure humor, until Sullivan's journey takes a harrowing twist. The frantic screwball romance *The Palm Beach Story* (1942) also featured McCrea, this time with Claudette Colbert, and without a hint of tragedy.

The real miracle of *The Miracle of Morgan's Creek* (1944) was how Sturges managed to get his suggestive script past the censorship board. After drinking spiked lemonade at a dance, Trudy Kockenlocker (Betty Hutton) wakes up married to an unknown soldier, and pregnant to boot. When she recruits 4-F Norval (Eddie Bracken) to save her reputation, nonstop absurdity ensues. "Here's the funniest picture ever made!" the ads announced, and it was hardly an exaggeration. *The Miracle of Morgan's Creek* is still considered one of the most hilarious movies Hollywood ever produced, by the American Film Institute (in its 100 Years . . . 100 Laughs list from 2000) and *Premiere* magazine (in "The 50 Greatest Comedies of All Time" from 2006).

Miracle takes place in Sturges's version of small-town America, a raucous, hard-hearted place, not exactly a Norman Rockwell painting. "If MGM's Andy Hardy series were a warm hug to their audience, the Sturges pictures were a jab in the ribs," screenwriter Douglas McGrath opined in a 2010 *Vanity Fair* piece. "Someday they're just gonna find your hair ribbon and an axe someplace—nothing else," William Demarest's blustering constable warns his fourteen-year-old daughter (Diana Lynn) in *Miracle*. Demarest was one of the Sturges company of regulars, appearing in nearly all of the director's films.

After crafting seven successful movies in a little over four years, Sturges fled Paramount and formed the independent California Pictures with Howard Hughes. Although the company gave prominent German director Max Ophüls his first job in Hollywood, it proved an unsuccessful venture that knocked Sturges off his winning streak. In less than a decade, he fell from the third-highest earner in the US to the brink of bankruptcy. A comeback might have been in the cards, had he not suffered a fatal heart attack in 1959.

Joel and Ethan Coen and Steven Spielberg are among the many latter-day filmmakers who have found inspiration in the glorious goofiness of Sturges. Spielberg has readily admitted that a good part of his directing education consisted of "sitting in a screening room and screening eight Preston Sturges films. He made some of the greatest movies ever made."

Barbara Stanwyck and Henry Fonda in The Lady Eve

MUST-SEE MOVIES

THE GREAT McGINTY (1940)

THE LADY EVE (1941)

SULLIVAN'S TRAVELS (1941)

THE PALM BEACH STORY (1942)

THE MIRACLE OF MORGAN'S CREEK (1944)

HAIL THE CONQUERING HERO (1944)

UNFAITHFULLY YOURS (1948)

Veronica Lake and Joel McCrea in Sullivan's Travels

KEY SCENE TO WATCH

"I wrote *Sullivan's Travels* to satisfy an urge to tell my fellow comedy directors that they were getting a little too deep-dish," Sturges later wrote, "and to leave the preaching to the preachers." A scene that expresses this message beautifully is the conversation between McCrea and Lake in their three-minute car ride. "There's nothing like a deep-dish movie to drive you out in the open," Lake says of educational pictures. "Film's the greatest educational medium the world has ever known," McCrea counters. "Take a picture like *Hold Back Tomorrow*. . . ." he suggests. "*You* hold it," she deadpans. Although Lake was becoming known for her blond peekaboo waves and her smoldering dramatic presence, Sturges drew a flawless comic performance from the eighteen-year-old newcomer.

PRESTON STURGES

ORSON WELLES

Years active: 1941–1984

A BOY WONDER, A GENIUS, A MAVERICK, A LEGEND. Many terms have been used to describe Orson Welles, the Hollywood antihero behind what is often considered the greatest movie ever made, *Citizen Kane* (1941). To the status quo Golden Age, Welles brought an

outsider's eye, an independent spirit, and an almost self-destructive insistence on following his own vision at any cost. Although his rebelliousness made his journey a difficult one, Welles was unstoppable, shooting films literally until the end of his life, even if they were never completed or distributed.

When Hollywood came knocking at his door in 1939, the twenty-four-year-old wunderkind of stage and airwaves had recently terrified the nation with his 1938 version of H. G. Wells's *The War of the Worlds*, an all-too-lifelike radio drama performed by Welles and his Mercury Theatre repertory company. This gave him the clout to negotiate an unprecedented deal with RKO: he would act in, write, direct, and produce one film a year for the

bargain price of $150,000. "I didn't want money; I wanted authority," he recalled, and he got it. Handing that much power to a newcomer (or to virtually any director) was unheard of. Welles wielded his power to the fullest on *Citizen Kane*, a story he conceived with screenwriter Herman J. Mankiewicz about a newspaper tycoon who, not coincidentally, resembled media mogul William Randolph Hearst.

Because he had, in his words, "the confidence of ignorance," he had the audacity to shoot from beneath floorboards to show the ceilings of rooms, to keep midscene cuts to a bare minimum, and to present a convoluted bildungsroman for the screen, filled with flashbacks and hinging on the mystery of "Rosebud." Following establishing shots of the

A THREAT TO THE SYSTEM

dilapidated Xanadu mansion, a snow-covered cottage is seen briefly, until a zoom out reveals it to be a snow globe held by a dying Charles Foster Kane (played by Welles), who is also covered, momentarily, in the same snowflakes inside the globe. It was (and still is) a bold way to begin a movie, and the ensuing scenes were just as striking. "I didn't know what you couldn't do," Welles said later in life. "I didn't deliberately set out to invent anything. It just seemed to me, why not?"

The tricks Welles and cinematographer Gregg Toland employed—layered narrative, deep focus photography—had been used before. But the way Welles commanded these artistic devices to craft a heightened cinematic reality—this was new. In 1941, theaters were reluctant to book the innovative movie for fear of igniting Hearst's wrath, making it a box office dud, though it won critical praise and an Oscar for Best Original Screenplay. Welles was branded a troublemaker, and was never again given the limitless creative freedom he enjoyed on *Kane*.

Orson Welles in The Lady from Shanghai

"Welles stands kind of above everybody's work. I think every filmmaker has some relation with Welles. If nothing else, he created the air we breathe in that regard. He's sort of the patron saint of indie filmmakers."

—RICHARD LINKLATER

The Magnificent Ambersons (1942) might have been a second *Kane*, had RKO not wrested control from Welles and made significant edits to the lengthy film, altering the direction of the story. Still, it remains a classic. The heartbreaking family saga bears the Welles touch in its meticulously choreographed scenes, exquisite sets, and the performances from his Mercury Theatre favorites, including Joseph Cotten and Agnes Moorehead. As the spinster Aunt Fanny, Moorehead delivers perhaps the most pitiable nervous breakdown captured on film, sinking to the floor with her back against a water heater, wailing, "I wouldn't mind if it burned me!"

In addition to his tendency to go over budget (*Ambersons* topped out at more than $1 million), Welles challenged the collaborative structure of 1940s American filmmaking by his "insistence on imprinting his own personality on his work," in the words of biographer Simon Callow. After RKO fired Welles in 1942, he was not hired as a director for years. The anti-Nazi mystery *The Stranger* (1946) was a mainstream effort to prove he could play by the rules, but even that was reedited against his wishes by the studio. He next lost control of *The Lady from Shanghai* (1947) to Columbia Pictures. A stylized, darkly ironic film noir full of confounding twists, *The Lady from Shanghai* was another failure that sadly seemed to mirror his failing marriage to leading lady Rita Hayworth.

Everything Welles touched seemed to become a financial disaster—except when he stuck to acting, such as portraying the dastardly Harry Lime in Carol Reed's *The Third Man* (1949). In 1957, Welles was set to play the portly police captain Quinlan in *Touch of Evil* (1958) when star Charlton Heston suggested to Universal that Welles direct the crime thriller. "I'll direct it, but if I also get to write it," Welles proposed, "every word of it." So, *Touch of Evil* became his chance for a comeback. When the studio saw a rough cut, though, they were "horrified," he recalled, at his unorthodox choices, such as long, unbroken tracking shots, and having no credits over the opening scene (commonly done today). During the editing phase of the picture, Welles was not only dismissed, but escorted from the Universal lot and not allowed to return.

144

MUST-SEE MOVIES

CITIZEN KANE (1941)

THE MAGNIFICENT AMBERSONS (1942)

JOURNEY INTO FEAR (1943)

THE LADY FROM SHANGHAI (1947)

OTHELLO (1951)

TOUCH OF EVIL (1958)

THE TRIAL (1962)

CHIMES AT MIDNIGHT (1965)

Rita Hayworth and Welles on the set of
The Lady from Shanghai. *Welles had
his wife's long auburn hair cropped and
bleached for the role.*

KEY SCENE TO WATCH

The denouement of *The Lady from Shanghai* is a dazzling, stupefying sequence in a maze of mirrors. Michael (Welles) is confronted by the double-crossing Elsa (Hayworth) in a fun house, their mirror images surrounding the couple. Nine reflections of Bannister (Everett Sloane) appear, and Elsa points her gun. "With these mirrors, it's difficult to tell; you are aiming at me, aren't you?" he asks. When he also takes aim, he admits, "Killing you is killing myself." Reflection upon reflection is fractured as a hail of gunfire shatters the glass in every direction. The sequence in the hall of mirrors has been appropriated so many times in film and television, it has almost become a visual cliché. The 1973 Bruce Lee film *Enter the Dragon* and Chad Stahelski's 2017 *John Wick: Chapter 2* are two features that paid tribute by staging their finales in mirror mazes.

By 1962, Welles was able to make a longtime dream come true: writing and directing his version of Franz Kafka's 1925 novel, *The Trial*, in Europe. And he was given complete artistic control by producer Alexander Salkind. After spending six months perfecting the script, Welles was back in his element, filming a book everyone said was unfilmable, and crafting a real work of art—his way. Much of it shot in an empty Paris railway station, Welles's *The Trial* is a surreal nightmare of vast, disorienting spaces and paranoia-inducing shadows. The *Hollywood Reporter* called it an "abstract film" that was "done with such dash and style that it is fascinating even while it is most opaque."

1965's *Chimes at Midnight* (titled *Falstaff* in Europe) was the movie Welles was proudest of, calling it his "least flawed" film. The actor-director's robust performance as the rascally Sir John Falstaff dominates the screen. A spin on several Shakespeare plays, the movie took over a year to make, as Welles had to stop to raise additional funds. His determination to be an independent auteur keeps Welles at the forefront of Hollywood history.

In the end, *Citizen Kane* remains his magnum opus, a stunning debut that was impossible to live down, or to live up to. "I started at the top and have been working my way down ever since," he quipped, only half joking. When Orson Welles died in 1985, he left behind several great movies, and many unfinished ones. His legendary renegade artistry remains a beacon of hope for aspiring directors everywhere.

Orson Welles as Charles Foster Kane in Citizen Kane

WILLIAM WYLER

Years active: 1925–1970

I COULD HARDLY CALL MYSELF AN AUTEUR, ALTHOUGH I'm one of the few American directors who can pronounce the word correctly," director and producer (and native French-speaker) William Wyler quipped when accepting the American Film Institute's Life Achievement Award in 1976. If ever

a director achieved a lifetime's worth of filmmaking prestige, it was Wyler. With an awe-inspiring succession of acclaimed movies, twelve Academy Award nominations for Best Director, and a total of thirty-eight Oscars for his body of work, no other director came close to his record.

Like most filmmakers of Hollywood's studio age, Wyler avoided the obvious stylistic or thematic trademarks of an auteur, making each film a stand-alone experience. From the filthy gutters of *Dead End* (1937) to the frothy flair of *Funny Girl* (1969), Wyler shunted his personality aside, thinking only of what served the picture best. Arriving in Hollywood from Alsace-Lorraine (on the Germany-Switzerland border) in 1922, Wyler worked his way

up from assistant to director-for-hire. He joined forces with producer Samuel Goldwyn in 1936. "We had sort of a love-hate relationship," he said of their stormy ten-year partnership that yielded, among others, the polished gem *Dodsworth* (1936), starring Walter Huston as Sinclair Lewis's middle-aged industrialist.

Wyler began his association with director of photography Gregg Toland on *These Three* (1936), an adaptation of Lillian Hellman's intense play *The Children's Hour.* That collaboration proved so effective, Hellman declared him "the greatest of all American directors." The depth-of-field cinematography Toland pioneered brought both background and foreground into sharp focus, lending realism

to Wyler's films, and allowing him to shoot longer scenes in a single take, uninterrupted by cuts. Notice a fluid scene in *The Westerner* (1940) when Judge Roy Bean (Walter Brennan) watches as Cole (Gary Cooper) walks away, mounts his horse, and rides into the horizon. We can still see Cole in the distance as the judge mutters, "By gobs, he stole my gun."

Movie queen Bette Davis credited Wyler with making her an A-list star in *Jezebel* (1938). "If Willy Wyler told me to jump in the Hudson River, I would," Davis once said. She trusted him professionally, and fell for him personally, later revealing,

"He was the love of my life." The feeling—at least, during their three films together—was mutual. For *Jezebel*, set in the antebellum South, Wyler surrounded Davis with period antiques and draped her in $30,000 worth of nineteenth-century gowns. On *The Little Foxes* (1941), Davis clashed violently with Wyler over her portrayal of icy Regina Giddens, and fainted from her heavy Orry-Kelly costumes and tight corsets. Rave reviews made the ordeal

William Wyler directs Samantha Eggar in The Collector, *1965*

A THREAT TO THE SYSTEM

> "William Wyler was my great idol, because he could take a bad script and make a mediocre picture. He could take a mediocre script and make a good picture. He could take a good script and make a great picture! This guy could never miss. His ability to tell a story on film was unparalleled."

—NORMAN JEWISON

worthwhile. *The Little Foxes*, critic Edwin Schallert wrote, "is one of those superfine things that the movies give birth to once in a dozen years."

Wuthering Heights (1939) starred Laurence Olivier, a stage-trained actor who remained grateful to Wyler for steering his talent in a more screen-appropriate direction. "I was overacting appallingly," Olivier recalled, until Wyler urged him to "come back to earth." Wyler exhausted actors with his multiple retakes, earning the sobriquet "Forty-take Wyler" (some even whispered "Ninety-take Wyler" behind the director's back). But no one could argue with the perfect results. Watch Wyler's long, unbroken take of Olivia de Havilland's Catherine as Montgomery Clift (as Morris) asks her forgiveness, and her hand in marriage, in *The Heiress*

MUST-SEE MOVIES

DODSWORTH (1936)

THE LETTER (1940)

THE LITTLE FOXES (1941)

MRS. MINIVER (1942)

THE BEST YEARS OF OUR LIVES (1946)

ROMAN HOLIDAY (1953)

BEN-HUR (1959)

THE COLLECTOR (1965)

FUNNY GIRL (1969)

KEY SCENE TO WATCH

After four years away at war, Al Stephenson (Fredric March) arrives at his home, surprising his family in *The Best Years of Our Lives*. His wife, Milly (Myrna Loy), hears the doorbell from the kitchen, and senses that Al has returned. She drops the dishes she was washing, and moves down a hallway toward Al, as he moves toward her, the couple finally connecting in a wordless loving embrace. Memorable, touching, and true to life, this scene was based on Wyler's actual return from World War II, when he and his wife, Talli, spotted each other at either end of a long hallway, and met in the middle. "We had to run to each other, so I thought I'd repeat that," Wyler explained. "It made the scene very effective."

(1949). A torrent of emotions rages behind her eyes, yet her body and face remain impassive. De Havilland won a Best Actress Oscar for the role. Under Wyler's direction, Audrey Hepburn and Barbra Streisand both took home gold statuettes for their Hollywood debuts.

Wyler's movies have proven their durability over the decades. His masterful ensemble piece *The Best Years of Our Lives* (1946) is set in a small American city post–World War II, yet it illustrates timeless, universal human problems: struggling to fit into society, marrying the wrong person, finding a good job. Ex-bombardier Fred (Dana Andrews) experiences traumatic war flashbacks in the film, while Homer

(Oscar-winner Harold Russell, an actual disabled veteran) adjusts to a disabling injury. Wyler himself had just returned from serving overseas, where he flew planes over enemy lines and suffered partial hearing loss. "I knew my subject. I had learned it the hard way," he later said of *The Best Years*.

In 1952, Wyler departed for Europe, where he made *Roman Holiday* (1953), the first Hollywood film shot entirely in Italy, and Wyler's first comedy in over a decade. Although a taskmaster on set, Wyler had a playful humor that shines through

Fredric March and Dana Andrews in The Best Years of Our Lives

A THREAT TO THE SYSTEM

in *Roman Holiday*, a sublime Cinderella-story-in-reverse that stands as perhaps the screen's most perfect romance, and one that made Audrey Hepburn an icon. A dozen years later, the stylish heist *How to Steal a Million* (1966) reunited Wyler and Hepburn for another European escapade, this time in Paris instead of Rome.

A grand remake of MGM's 1925 silent biblical epic, Wyler's *Ben-Hur* (1959) raked in a record eleven Oscars (unequaled until James Cameron's *Titanic* tied in 1998). But shooting it wasn't easy. The veteran director spent almost a year managing the massive cast, the bulky 70-mm film, the nine-minute chariot race (which took ten weeks to shoot), and the pressure of *Ben-Hur*; as the most expensive film ever made at the time, the fate of MGM was riding on its success. The studio was in good hands. The widescreen Technicolor feat became the second-highest-grossing film in history (after *Gone with the Wind* [1939]) and remains an all-time favorite.

As he grew older, Wyler's films became darker and edgier. *The Collector* (1965) was the tale of a brutal kidnapping that Wyler spun into a tragic, perverse love story. His last film, *The Liberation of L. B. Jones* (1970), was a diatribe against racism in the American South. Wyler's liberal social beliefs had been seeping subversively into his pictures for years (1951's *Detective Story* was a veiled indictment of intolerance), and now that the 1960s counterculture revolution allowed it, Wyler's ideology was on full display. Critic Andrew Sarris called *The Liberation of L. B. Jones* "the most provocative brief for Black Power ever to come out of a Hollywood studio." It was the last word from a man whose forty years of excellence left a lasting impression on cinema.

Charlton Heston in Ben-Hur's *famous chariot race*

WILLIAM WYLER

DARK UNDERCURRENTS

Flashbacks, voiceover narration, and dark, expressionistic lighting were the hallmarks of film noir—some deliberate artistic flourishes, others necessitated by lean budgets. "Cary Grant and all the big stars at RKO got all the lights," laconic noir legend Robert Mitchum once joked. "We lit our sets with cigarette butts." Often, the forces behind these films were not A-list directors, but below-the-radar masters who made the most of the bleak crime stories they were assigned.

Canadian-born editor-turned-director **Edward Dmytryk** was known as "Mr. RKO" for his run of successful pictures for the studio. *Murder, My Sweet* (1944) explored the nocturnal underworld of pulp novelist Raymond Chandler's Los Angeles, even quoting Chandler's prose in

Dick Powell's narration; *Cornered* (1945) also featured Powell as a war-hardened veteran. *Crossfire* (1947) was a tightrope of suspense, the first Hollywood movie to target anti-Semitism, earning Dmytryk a Best Director nomination.

From the ominous atmosphere of *My Name Is Julia Ross* (1945) to the sexually charged thrill ride *Gun Crazy* (1950), **Joseph H. Lewis** made his mark on the dark side. A stylish, creatively shot Bonnie-and-Clyde love story, *Gun Crazy* is usually considered his masterpiece, but Lewis also delivered the intense *So Dark the Night* (1946) and the jazz-infused *The Big Combo* (1955), among other well-crafted B-movies.

Virginia Huston and Robert Mitchum in Jacques Tourneur's Out of the Past

German émigré **Robert Siodmak** arrived in Hollywood in 1939, but hit his stride in the 1940s at Universal, starting with the low-budget classic *Phantom Lady* (1944). The haunting *The Spiral Staircase* (1945)—which he was able to edit to his own standards, due to an editors' strike—and the hard-boiled Hemingway tale *The Killers* (1946) may be the pinnacle of Siodmak's career; the dismal-but-sensuous *Criss Cross* (1947) earns honorable mention.

Jacques Tourneur is most famous today for the quintessential tough guy–meets–femme fatale flick *Out of the Past* (1947), starring Robert Mitchum as the trench-coated private eye who falls for the wrong dame (Jane Greer). Before that, Tourneur cut his teeth at RKO, helming the intoxicating *Cat People* (1942) and *I Walked with a Zombie* (1943) for producer Val Lewton. His elegant *Experiment Perilous* (1944) was an exercise in gothic intrigue with Hedy Lamarr.

Learning his craft by assisting F. W. Murnau, Austrian-American **Edgar G. Ulmer** knew how to set a mood with striking imagery. If the thriller *The Black Cat* (1934) earned Ulmer attention, the threadbare noir *Detour* (1945) is the movie he's most remembered for. Shot in two weeks for $100,000, *Detour* was a doom-laden hard-luck story for Poverty Row studio PRC. Ulmer stayed in the shadows with *The Strange Woman* (1946), *Ruthless* (1948), and *Murder Is My Beat* (1955).

THE ARCHERS

Through his alliance with screenwriter, coproducer, and codirector **Emeric Pressburger**, director **Michael Powell** made some of the greatest motion pictures to emerge from postwar England. After dabbling in black and white, the Archers (as the Powell-Pressburger team called themselves) used Technicolor to radiant effect in their epic tale of love and war, *The Life and Death of Colonel Blimp* (1943), and their 1946 romantic fantasia *A Matter of Life and Death* (also known as *Stairway to Heaven*). When ballerina Victoria Page (Moira Shearer) performed "The Ballet of the Red Shoes" in the color-saturated spectacle *The Red Shoes* (1948), Powell and Pressburger pioneered

a subjective, impressionistic rendering of dance on film. With Oscar-winning cinematographer Jack Cardiff by their side, the Archers delivered the darkly engrossing *Black Narcissus* (1947) and the fanciful *Tales of Hoffman* (1951) before parting ways in 1957. In the 1940s, Powell and Pressburger's movies made an impact in America, where they influenced Vincente Minnelli, Martin Scorsese, George A. Romero, and other Hollywood filmmakers— and filmmakers-to-be.

Robert Helpmann and Moira Shearer in The Red Shoes

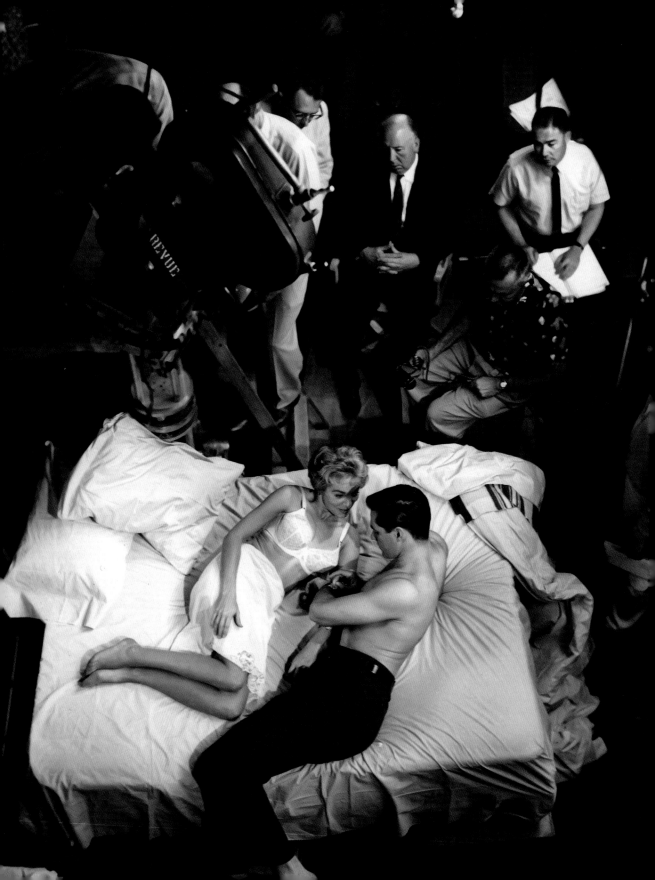

Chapter Four

THE DIRECTOR AS STAR

In 1950, Americans started buying television sets in record numbers. To outshine the small screen, movies grew supersized via new processes like CinemaScope and Cinerama. Drive-in theaters popped up everywhere, allowing audiences to relax in their cars and enjoy movies projected to enormous proportions. While indoor theaters featured screens no more than 40 feet wide, drive-in screens might be as massive as 80 feet.

If movies in the 1950s were large, the people who made them were larger than life. Big-name directors Cecil B. DeMille and Alfred Hitchcock often appeared in their own trailers. DeMille even narrated *The Ten Commandments*, while Hitchcock made in-joke cameos in his films, and Otto Preminger costarred as the prison commandant in Billy Wilder's *Stalag 17*. Once an invisible force behind the camera, the director could now attain a movie-star level of fame. Ida Lupino, in fact, *was* a movie star who made the leap to directing, feeling more empowered in the director's chair than she did acting.

As television encroached on the industry's profits, postwar Hollywood erupted in a last hurrah of glitz and glamour, of extravagant studio epics. But the '50s came with a dark side: the purging of suspected Communists in the film capital derailed some of the industry's best and brightest. As filmmakers fought against the constrictive atmosphere, the old studio system slowly fell apart at the seams; the Production Code even loosened a bit, making exceptions for slightly more explicit sexual innuendo and language—a harbinger of things to come.

Alfred Hitchcock and crew shoot the opening scene of Psycho, *1959.*

ALFRED HITCHCOCK

Years active: 1922–1976

R ACKING UP A PHENOMENAL FILMOGRAPHY OF sophisticated thrillers over the course of fifty years, Alfred Hitchcock earned his title, the "Master of Suspense." The man behind such unforgettable, edge-of-your-seat classics as *Rear Window* (1954), *Vertigo* (1958),

Psycho (1960), and *The Birds* (1963) tantalized millions and inspired countless imitations of his tense and morbidly witty style, commonly known as Hitchcockian. The tremendous scope and impact of his movies surpasses virtually all of his fellow twentieth-century directors.

The American press was already affectionately referring to the Essex, England, native as "Hitch" in 1940, when his Hollywood contract with producer David O. Selznick yielded its first effort, the Best-Picture–awarded mystery *Rebecca*. It was *The Lady Vanishes* (1938) that had brought him to the attention of Selznick. The clever espionage puzzle waxes and wanes between drama, comedy, and suspense, a tone Hitchcock had mastered in

The 39 Steps (1935)—which initiated his standard form of fear inducement: the dreadful twist of fate that could befall any average person in commonplace surroundings. This theme continued with his personal favorite, *Shadow of a Doubt* (1943)—a sinister sliver of small-town terror shot on location in sleepy Santa Rosa, California—and with *Strangers on a Train* (1951), *The Man Who Knew Too Much* (1956), and *North by Northwest* (1957).

Hitch loved to lace his thrillers with sex appeal and humor. Despite its Freudian trappings, *Spellbound* (1945) was a high-gloss Hollywood romance; the voyeuristic *Rear Window* was loaded with dark comedy, as housebound hero Jeff (James Stewart) surveys a sampling of unhappily-ever-after couples

THE DIRECTOR AS STAR

through his zoom lens; *To Catch a Thief* (1955) was as much an escapist rom-com as it was a cat-and-mouse game.

Avoiding traditional whodunits, Hitchcock crafted his own subtype of suspense, told through clear, carefully plotted visuals. "I deal in nightmares, and nightmares have to be awfully vivid," he once said. He worked closely with storyboard artists to preplan key shots for maximum efficiency. In the opening scenes of *Rear Window*, Hitchcock and cinematographer Robert Burks feed us the whole setup using only props and camera movement; we see Jeff's courtyard, his sweaty brow, the cast on his leg, and his photographs, and know he's an injured photographer stuck in his apartment in summer. In his sublime spine-tingler *Vertigo*, Hitch spends ten minutes following Scottie (Stewart), who is following an enigmatic blonde (Kim Novak). We see everything Scottie sees through a series of obsessive point-of-view shots, no dialogue needed.

Alfred Hitchcock with bound scripts from his films, 1966

"Alfred Hitchcock was, along with DeMille, Hawks, and Ford, one of the few directors whose name was generally known to the public at large. His is a filmography second to none, and under his own terms, he was one of the most influential artists of his era. His late-career triumph *Psycho* changed the psyche of the entire world, cinematically and sociologically. And every time I set up a point-of-view shot I think of Hitchcock."

—JOE DANTE

Hitchcock has been taken to task for saying, "Actors should be treated like cattle," but this was a wry exaggeration. What he meant, no doubt, was that his visual storytelling was the primary element in a Hitchcock film, and actors were secondary. On the first day of *Psycho*, he gave one piece of direction to Janet Leigh: "My camera has to be the focal point. When my camera moves, you have to move." Simply hiring a performer was a display of his trust in that performer. "If he didn't have faith, I don't think you'd be working with him," observed screenwriter Joseph Stefano, who adapted Robert Bloch's novel *Psycho*.

Paramount Pictures declined to finance the director's first true horror effort, so he raised $800,000 and produced *Psycho* himself as an independent film. The twisted tale of a woman on the run (Leigh) and the lonely motel-owner she encounters (Anthony Perkins) arguably represents the pinnacle of Hitchcock's skill, artistry, and knack for promotion, as theaters drew around-the-block lines by refusing anyone entrance after the film had started. But it was the strength of the movie itself—not merely the marketing or the shocking shower scene—that earned $9 million at the box office and Hitchcock a Best Director Oscar nomination. "It wasn't a message that stirred the audiences, nor was it a great performance," Hitchcock told filmmaker (and fan) François Truffaut. "They were aroused by pure film." And pure Hitchcock; *Psycho* was solely his vision, not Selznick's, not Paramount's. A

brilliantly stark, sexy, and economical plunge into split-personality psychosis, *Psycho* shattered the conventions of Hollywood filmmaking in 1960, causing the *Village Voice*'s Andrew Sarris to declare Hitchcock "the most daring avant-garde filmmaker in America today."

After the black-and-white thrills of *Psycho*, the bloody Technicolor trauma of *The Birds* was a notch more sadistic. For the scene in which Tippi Hedren's Melanie is assaulted by crows in an attic, the mechanical birds Hitchcock planned to use malfunctioned, so Hedren spent seven days in a cage with "handlers hurling live birds at me," she recalled in 2016. "It was brutal and ugly and relentless." The first-time film actress required five days of doctor-ordered bed rest to recover.

Cool, refined leading ladies—usually blondes—were a Hitchcock staple. When his favorite fair-haired female Grace Kelly married Prince Rainier and retired to Monaco in 1956, Eva Marie Saint, Kim Novak, and Tippi Hedren took up the mantle. He ascribed his penchant for blondes to "the tradition of the cinema" dating back to silent days, when "the hero was always a dark man and the heroine was always a blonde." Since Hitchcock's death, Hedren's accusations of sexual harassment have haunted his legacy, whereas Kelly described the filmmaker in 1976 as "someone I love and respect . . . a warm and understanding human being."

James Stewart and Grace Kelly in Rear Window

MUST-SEE MOVIES

REBECCA (1940)

SHADOW OF A DOUBT (1943)

NOTORIOUS (1946)

STRANGERS ON A TRAIN (1951)

REAR WINDOW (1954)

NORTH BY NORTHWEST (1957)

VERTIGO (1958)

PSYCHO (1960)

THE BIRDS (1963)

Ingrid Bergman in a key scene in Notorious

KEY SCENE TO WATCH

Hitchcock demonstrates his flair for building suspense via imagery when Ingrid Bergman (as Alicia) purloins a key from Claude Rains (as Alex) in *Notorious*. As they dress for a party, the spying Alicia sneaks the wine cellar key from Alex's keyring, planning to search for hidden uranium. The scene that follows kicks off with an awe-inspiring crane shot that swoops from the ceiling down a staircase and across a grand foyer to finally land on a close-up of Bergman's hand clasping the key. "That's like saying," Hitchcock later revealed, "in this vast area, everybody's having a good time, but the key to the entire evening is contained in somebody's hand." Bergman's costar Cary Grant swiped the key from the set and gave it to Bergman, who kept it as a good luck charm until 1979, when she presented it to Hitchcock at his American Film Institute Life Achievement Award ceremony.

By 1966, an interviewer asked the living legend, "Why do you use stars at all? Hitchcock *is* a star." His rotund figure and macabre deadpan humor made him an icon to viewers who spotted him in his movie cameos and watched his long-running TV series *Alfred Hitchcock Presents*. Across North America, England, and Europe, the Hitchcock brand was known to all. The "Master of Suspense" was assisted by a top-tier team, including movie-credit innovator Saul Bass; Bernard Herrmann and his evocative scoring; eight-time Oscar-winning costume designer Edith Head; and Hitch's most important collaborator, critic, and creative influence: his ever-present wife and editor, Alma Reville. "The Hitchcock touch had four hands," wrote critic Charles Champlin in 1982, "and two of them were Alma's."

Gauging Hitchcock's influence on filmmaking and culture is a monumental task. From Stanley Donen's *Charade* (1963) to Brian De Palma's *Dressed to Kill* (1980) to Martin Scorsese's *Cape Fear* (1991)—modeled after director J. Lee Thompson's Hitchcock-inspired 1962 original—dozens of thrillers have taken a Hitchcockian turn for decades now. "My films are inspired by Hitchcock, of course," De Palma has said. "Hitchcock is the grammar of cinema; he's made all the connections. Of course, he's done it better than anyone. He's the giant."

Over forty years after his death, his work remains popular, relevant, and widely referenced throughout the world.

Tippi Hedren fights off a seagull in The Birds.

ELIA KAZAN

Years active: 1945–1976

A S THE ESTABLISHED ORDER OF THE STUDIO SYS-
tem began to decay in 1950s Hollywood, Elia Kazan was a key player
in blazing the trail toward a new kind of filmmaking. Truthful and emotionally raw, Kazan's movies often critiqued American societal ills such

as anti-Semitism (*Gentlemen's Agreement* [1947]), racism (*Pinky* [1949]), and the political power of the
media (*A Face in the Crowd* [1957]). Some of his
most timeless work, however, addressed universal
conflicts inherent in the human experience: the
showdown between reality and illusion in *A Streetcar
Named Desire* (1951), the harsh family dynamics in
East of Eden (1955).

Known as "Gadge" to his friends (for "Gad-
get," as he was small and handy to have around),
Kazan got his start as an actor with the innovative
Group Theatre in 1930s New York City, the birth-
place of Lee Strasberg's Method, which taught
actors to summon emotional memories from their
lives. He worked his way up to director, a path

that led to an outstanding debut film with *A Tree
Grows in Brooklyn* (1945). Kazan, screenwriter Budd
Schulberg, and cameraman Leon Shamroy transformed Betty Smith's poignant coming-of-age novel
into a child-centered drama without a trace of sac-
charine. From there, Kazan addressed weightier
issues; *Gentleman's Agreement* marked the first time the
word "Jew" was used in a major Hollywood movie,
while *Panic in the Streets* (1950) was a startling quasi-
documentary about an airborne virus that ter-
rorizes the population of New Orleans. In 1951,
Kazan set the bar for screen drama a few notches
higher with his film version of a Tennessee
Williams play he helmed on Broadway: *A Streetcar
Named Desire.*

Kazan cast a young Method actor named Marlon Brando in the role of blue-collar brute Stanley Kowalski, kicking off the career of one of cinema's most enduring icons. When Vivien Leigh's fragile Blanche DuBois was confronted with Brando's fiery Stanley, a torrent of rage was unleashed on the screen. Although several of the film's lustier scenes were cut to comply with the Production Code (a battle Kazan fought and lost), filmgoers were blown away by the primitive power of Brando, and saw a whole new side to Leigh. "I was full of admiration for the lady," Kazan said of his leading actress, who was determined to deliver greatness. "She'd have crawled over broken glass if she thought it would help her performance." Leigh, Kim Hunter, and Karl Malden all took home Oscars for *Streetcar*.

In 1952, Kazan was called to testify before the House Un-American Activities Committee

Eliza Kazan on the set of Baby Doll, *1956*

(HUAC), and willingly provided the names of eight actors suspected of Communist ties. Many saw HUAC's Hollywood investigation as a no-win situation. If accused artists remained silent, they might never work again; if they informed, they were shunned by their peers. In the ensuing years, Kazan admitted to feelings of guilt, yet clung to the conviction that he had made the right decision. The blot on his legacy was long-lived, following him to the 1999 Oscars ceremony, where he was met with protests as he accepted his honorary award.

A Schulberg-penned story of union corruption among New Jersey dockworkers, *On the Waterfront* (1954) starred Brando in a now-legendary role as tormented ex-boxer Terry Malloy. "It was so cold and so miserable and we worked so long," Brando recalled of *Waterfront*, shot on location during a freezing Hoboken winter. "I was never more miserable in my life and never more sur-

Vivien Leigh and Marlon Brando in A Streetcar Named Desire

MUST-SEE MOVIES

A TREE GROWS IN BROOKLYN
(1945)

A STREETCAR NAMED DESIRE
(1951)

ON THE WATERFRONT (1954)

EAST OF EDEN (1955)

BABY DOLL (1956)

A FACE IN THE CROWD (1957)

WILD RIVER (1960)

SPLENDOR IN THE GRASS
(1960)

AMERICA AMERICA (1963)

KEY SCENE TO WATCH

With orders from Johnny Friendly, Charley (Rod Steiger) pulls a gun on Terry (Marlon Brando) to try to stop him from testifying as they ride in the back of a car in *On the Waterfront*. Instead of fear, Brando reacts with a look of disappointment, shaking his head as he pushes the gun away. He then defends himself against Charley's betrayals, past and present, with the memorable lament: "I coulda had class. I coulda been a contender. I coulda been somebody, instead of a bum, which is what I am." With these heartbreaking words, Terry shames his brother into backing down, a move that seals Charley's fate.

Elia Kazan directs Marlon Brando in On the Waterfront.

> ## "*On the Waterfront* has a very special place in my heart. . . . Kazan and Budd [Schulberg] had problems making this film. The studio was like, 'Who wants to see a film about sweaty longshoremen?' But they got it done. And it's one of the greatest films ever made, in my opinion."
>
> —SPIKE LEE

prised by the results," he said of the unpleasant conditions that contributed to "the best performance I've ever seen by a man in films," in the words of Kazan. The actor expressed a range of understated emotions in his close-ups, and brought improvisational energy to the action, such as the park scene when Edie (Eva Marie Saint) drops a white glove and Terry puts it on. The Academy voted the film eight Oscars, including Best Picture, and it continues to appear on lists of the greatest movies ever made. *On the Waterfront*'s success earned Kazan the respect he felt he'd been missing since the HUAC scandal, and was interpreted by many as an attempt to justify his testimony, in the form of Terry heroically informing on a shady union boss (Lee J. Cobb).

In his quest for cinematic realism, Kazan favored unknown actors over established movie stars. Eva Marie Saint, Andy Griffith, and Carroll Baker were among the new faces that Kazan elevated to fame. He also gave the intuitive, unpredictable newcomer James Dean the lead in *East of Eden*, and in 1960's *Splendor in the Grass*, he cast Warren Beatty in his first major role while providing Natalie

Wood the chance to do some of her best acting in the explosive bathtub scene. Gadge had a way of wringing great performances from actors by any means necessary; when Dean had trouble with the rooftop sequence in *East of Eden*, Kazan took the actor to an Italian restaurant and filled him with Chianti, allowing him to nail the scene.

With all the passion Kazan put into his stage and screen work, he seemed to run out of steam early. In 1963, he wrote, produced, and directed *America America*, the touching true story of his Greek family's immigration from Istanbul to America when he was a child, and in 1976 he directed his final film, *The Last Tycoon*, set in Golden Age Hollywood and based on F. Scott Fitzgerald's unfinished novel.

Although he lived into the twenty-first century, Kazan is most associated with the 1950s. In a sense, he bridged the gap between the old studio system of the 1940s and the New Hollywood that emerged in the late 1960s. By tackling controversial subjects and striving for naked realism, Kazan impacted millions with the depth and humanity of his films.

THE DIRECTOR AS STAR

IDA LUPINO

Years active: 1949–1966

A S 1950s HOLLYWOOD'S ONLY COMMERCIALLY SUC-
cessful actress to become a commercially viable director, Ida Lupino
blazed a trail other women are still following, from Kasi Lemmons
to Angelina Jolie. Lupino, a contract star at Warner Bros., was often

suspended for refusing roles she felt were demeaning. Instead of sitting idly at home, curiosity about filmmaking led her back to the studio, where "I used to ask if I could sit in the cutting room and see how a film is put together," she recalled.

Born into a prominent English theater family, Lupino began acting in films as a teenager. During the '40s, she grew increasingly restless as an actress. Although she gave stellar performances in Raoul Walsh's *The Man I Love* (1947) and Jean Negulesco's scintillating noir *Road House* (1948), the itch to direct had taken hold. But breaking into the field was a hurdle. "There was an absolute and ironclad caste system in the film capital in the 1940s and 1950s which, it seems to me, had its primary purpose to exclude females," she observed.

Her shot came in 1949, when she and her husband, Collier Young, formed an independent production company, and Lupino picked up the reins on *Not Wanted* (1949) after director Elmer Clifton suffered a mild heart attack. The film's controversial topic of unwanted pregnancy resulted in box office action, but even given her acceptance into the Directors Guild (as the only woman among 1,300 men), she struggled to be taken seriously. "Believe me," she remembered, "I *fought* to produce and direct my own pictures." Wily and tenacious, Lupino achieved an incredible level of success in the totally male-dominated industry of the '50s. She managed to juggle acting, writing,

167

directing, producing, and motherhood, costarring in Nicholas Ray's *On Dangerous Ground* (1951), turning out a taut sports drama with *Hard, Fast and Beautiful!* (1951), and giving birth to a daughter—all in the span of a single year. As tough as Lupino had to be in her dealings, she gained her crew's respect by being maternal and kind, preferring to be called "Mother" on set.

Her polio-themed *Never Fear* (1949) so impressed RKO chief Howard Hughes that he secured Lupino and Young a deal to finance and distribute their indie efforts. Lupino was offered another long-term acting contract, but turned it down. "I was now able to tell Warner Bros. to go to hell!" she said

Ida Lupino on set, 1957

THE DIRECTOR AS STAR

of her power upgrade. Her goal was to spotlight issues affecting women, which many male directors wouldn't touch. She bucked Hollywood standards with the insightful *Outrage* (1950), an honest story about rape, or as the *New York Times* put it, "a sex crime, which, heretofore, 'nice' producers didn't make movies about." Under the Production Code, Lupino was forbidden to include the word *rape* in the film. But her message came through loud and clear anyway, in the look of turmoil in Mala Powers's eyes as she battles judgments and double standards, struggling to recover from the trauma of attack.

With her surprisingly sensitive exposé of adultery, *The Bigamist* (1953), Lupino became the first woman in the sound era to direct herself onscreen. Always up for a challenge, Lupino jumped from female-centered dramas to a hard-edged film noir with an all-male cast, *The Hitch-Hiker* (1953). She and Young completely rewrote Robert Joseph's script about two men (Edmond O'Brien and Frank Lovejoy) who pick up a psychotic killer (William Talman) while on a fishing trip, adding a ripped-from-the-headlines urgency and paring down the nightmare to an intense seventy minutes. "*The Hitch-Hiker* is a suspenseful, wire-tight little melodrama that can stand on its own merits," *Film*

Ida Lupino directs Carleton G. Young and Claire Trevor in Hard, Fast and Beautiful!, *1951.*

> "What is at stake in Lupino's films is the psyche of the victim. They addressed the wounded soul and traced the slow, painful process of women trying to wrestle with despair and reclaim their lives. Her work is resilient, with a remarkable empathy for the fragile and the heart-broken. It is essential."

—MARTIN SCORSESE

Bulletin raved in 1953. "An example of intelligent, economical filmmaking at its best." Shooting in the rocky hills of Lone Pine, California, on a budget of barely over $100,000, Lupino made lonely roads and desolate landscapes key players in what arguably remains her best film. In 1998, *The Hitch-Hiker* was recognized by the Library of Congress as a defining entry in the noir canon.

This actress turned director was a self-taught wonder, boldly taking charge with none of the training, apprenticeships, or encouragement that most male directors had. Other movie stars followed in her footsteps. After Lupino broke the ice, Claudette Colbert announced her aim to direct in 1949, but her picture deal never materialized. Actress Lee Grant was inspired by Lupino to become a documentary filmmaker in 1973. When Clint Eastwood was a cast member of the TV series *Rawhide* in 1959, he visited the set next door to watch Lupino helm an episode of *Have Gun—Will Travel*, and saw her riding a horse alongside the cameraman to get action shots. "I believed that if an actress could become a director, it kind of made me think I could be a director," Eastwood later said.

Lupino showed her range by shifting from shoot-'em-up TV westerns to a convent setting for *The Trouble with Angels* (1966), her first feature in thirteen years. The low-budget filmmaker relished the chance to work in color for a change, and crafted a warm and perceptive coming-of-age dramedy starring Oscar-winning youngster Hayley Mills playing against type as a mischievous hell-raiser with an unexpectedly poignant character arc.

Ultimately, television proved more welcoming than film, giving Lupino the chance to helm over one hundred episodes in the late 1950s and 1960s. She not only served as *The Twilight Zone*'s sole female director, but piloted one of its most memorable outings, 1964's grotesquely shocking "The Masks." The powerhouse talent continued acting into her sixties. But it was her years behind the camera as Hollywood's only woman director that made Ida Lupino the mother of independent filmmakers everywhere.

MUST-SEE MOVIES

OUTRAGE (1950)

HARD, FAST AND BEAUTIFUL!
(1951)

THE HITCH-HIKER (1953)

THE BIGAMIST (1953)

THE TROUBLE WITH ANGELS
(1966)

*Frank Lovejoy, William Talman, and
Edmond O'Brien in* The Hitch-Hiker

KEY SCENE TO WATCH

Held hostage by gun-toting criminal Emmett Myers, Roy and Gilbert bed down for the night outdoors near a brook in *The Hitch-Hiker*. "You guys are gonna die," the hitchhiker tells the men at gunpoint. As the rushing water throws moonlight upon Emmett, we see a cold expression on his face, and a dead look in his right eye. "I got one bum eye," he says. "It won't stay closed." All night, Emmett's eye remains open, making it impossible to tell whether he's asleep or awake. Lupino had entered San Quentin State Prison's death row to visit Billy Cook, the murderer on whom *The Hitch-Hiker* was based. "Billy Cook had 'Hard Luck' tattooed on the fingers of his left hand and a deformed right eyelid that would never close completely," she observed, and included the eyelid detail in the film.

JOSEPH L. MANKIEWICZ

Years active: 1946–1972

"I CAME IN WITH TALK," JOSEPH LEO MANKIEWICZ SAID of his Hollywood entrance. Like his older brother, *Citizen Kane* (1941) screenwriter Herman Mankiewicz, he embarked on the picture business when sound exploded and witty wordsmiths were required. He arrived in 1929 and went to

work turning out talkies for Paramount. Herman was his mentor, but Joe was a fast learner, developing his own wry and sophisticated screenwriting voice—even coining the phrase "my little chickadee" for W. C. Fields. By 1944, he had signed on not only to write, but to produce and direct at Twentieth Century-Fox. His career ignited as his brother's declined.

Ernst Lubitsch was set to direct the Gene Tierney vehicle *Dragonwyck* (1946) when a heart attack stopped him and Mankiewicz stepped in, making his spur-of-the-moment directorial debut. He and Tierney reteamed the following year for the sublime supernatural romance *The Ghost and Mrs. Muir*. Mankiewicz crafted a tense trio of noirs

with *Somewhere in the Night* (1946), *House of Strangers* (1949), and *No Way Out* (1950). Whereas the first two were potent and atmospheric, *No Way Out* was an unflinching indictment of racism, boasting the knockout film debut of Sidney Poitier. With these projects, Mankiewicz refined a simple but effective directorial style, avoiding flourishes like obvious camera movements or elaborate setups. "The perfect film," he once said, "keeps the audience riveted from start to finish in what is happening, participating in it, without knowing that it's ever been directed."

A Letter to Three Wives (1949) marked the first time he had the satisfaction of seeing "screenplay and direction by Joseph L. Mankiewicz" on the

screen (though Vera Caspary contributed to the script). With his urbanely written romance-comedy-drama of three suburban women (Jeanne Crain, Linda Darnell, and Ann Sothern) prompted to reassess the strength of their marriages by a note from the town flirt, Mankiewicz officially arrived as a writer/director of acclaim. *Variety* called *Three Wives* "A standout in every aspect," praising the dialogue, acting, and story, particularly the direc-

tor's trick of never showing the audience the mystery woman who wrote the titular letter.

In 1950 and '51, Mankiewicz made history by winning back-to-back double Academy Awards for writing and directing—a feat no one has accomplished since—for *A Letter to Three Wives* and *All*

Joseph L. Mankiewicz directs Ava Gardner in The Barefoot Contessa.

173

> "It's an astonishment every time you see *All About Eve*. The story of this young ingénue creeping into an older woman's life and taking over is absolutely fascinating to me. It was definitely a model for *The Favourite.*"
>
> —DEBORAH DAVIS, SCREENWRITER

About Eve (1950), also nabbing a Golden Globe and other laurels for *Eve*'s exquisite screenplay. The perennial classic is chock-full of legendary lines; Bette Davis's haughtily delivered "Fasten your seatbelts, it's going to be a bumpy night" is only one of many quotable quips that Mankiewicz formulated in adapting Mary Orr's short story "The Wisdom of Eve." The bitter rivalry between stage star Margo Channing (Davis) and her protégée Eve Harrington (Anne Baxter) served as a thinly veiled statement about Joe and Herman's competitive fraternal relationship. Acid-tongued columnist Addison DeWitt (George Sanders) voiced some of the author's own opinions on, for example, the brand-new medium of TV: "That's all television is, my dear, nothing but auditions," he tells an aspiring actress played by a prefame Marilyn Monroe.

Eve had an unconventional structure, unfolding in flashbacks from three different characters' perspectives. Confident in the strength of his original script, Mankiewicz never barked commands at actors, but whispered gentle hints of direction in their ears and trusted them to handle the rest. "*Eve*

was the only picture where everybody working on it was in seventh heaven, and it all came out right," Davis recalled of the iconic role that reignited her lagging career. "You just *knew* it had to be great and that it would be great for all of us." The film set a record with fourteen Oscar nominations, and has since inspired books, stage adaptations, and a Broadway musical.

Mankiewicz gravitated to women as a subject matter. "Female roles, writing females, directing females, has always been infinitely more exciting, infinitely more rewarding, and infinitely easier than men," he revealed. The fact that he was married to an actress who suffered from depression, Rose Stradner, aided his understanding of the complex Margo Channing and the doomed diva Maria Vargas (played by Ava Gardner) in 1954's *The Barefoot Contessa*, his first independent venture after forming his own East Coast production company. Besides beautiful starlets and sparkling wit, plunges into the dark side of the human psyche characterized his films, particularly in *Suddenly, Last Summer* (1959), a Tennessee Williams and Gore Vidal–scripted

MUST-SEE MOVIES

THE GHOST AND MRS. MUIR
(1947)

A LETTER TO THREE WIVES
(1949)

NO WAY OUT (1950)

ALL ABOUT EVE (1950)

JULIUS CAESAR (1953)

THE BAREFOOT CONTESSA
(1954)

GUYS AND DOLLS (1955)

CLEOPATRA (1963)

SLEUTH (1972)

Eve (Anne Baxter) and Margo (Bette Davis) square off in All About Eve.

KEY SCENE TO WATCH

"Bill's welcome-home birthday party; a night to go down in history," Bette Davis says prior to the famous party scene in *All About Eve*. Before the guests arrive, actress Margo and her beloved director Bill (Gary Merrill) have an argument in the empty living room while she checks that the cigarette boxes and candy dishes are full. As originally scripted, the couple fenced words without any props, but Davis asked Mankiewicz for something to do with her hands. "As you get angry, you want a piece of candy," the director told her. "The angrier you get, the more desperately you want candy. You look toward the candy jar on the piano. And then finally, passionately, you eat the candy." Margo trying repeatedly to resist a chocolate before ultimately surrendering gives the talky scene a subtext that's both humorous and relatable.

JOSEPH L. MANKIEWICZ

imbroglio that tackled the then-taboo topics of homosexuality and mental illness.

In 1961, Mankiewicz agreed to helm an epic of ancient Egypt featuring Elizabeth Taylor as Queen of the Nile. It was a decision he lived to regret. "*Cleopatra* was conceived in emergency, shot in hysteria, and wound up in blind panic," he recalled with chagrin. Between Taylor's illnesses, her scandalous affair with costar Richard Burton, and an out-of-control budget that hit $44 million, *Cleopatra* (1963) became a two-year ordeal that nearly bankrupted Fox and brought Mankiewicz's career to a screeching halt.

Sleuth (1972), a cunning thriller with Laurence Olivier and Michael Caine, served as both a welcome return and a graceful exit for the veteran filmmaker. As one of Hollywood's most literate voices, Joseph Mankiewicz jumped ship soon after the Production Code was abolished and, with it, much of the polished verbiage for which he was known. His movies, especially *All About Eve*, remain exceptional examples of screenwriting at its finest.

Elizabeth Taylor gets into costume for Cleopatra, *with the help of designer Irene Sharaff.*

OTTO PREMINGER

Years active: 1931–1979

ONE OF SEVERAL EUROPEAN EXILES WHO SUPPLIED
1940s–1960s Hollywood with a dark, noirish sensibility, Austrian-born
actor/director/producer Otto Preminger courted controversy during
his career, becoming the first filmmaker to openly defy the Production
Code that had been in place since 1934. But behind
the provocative persona was a talented director who
turned out more than his share of great movies.

After a few forgettable films at Fox, the spellbinding mystery *Laura* (1944) was Preminger's first
masterwork. "I took one story nobody else wanted
called *Laura* and got Zanuck to let me produce
it," Preminger recalled; he also convinced Darryl Zanuck to let him replace Rouben Mamoulian as the film's director. Brandishing dreamlike
flashbacks, a haunting score by David Raskin, an
enigmatic painting of the beautiful Laura Hunt
(Gene Tierney's signature role), Joseph LaShelle's
Oscar-winning cinematography, and a poised performance by Dana Andrews as the obsessed detective, Preminger crafted a beloved whodunit that no
one else had faith in at the time. *Laura* launched him
into the big leagues.

Again casting Andrews (who would appear in
a total of four Preminger films), this time as a con-
man who preys on both Alice Faye and Linda Darnell, Preminger fashioned *Fallen Angel* (1945) as a
gritty, somberly romantic noir. Soon, he was churning out crime films, dramas, and comedies quickly,
efficiently, and under budget. It took him less than
a million dollars and only eighteen shooting days
to make the femme fatale–driven *Angel Face* (1953),
with its stunning finale that critic Dave Kehr called
"one of the most audacious endings in film history."

The Moon Is Blue (1953) was a seminal motion

Otto Preminger directs Dorothy Dandridge in Carmen
Jones, *1954.*

picture, the first to deliberately break the Production Code by being released without earning its seal of acceptance. It hit the public uncensored and unapproved, a bold move by Preminger. The film itself is a trifle, a lightweight sex comedy about a virgin (Maggie McNamara) determined to resist the amorous attentions of two competing suitors, played by William Holden and David Niven. The only thing revolutionary about it was the use of the words "virgin" and "seduce," both prohibited by the Code.

Preminger struck out as an independent to bring Oscar Hammerstein II's jazz opera *Carmen Jones* (1954) to the screen. Its all-Black cast and its "over-emphasis on lustfulness" (in the words of Code-enforcer Joseph Breen) made the ambitious musical drama a risky venture for 1950s America,

THE DIRECTOR AS STAR

but when Dorothy Dandridge hit theaters as the irresistibly sexy Carmen, she shot to stardom. With the married Preminger as her mentor and lover, she became the first African American woman to earn a Best Actress Oscar nomination, and the first to grace the cover of *Life* magazine—though her career slowly declined under his control. After the two separated, they worked together on the fraught *Porgy and Bess* (1959), Preminger's lavish big-screen musical based on the opera by George and Ira Gershwin and DuBose Heyward. Following a successful theatrical run, the controversial all-Black opus was shelved and never released for home viewing, many believing its portrayal of African Americans to be regressive.

Preminger continued to push limits with *The Man with the Golden Arm* (1955). Kicking off with Elmer Bernstein's electrifying jazz score and Saul Bass's modern-artsy opening credits, the film follows heroin addict Frankie through his highs and lows. Frank Sinatra played the lead with a twitchy authenticity that remains riveting today, long after drug use has ceased to be a shocking topic. *The Hollywood Reporter* described Sinatra's performance as "a tortured realistic masterpiece," and Kim Novak matched him with one of her finest characterizations as the nightclub hostess who helps him kick the habit. Preminger took on the Code again by distributing *The Man with the Golden Arm* before it was approved. The rave reviews and box office success led the Motion Picture Association of America to relax some of the Code's restrictions.

Sammy Davis Jr. and Dorothy Dandridge in Porgy and Bess

"Preminger was delightful, full of irony, and hip. He was a gutsy director and a great actor, too. He took most of his projects because he wanted to do them."

—PAUL MAZURSKY

The director discovered seventeen-year-old Jean Seberg for the lead in the critically panned *Saint Joan* (1957) and cast her again in *Bonjour Tristesse* (1958), a flawed film, but an innovative one in its use of black-and-white mixed with color. The look and feel of Preminger's films evolved with the times, from the shaded noir landscape of *Daisy Kenyon* (1947) to the brighter, starker spaces of *Anatomy of a Murder* (1959), but most of his movies shared fluid camera movements, a minimum of cuts, and efforts at realism, whether in lighting or acting.

A new standard in courtroom drama, the fact-based *Anatomy of a Murder* represents to many the height of Preminger's prowess as an independent director/producer. His first film shot entirely on location (in Marquette, Michigan, where the actual events occurred), *Anatomy* was a frank dissection of rape and murder through a legal lens. Sam Leavitt's cinematography and Duke Ellington's score enliven the film's engrossing 160-minute mystery, informed by the trials his lawyer father allowed Preminger to attend in his youth.

Preminger was well known in Hollywood as a bombastic, autocratic presence. "Otto Preminger was the kind of guy that didn't care that people called him loudmouth or braggart or anything as long as they called him something," critic Peter Travers of *Rolling Stone* has opined. But Preminger's persona seemed semi-contrived, a savvy attention-grabber that worked to his advantage as an actor—his bald head cropping up in Billy Wilder's POW dramedy *Stalag 17* (1953) and as chilly villain Mr. Freeze in the 1960s TV series *Batman*—and as a director, generating more interest in his films.

Preminger pressed onward and upward into the 1960s, gaining prestige with the big-budget epic *Exodus* (1960)—a film that Preminger credited to blacklisted screenwriter Dalton Trumbo, breaking the power of the blacklist—and another courtroom classic, *Advise & Consent* (1962), a landmark in its openness about homosexuality and its bandying of the word *bitch*. Still riding high in 1965, he presented *Bunny Lake Is Missing*, a visually evocative, ahead-of-its-time psychological thriller. It wasn't until 1968's misguided hippie comedy *Skidoo* that Preminger seemed to go off the rails, losing much of the artistic reputation he had spent years earning. His films from the late 1940s through the mid-1960s endure as emblems of his vision and artistry.

MUST-SEE MOVIES

LAURA (1944)

WHERE THE SIDEWALK ENDS (1950)

ANGEL FACE (1953)

CARMEN JONES (1954)

THE MAN WITH THE GOLDEN ARM (1955)

ANATOMY OF A MURDER (1959)

EXODUS (1960)

ADVISE & CONSENT (1962)

KEY SCENE TO WATCH

When James Stewart's attorney Biegler opens his office door and finds Mrs. Laura Manion (Lee Remick) lounging on the sofa, listening to a jazz record, in *Anatomy of a Murder*, he's slightly thrown off-kilter. Sporting fitted slacks and a low-cut top, Laura recounts the story of her alleged rape, including such details as the "panties and a bra" she was wearing underneath. Casually puffing on a cigarette, Remick underplays Laura with a fresh directness that ruffles staid Stewart's feathers—typical of the way Preminger liked to plant explicit content in his films to make the audience squirm.

James Stewart and Lee Remick in Anatomy of a Murder

NICHOLAS RAY

Years active: 1948–1979

PERHAPS THE MOST SUBVERSIVE FILMMAKER TO ascend the ranks in 1950s Hollywood, Nicholas Ray was a trained Method actor who brought a dark urgency to midcentury movies. With such titles as his remarkable debut *They Live by Night* (1948), the introspective noir *In*

a Lonely Place (1950), and the quintessential delinquent drama *Rebel Without a Cause* (1955), Ray became the reigning king of misfits, outsiders, and tortured souls.

He began as an unruly Wisconsin kid who briefly studied architecture before drifting onto the stage, where he was taken under the wing of Elia Kazan in New York's Group Theatre. His understanding of actors let him forge a deep rapport with Humphrey Bogart and a simpatico bond with James Dean, and to finesse tender-but-tough performances from Farley Granger and Cathy O'Donnell as two young lovers in *They Live by Night*, a visceral journey into the seedy world of crime in rural Oklahoma.

While filming the romantic whodunit *A Woman's Secret* (1949), Ray developed such a passion for sultry blond starlet Gloria Grahame that they married, but separated at an inconvenient moment: just as shooting began on *In a Lonely Place*, Grahame's breakout coleading role with Bogart. The dissolution of Ray and Grahame's union informed the film's somber final scenes, in which Dix (Bogart) and Laurel (Grahame) let suspicions destroy their relationship. Loosely based on Dorothy B. Hughes's chilling novel, *In a Lonely Place* gave Bogie new dimension as a moody screenwriter accused of strangling a woman in a fit of rage. "I took the gun out of Bogart's hands," Ray noted of the star. "The guy is amazing when you don't give him any props,

just strip him to his own emotional core." Ray lit Bogart's eyes in way that suggests mania waiting to erupt at any time.

His follow-up *On Dangerous Ground* (1951) was a beautifully nuanced noir in which darkness served to depict the mind-set of Robert Ryan's vitriolic cop, and to suggest the blindness experienced by the woman who touches his soul, played by Ida Lupino. When Ray undertook a color western with

Johnny Guitar (1954), the result was a neurotic, melodramatic tour de force for Joan Crawford, now a cult classic and one of the most unconventional Old West tales ever told.

As rock-and-roll hit the music charts in 1955, Nicholas Ray presented *Rebel Without a Cause*,

Nicholas Ray directs Humphrey Bogart and Gloria Grahame in In a Lonely Place.

cementing twenty-four-year-old James Dean, who died in a car crash one month before the film's release, as the icon of angst for an entire generation. When Warner Bros. saw early footage, they upgraded the black-and-white production to WarnerColor—the better for Ray to convey meaning through visual cues: the bright red of Jim's windbreaker, Judy's lipstick, and Plato's one sock; the blue-red explosion of the Earth at the planetarium show.

A decade before Mike Nichols stylistically expressed '60s youth culture with *The Graduate* (1967), Ray used unorthodox camera setups to express the alienation of suburban teenagers. At the police station, he subtly split the screen into three parts with glass office partitions, simultaneously showing Dean's Jim, Natalie Wood's Judy,

Ward Bond, Ida Lupino, and Robert Ryan in On Dangerous Ground

MUST-SEE MOVIES

THEY LIVE BY NIGHT (1948)

IN A LONELY PLACE (1950)

BORN TO BE BAD (1950)

ON DANGEROUS GROUND (1951)

JOHNNY GUITAR (1954)

REBEL WITHOUT A CAUSE (1955)

PARTY GIRL (1958)

KING OF KINGS (1961)

Ann Doran, James Dean, and Jim Backus in Rebel Without a Cause

KEY SCENE TO WATCH

When Jim's parents (Ann Doran and Jim Backus) confront him after the fatal "chickie run" in *Rebel Without a Cause*, Mr. Stark lectures Jim from below, while Mrs. Stark cuts him off at the top of the stairs, Jim between them on the landing. Threatened by his mom, Jim begs his father for support. "Dad, stand up for me." When he remains silent, Jim explodes in fury, dragging his father by the lapels, choking him before running out the door. This scene originally took place in Jim's mother's bedroom, but as Ray and Dean rehearsed, Ray realized it would be more dramatic if staged on the staircase, suffusing the dialogue with added meaning by physically placing Jim and his parents on different levels.

> "I think in all of Nick Ray's films, there's the interior of the person, the character, and the exterior of the world. And they don't align. And the world causes pain and disillusionment and betrayal, and yet he's so sympathetic to the interior of his characters."
>
> —JIM JARMUSCH

and Sal Mineo's Plato. At Jim's house, Ray shot upside down to indicate Jim's supine perspective, turning the camera 180 degrees as his mother (Ann Doran) enters and Jim sits up. Although it riled reviewers at the time, *Rebel Without a Cause* has since been recognized as "a masterpiece," to quote author William Faulkner, "the American cinema's only Greek tragedy."

Bold colors and shadowy lighting were used to great effect in *Bigger Than Life* (1956), starring James Mason (who also produced and cowrote the film) as a teacher whose mind is increasingly deranged by the cortisone he takes to save his life. By starting with bright sunshine and light hues, and gradually darkening the scheme as Mason descends into madness, Ray peeled back the veneer of nifty-fifties conformity to expose the monsters lurking in the closet.

Ray's films had a major impact on the directors of the French New Wave movement, who spotted a European sensibility in his artistic experimentation; Jean-Luc Godard went so far as to declare "The cinema is Nicholas Ray." Director Curtis Hanson was profoundly influenced by Ray's work, especially as he crafted his 1950s-set neo-noir *L.A. Confidential* (1997). "Even though Ray's characters are alienated from society, the demons they struggle the hardest with come from within," Hanson observed in 2002.

A sensitive, even tormented man, Ray struggled with his own demons in the forms of alcohol, drugs, and his disillusionment with the film business. "The terrible evil of the Hollywood system," producer and friend John Houseman once speculated, "affected Nick more than other people." With the help of *Rebel* cast member Dennis Hopper, Ray secured teaching positions when directing work dried up, mentoring indie filmmaker Jim Jarmusch as Kazan had mentored him years before.

When Nicholas Ray succumbed to lung cancer in 1979, writer/producer Myron Meisel eulogized the iconoclast in the *Los Angeles Times*. "He could make films so intense, so visually expressive, and so thematically compelling that for all the brevity of his directing career, he was undeniably one of the greatest artists ever to work in film."

DOUGLAS SIRK

Years active: 1935–1959

L IKE SO MANY GREAT FILMMAKERS BEFORE HIM, Douglas Sirk originally hailed from Germany, fleeing the Nazi regime to land in Golden Age Hollywood. By the 1950s, he had earned the moniker "Master of Melodrama" for his aesthetically lush tearjerkers that immersed Eisenhower-era audiences in a world of gilt-edged passion, enriched by his signature use of oversaturated Technicolor.

On the surface, Sirk made emotionally charged romances, referred to as "women's pictures" at the time. But scratch the exterior shellac and a stream of subtext comes rushing out, a "cataloguing," as critic Dave Kehr described it in 1999, "of the fears and anxieties, the frustrations and contradictions, of an America then at the height of its postwar power and prestige." Every facet of a Sirk film was intricately planned to evoke a feeling or express a silent critique: Agnes Moorehead's ice-blue dress contrasting the blood-red gown Jane Wyman wears in *All That Heaven Allows* (1955); the surreal fuchsia hallway panels in *Written on the Wind* (1956); the lustrous rhinestones cascading over the opening credits of *Imitation of Life* (1959). It all made for magnificent drive-in fare, blazing across the big screen like fever dreams in sumptuous CinemaScope.

Although he had a few 1940s hits under his belt, it was Sirk's seven-year contract with Universal Studios (signed in 1950) that yielded his most ambitious and indelible work. *Magnificent Obsession* (1954) was first adapted from the Lloyd C. Douglas novel in 1935, but Sirk breathed new life into the well-worn yarn about a millionaire playboy who, through a series of incredible coincidences and chance accidents, ends up performing a life-saving operation on the widow whose blindness he caused.

His gift for expressive mise-en-scène—and the sincere performances by Jane Wyman and Rock Hudson—allowed Sirk to transcend the material.

Edwin Schallert of the *Los Angeles Times* called *Magnificent Obsession* "a deeply moving experience," but admitted that some "will dismiss it as plain hokum." Many reviewers shrugged off Sirk's films as cinematic soap operas. The *New Yorker*'s Pauline Kael commonly designated them as "trash" while admitting that she still enjoyed them. Of *The Tar-*

nished Angels (1957), she wrote, "It's the kind of bad movie you know is bad, and yet you're held by the mixture of polished style and quasi-melodramatics achieved by the director." Sirk never denied such allegations. He described the source story for *Magnificent Obsession* as "a combination of kitsch, and craziness, and trashiness," but maintained: "There

Douglas Sirk, Jane Wyman, and Rock Hudson on the set of All That Heaven Allows

"Douglas Sirk was a major, major influence, certainly with the early films that I did, and as I began to shape myself as a filmmaker. . . . *Written on the Wind* is kind of a psycho-sexual melodrama that is almost like a dream state of something incredibly passionate and erotic and evocative. It seduces you and takes you in."

—KATHRYN BIGELOW

is a very short distance between high art and trash."

All That Heaven Allows leaned more toward art than trash. Its very title is revealing: a searing comment on what 1950s suburbia allowed women to be—and not to be. Newly widowed Cary (Wyman) is discouraged from expressing her sexuality, scandalized for falling in love with a younger man (Hudson), and prodded by her well-intentioned kids into getting a television set instead. When the console TV is wheeled into her living room, Cary sees herself reflected in its screen, alone. Sirk deftly used mirror images to show another side of a character, or the self that they keep hidden.

Sirk's exploration of a wealthy spoiled American family, *Written on the Wind* deliberately exaggerated alcoholic binges by an oil tycoon's son (Robert Stack) and the sexual antics of his sister (Dorothy Malone) to deliver a heightened fantasy-nightmare of excess that left the middle-class characters (Lauren Bacall and Hudson) all the more eager to lead average lives. The *Los Angeles Times* suggested that Malone deserved an Oscar for her

"brilliant portrayal of sensuality on all counts," and she did indeed snare the gold for Best Supporting Actress. Malone, Hudson, and Stack reunited for *The Tarnished Angels*, a tempestuous love triangle in crisp black and white, both grittier and more abstract than Sirk's earlier work.

The filmmaker ended on a high note, with the wildly successful *Imitation of Life*, a '50s update of Fannie Hurst's novel and John M. Stahl's 1934 film. Producer Ross Hunter and Sirk packed a wallop of emotional truth behind the glossy finish. "I tried to make it into a picture of social consciousness," said Sirk, "not only of a White social consciousness but of a Negro one, too. Both White and Black are leading imitated lives." Sarah Jane (Susan Kohner) is a young Black woman who renounces her past and her mother (Juanita Moore) by passing for White; Lora (Lana Turner) chooses an artificial life of movie stardom in lieu of an authentic connection with her daughter (Sandra Dee). The soul-stirring story of these four women became Universal's biggest moneymaker of 1959, and remains "the toughest-minded, most irresolvable movie ever made about race in this country," according to the *Village Voice*'s Charles Taylor in 2015.

The lavish, devastating funeral at the end of *Imitation of Life* served as a fitting farewell to Sirk, who was planning his departure from Hollywood while shooting. "I had had enough," he recalled in 1970. "I had outgrown this kind of picture-making." And, like one of his characters at the end of a movie, he slipped away to Switzerland, leaving a legacy that continues to inspire. Oscar-winning director Kathryn Bigelow has been influenced by Sirk's movies, as have filmmakers Pedro Almodóvar, Rainer Werner Fassbinder, and Lars von Trier. In his 2002 drama *Far from Heaven*, Todd Haynes paid homage to *All That Heaven Allows*, complete with set design and cinematography in a close approximation of the Sirkian style.

Contemporary reassessments of Douglas Sirk appreciate him as a singular talent. The romantic clichés found in his melodramas are intrinsic to classic-era Hollywood, and have been obsolete for so long that we can look at them afresh, finding new meaning with every re-watching. Because Sirk retired in 1959, his body of work stands as an emblem of its era, a time capsule of midcentury values and aesthetics that, like vintage wine, grows richer with time.

Juanita Moore and Susan Kohner in Imitation of Life

MUST-SEE MOVIES

LURED (1947)

MAGNIFICENT OBSESSION (1954)

ALL THAT HEAVEN ALLOWS (1955)

WRITTEN ON THE WIND (1956)

BATTLE HYMN (1957)

THE TARNISHED ANGELS (1957)

A TIME TO LOVE AND A TIME TO DIE (1958)

IMITATION OF LIFE (1959)

KEY SCENE TO WATCH

"This room!" Jane Wyman's Cary exclaims, awed by the old mill her ex-fiancé renovated in *All That Heaven Allows*. "The beauty that Ron's put into it . . . and the love." As Ron lies asleep with a concussion, Cary stands near a big picture window. Sirk and cinematographer Russell Metty simulated winter moonlight by casting a blue light on Wyman's face, which also conveys her sadness. When Ron wakes in the morning, the filmmakers frame Cary with a snowy view outside the window, an obvious matte painting that recalls animated Disney fare—a deer even appears, symbolizing hope and renewed life. "The angles are the director's thoughts," Sirk once said, "the lighting is his philosophy."

Rock Hudson and Jane Wyman in All That Heaven Allows

NEOREALISM MAESTROS

Italian filmmaking erupted in a golden age after the toppling of Benito Mussolini's fascist regime in World War II. Bereft of funds and studio space, auteurs took to the war-torn streets, shooting vividly natural, documentary-style movies that came to be termed neorealism. Although the movement was short-lived, its frankness impacted the freewheeling New Wave in France, and the gritty crime films of postwar Hollywood.

Giuseppe De Santis exposed Italy's abysmal living conditions with his impressive debut film, *Tragic Hunt* (1946). His sexed-up statement about American capitalism, *Riso amaro* (*Bitter Rice* [1950]), was a breakout success, earning an Oscar nomination. With *Rome 11:00* (1952), De Santis delivered a harrowing drama based on a real-life disaster, when so many unemployed women applied for the same job that a staircase collapsed, injuring dozens.

When stage and screen actor **Vittorio De Sica** jumped to directing, he eventually became a leading figure of Italian cinema. In 1946, he helmed *Shoeshine*, a heartbreaking (and Academy Award–winning) tale of two wayward shoeshine boys sent to jail. De Sica earned a second Oscar for his 1948 masterpiece *Bicycle Thieves*, a brutal illustration of postwar Rome's desperate circumstances, with nonactors Lamberto Maggiorani and Enzo Staiola as father and son searching for a stolen bicycle. He crafted another masterwork with the touching *Umberto D.* (1952), and garnered international acclaim for the Sophia Loren–Marcello Mastroianni vehicle *Marriage Italian Style* (1964) and the period piece *The Garden of the Finzi-Cotinis* (1970).

As the son of a cinema owner, **Roberto Rossellini** was raised on movies. Thanks to his early training in documentaries, Rossellini put the real in neorealism, kicking the movement into high gear with his authentic slice of Nazi-ruled life, *Rome, Open City* (1945). *Paisan* (1946) and *Germany, Year Zero* (1948) rounded out his antifascist trilogy, while 1950's *Stromboli* marked his first film with soon-to-be-wife Ingrid Bergman, as a despondent fisherman's wife. After the couple collaborated again on *Europa '51* (1952), their loosely scripted third film together, *Journey to Italy* (1954), sparked the New Wave movement in France.

Though **Luchino Visconti** was a count and a member of the Italian aristocracy, his first film—which also happens to be the first neorealist film—was a seedy, unauthorized adaptation of James M. Cain's *The Postman Always Rings Twice*. The sexually frank *Ossessione* (1943) was censored by Italy's government and rarely shown in America due to copyright violation of Cain's novel.

Visconti soon moved away from neorealism, embracing a more genteel filmmaking style with 1963's *The Leopard* and the Oscar-nominated *The Damned* (1969).

Roberto Rossellini directs Ingrid Bergman in Europa '51.

BILLY WILDER

Years active: 1934–1981

WHETHER HE ATTACKED COMEDY, DRAMA, OR film noir, Billy Wilder's cynical humor permeated every frame of his films. From the verbal sparring of Fred MacMurray and Barbara Stanwyck in the suspense-fest *Double Indemnity* (1944) to the

sexual double entendres in the riotous *Some Like It Hot* (1959), Wilder had a way of injecting doses of hilarity into every movie, at just the right spots. Take his expert mélange of comedy and drama, *The Apartment* (1960), for example: at the moments when things turn dire and dismal, a perfectly timed joke—sometimes a very dark one—forces us to laugh even as we wipe our tears. It was a gift he learned from his mentor, Ernst Lubitsch.

"Lubitsch was my influence as a director," Wilder has said. "For many years, I had that sign on my wall: HOW WOULD LUBITSCH DO IT? I would *always* look at it when I was writing a script or planning a picture." After coscripting Lubitsch's *Ninotchka* (1939) and Howard Hawks's *Ball of Fire*

(1941) with his longtime collaborator Charles Brackett, Wilder ventured into directing with the frothy farce *The Major and the Minor* (1942). Featuring an inspired performance from Ginger Rogers as a grown woman passing for a twelve-year-old, *The Major and the Minor* set Wilder off on a decade of great features for Paramount Pictures.

The Austrian-born Wilder had learned English from watching American movies, giving him an outsider's appreciation of US culture. In his prototypical LA noir, *Double Indemnity*, Wilder and cowriter Raymond Chandler gave us likeable-yet-hard-boiled antihero Walter Neff (MacMurray), an insurance salesman who grabs a beer on his way to the bowling alley and calls the woman

he's willing to kill for (Stanwyck) "Baby." After the crime, the lovers meet up in the canned-goods aisle of a grocery store. "Not for cinema gourmets" is how Wilder described the tone of his films. "I don't do cinema," he said. "I make movies—for amusement . . . for a middle-class audience, for the people that you see on the subway."

In 1950, movies suddenly became self-referential as Hollywood produced a spate of showbiz stories: Wilder's *Sunset Boulevard*, Nicholas Ray's *In a Lonely Place*, and Joseph L. Mankiewicz's *All About*

Billy Wilder directs Barbara Stanwyck and Fred MacMurray in Double Indemnity.

Eve, all premiering within three months of each other. *Sunset Boulevard*, hailed by the *Los Angeles Times* as being "Hollywood's definitive look at itself," may have been the bitterest in its scornful pity for washed-up silent icon Norma Desmond, played to the hilt by actual '20s star Gloria Swanson. But *Sunset Boulevard* was also a scathing joke at Hollywood's expense, achieved through William Holden's caustic quips ("They'll love it in Pomona.") as disillusioned screenwriter Joe Gillis and Swanson's gloriously over-the-top performance, filled with egotistical zingers ("We didn't need dialogue. We had faces.") and theatrical gestures. Gillis was a typical Wilder character, selling his soul for money and hating himself for it.

Stalag 17 (1953) was a biting comedy set in a Nazi POW camp during World War II, starring Holden in an Oscar-winning role. In *Sabrina* (1954), once again, irreverent humor saved the day, drowning out the sorrows of the eponymous chauffeur's daughter. Who else but Wilder could illicit laughter while lovely Audrey Hepburn chokes on car exhaust fumes in an enclosed garage, hoping to kill herself?

The jewel in Wilder's comedy crown was the seminal cross-dressing escapade *Some Like It Hot*, one of the most ferociously funny films ever made and one of Marilyn Monroe's last and most enduring screen performances as sultry singer Sugar Kane. Wilder (who had worked with Monroe in *The Seven Year Itch* [1955]) made magic with the iconic blonde, this time flanked by the comic duo of

Tony Curtis and Jack Lemmon as jazz musicians disguised as ladies. For the famous finale, when Lemmon pulls off his wig and reveals, "I'm a man," Wilder and cowriter I. A. L. Diamond struggled to find a response for Joe E. Brown's smitten millionaire, Osgood Fielding. At one point, Diamond blurted out, "Nobody's perfect." Wilder added it to the script as a placeholder, thinking, "Then we're going to *really* sit down and make a *real* funny last line. We never found the line, so we went with 'Nobody's perfect.'" This classic (and, as it turns

Jack Lemmon and Joe E. Brown in Some Like It Hot

196

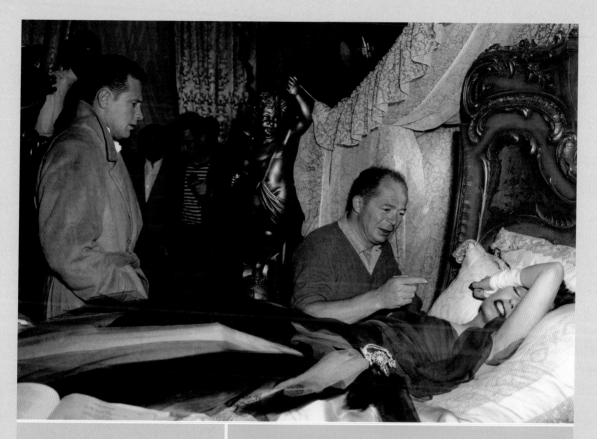

MUST-SEE MOVIES

DOUBLE INDEMNITY (1944)

THE LOST WEEKEND (1945)

SUNSET BOULEVARD (1950)

ACE IN THE HOLE (1951)

STALAG 17 (1953)

SABRINA (1954)

THE SEVEN YEAR ITCH (1955)

SOME LIKE IT HOT (1959)

THE APARTMENT (1960)

Billy Wilder directs Gloria Swanson and William Holden in Sunset Boulevard.

KEY SCENE TO WATCH

When Joe first meets Norma in *Sunset Boulevard*, she and Max (Erich von Stroheim) mistake him for an undertaker they called to bury her dead monkey, adding a morbid twist to the scene. The eccentric relic from Hollywood's bygone past removes her sunglasses and orders Joe to leave. But he stays, recognizing her. "You're Norma Desmond," he says, "used to be in silent pictures, used to be big." Swanson stands up tall and arches her eyebrows before delivering one of *Sunset Boulevard*'s most referenced lines: "I *am* big. It's the pictures that got small." A bittersweet clash between Norma's grandiose delusions and Joe's slick modernity, the scene could be interpreted as symbolizing the fraught talkie takeover and the destruction it wreaked on silent cinema.

> "Part of the great fun of being a fan of Billy Wilder is that your favorite Wilder pictures change over the years. For me, sometimes it's *Love in the Afternoon*; other times it's *A Foreign Affair*; but usually I return to *The Apartment*. The characters, the score, the melancholy, and the perfection of the script and performances. . . . It's hard to top. Though the fizzy comic wallop of *Some Like It Hot* sure gives it a run for its money."
>
> —CAMERON CROWE

out, perfect) punchline is now etched into Billy Wilder's gravestone.

With Best Picture–winner *The Apartment*, he became the first person to receive triple Academy Awards as writer, director, and producer. The movie benefited from another memorable last line, this one from Shirley MacLaine's elevator operator, Fran Kubelik, to Lemmon's office drone, C. C. Baxter, who lays his cards on the table—literally and figuratively—shuffling a deck and opening his heart: "I love you, Miss Kubelik." Her reply? "Shut up and deal." A reciprocal declaration of love and a kiss "would have been too romantic; too sweet," noted Wilder. Of the director she called "the great master," MacLaine later revealed, "I learned more from him than anyone else." Again pairing MacLaine and Lemmon, *Irma la Douce* (1963) was not only Wilder's first color film but the biggest box office bonanza of his career, earning $25 million.

Known for his acerbic humor in real life (he told Walter Matthau while making 1964's *The Fortune Cookie*, "We're on the track of something absolutely mediocre."), Wilder had a way of cutting to the core of human nature, finding the painful truths we hide, and parading them as comedy. We not only smile at Joe Gillis's wisecracks but identify with the poor sap, the flawed everyman who ends up floating facedown in Norma Desmond's swimming pool; we're both charmed and repulsed by Kirk Douglas's glib reporter in *Ace in the Hole* (1951), prolonging an injured man's misery to nail a front-page story.

Billy Wilder spent his later years collecting a carload of lifetime achievement honors, or what he referred to as "Quick, before they croak" awards. But it was the sixty-two movies he crafted—either as writer, director, or both—that certify Wilder as a world-class comic mind whose work still resonates and inspires today.

ROBERT WISE

Years active: 1944–2000

ROBERT WISE MAY BE THE MOST UNDERAPPRECIATED filmmaker from studio-era Hollywood. Sometimes dismissed as a worka-day craftsman, Wise in fact built a filmography of great style, consistent integrity, and profound variety. With his meticulous focus on quality, he

achieved an admirable longevity, both in his career span and in the lingering popularity of his films. He made durable entertainment to last through the decades—and that's exactly what *The Day the Earth Stood Still* (1951), *West Side Story* (1961), *The Sound of Music* (1965), and other Wise classics have done.

In 1933, the movie-crazed boy from a small Indiana town crashed Hollywood, landing in RKO's editing department as a film porter who transported reels to the cutting rooms. By 1941, he was editing *Citizen Kane* for Orson Welles. Wise was a hardworking, efficient editor turned director who thoroughly researched his subjects. In preparing for *The Set-Up* (1949), he observed third-rate fighters night after night, soaking up every nuance until he

was able to invoke a powerful plausibility in the tale of a worn-out boxer (Robert Ryan) striving for one last shot at glory. He returned to the boxing ring with 1956's more upbeat *Somebody Up There Likes Me*, a breakthrough role for young Paul Newman as plucky champ Rocky Graziano.

After he left RKO for Twentieth Century-Fox, Wise made one of the first—and still one of the best—man-from-space movies, *The Day the Earth Stood Still*. With spot-on performances from Michael Rennie as affable alien Klaatu and Patricia Neal as the visitor's only friend on Earth, this renowned entry in the genre offers thrills, suspense, and a level of intelligence rare in '50s flying-saucer fare. Later in his career, the director circled back to sci-fi with

THE DIRECTOR AS STAR

The Andromeda Strain (1971) and Star Trek: The Motion Picture (1979).

Like Howard Hawks, Wise tried his hand at every genre, and fashioned unforgettable movies in each: film noir, science fiction, musical, thriller, western, war, and his wrenching biopic of real-life executed gun moll Barbara Graham, I Want to Live! (1958). Without openly criticizing the death penalty, Wise shrewdly leads the audience to conclude that the practice is inhumane by forcing us to endure the prisoner's agonized final moments before the gas chamber, punctuating the message with Barbara's searing last words: "Good people are always so sure they're right." Susan Hayward collected the only Academy Award of her career for playing the untamed but not unsympathetic Graham. Wise often addressed social issues in his movies, taking stands against nuclear war (in The Day the Earth Stood Still), racism (in Odds Against Tomorrow [1959]), and American imperialism (in The Sand Pebbles [1966]).

An impassioned plea for peace set to Leonard Bernstein's syncopated score, West Side Story was a two-year journey for Wise, working as pro-

Robert Wise sets up a shot for West Side Story.

ducer and codirector (stage director–choreographer Jerome Robbins helmed the dance sequences) of the 70 mm Panavision production. Wise and Robbins decided to shoot in actual Manhattan locations, yet retain the stylized staging of the Broadway show. "It was the first film I remember where tests were done, way in advance of the shooting, of ways to make the look of the film different from any film that had ever been done before," costar Rita Moreno remembered. The contrast of impressionistic dance against a backdrop of brick tenements stunned the senses of the world, leading the *New York Times* to instantly pronounce *West Side Story* "a cinema masterpiece." It was the sensation of 1961, earning triple its $6 million budget and sweeping the Oscars with ten wins, including Best Picture and Best Director. Its 2021 update by Wise fan Steven Spielberg keeps *West Side Story* on the public's radar.

The supernatural and psychological thriller *The Haunting* (1963) was based on Shirley Jackson's *The Haunting of Hill House*, a book Wise devoured and yearned to bring to the screen. As a hands-on director-producer, he supervised every aspect, including Nelson Gidding's adapted screenplay, Julie Harris's eerily credible performance, and Davis Boulton's photography, which was novel in its absence of shadows. The result was an almost clinical examination of a paranormal-fueled mental breakdown that managed to horrify while defying horror stereotypes.

Never wanting to repeat himself, Wise hesitated before agreeing to *The Sound of Music* because he had already done a musical. But once he jumped on

Robert Wise demonstrates the dance Susan Hayward performs in I Want to Live!

board, he gave the production his all, even strap-ping his cameraman to a helicopter to capture the iconic opening scene of Julie Andrews surrounded by the awe-inspiring Alps. Until they nailed it per-fectly, Wise shot and reshot, sending the chopper swooping down as Andrews twirled, lip synching, while hi-fi speakers blasted the Rodgers and Ham-merstein song from the trees.

With an array of such memorable shots, *The Sound of Music* earned Wise another matching set of Best Picture and Best Director Oscars, and sur-passed *Gone with the Wind* (1939) as the highest-grossing movie of all time (a status it held until George Lucas's *Star Wars* eclipsed it in 1977). *Time* magazine revisited the musical at its fiftieth anni-versary in 2015. "In an era of Marvel superheroes

with personality disorders, and when the few mega-hit heroines are warrior princesses, the notion of a would-be nun outwitting the Nazis with the weapon of melody is so old-fashioned it's almost radical," Richard Corliss wrote, calling the film "the last gasp of the studio system's belief in G-rated oper-ettas of inspirational uplift." Its hopeful simplic-ity has made *The Sound of Music* beloved across the world, delighting three generations that have grown up singing along with the timeless treasure.

Although highly regarded in the industry—Wise served two terms as president of the Acad-emy of Motion Picture Arts and Sciences—he was often accused of lacking a distinct artistic finger-print. "Some of the more esoteric critics claim that there's no Robert Wise style or stamp," he told a reporter in 1998. "My answer to that is that I've tried to approach each genre in a cinematic style that I think is right for that genre. I wouldn't have approached *The Sound of Music* the way I approached *I Want to Live!* for anything, and that accounts for a mix of styles."

Within the preestablished boundaries of Hol-lywood filmmaking, Wise carved out a résumé rife with prestige and perfection. By focusing on the material and wielding the techniques he believed necessary to make each project outstanding, he achieved his own brand of greatness.

Julie Andrews in Bavaria for the opening shot of The Sound of Music

MUST-SEE MOVIES

BORN TO KILL (1947)

THE SET-UP (1949)

THE DAY THE EARTH STOOD STILL (1951)

EXECUTIVE SUITE (1954)

I WANT TO LIVE! (1958)

WEST SIDE STORY (1961)

THE HAUNTING (1963)

THE SOUND OF MUSIC (1965)

THE SAND PEBBLES (1966)

Klaatu (Michael Rennie) arrives on Earth with his robot, Gort.

KEY SCENE TO WATCH

When Professor Barnhardt (Sam Jaffe) asks Klaatu for "a demonstration of force" that will prove his credibility to the scientific community, the alien neutralizes all electricity on the planet, bringing machines, cars, and trains to a grinding halt in *The Day the Earth Stood Still*. This scene not only fulfills the promise of the movie's title but provides an arresting visual without the use of elaborate special effects. Notice the simple but effective moment between Klaatu and Helen in the dark elevator, with dim strips of light illuminating Helen's awestruck eyes. Even in a sci-fi film, Wise placed people front and center, keeping the audience invested in the characters rather than overloading their senses with visual fireworks.

FRED ZINNEMANN

Years active: 1942–1982

AN INTELLIGENT, CULTURED FILMMAKER WITH UNCOM-
promising standards of excellence, Fred Zinnemann had no qualms
about rejecting projects he felt were subpar. As a result, he left behind a
rich forty-year legacy of handsomely crafted films, many of which con-

cern individuals forced to choose between com-
promising their moral integrity and following their
consciences. Without being heavy-handed, he made
one thing clear: in a Zinnemann movie, the consci-
entious choice is always the right one.

The techniques Zinnemann mastered in his
apprenticeship with documentarian Robert Flaherty are apparent in his early features. *The Seventh
Cross* (1944) was an honest look at a concentration
camp refugee (Spencer Tracy), while 1948's *The
Search*—actually shot on location in Germany—
marked Montgomery Clift's first screen appearance
as a US soldier who cares for a young Auschwitz
survivor. As his mother and father were both killed
in the Holocaust, the atrocities of Nazi Germany

impacted Zinnemann personally, perhaps driving
him to examine morality via his movies. "A man's
character is his destiny," he said, was the theme of
his streamlined, suspenseful masterpiece *High Noon*
(1952), a collaborative effort with screenwriter Carl
Foreman and producer Stanley Kramer.

With an iconic performance by Gary Cooper as
a retired small-town marshal forced to face the bad
guys alone, *High Noon* is notable for its unique aesthetic; unlike most westerns, there is no heroic cowboy riding into the sunset, no picturesque prairies.
Zinnemann and cinematographer Floyd Crosby
wanted "to show a film set in 1880 that would look
like a newsreel—if there had been newsreels and
cameras in those days," the director noted. The film

garnered Oscars for its memorable Dimitri Tiom-
kin score and for Cooper, among other laurels. Foreman's Writers Guild Award–winning script alluded
to his own blacklisting for refusing to provide names
of Communists to the House Un-American Activities Committee. The director, too, viewed *High Noon*
as a statement against the oppressive forces that had
seized Hollywood.

"I just like to do films that are positive in the
sense that they deal with the dignity of human
beings and have something to say about oppression,
not necessarily in a political way but in a human
way," Zinnemann once said. But the trick was to
also entertain, to sugarcoat the message a little,

as he did in his wildly popular 1953 rendition of
James Jones's novel *From Here to Eternity*. One of the
highest-grossing and most critically lauded hits of
the decade, this intense tapestry of a movie is often
remembered for its "kiss on the beach scene," in
which Burt Lancaster and Deborah Kerr take a
risqué roll in the surf.

Oklahoma! (1955) was a unique adventure for
Zinnemann: a colorful, feel-good musical that
stands out in a career of serious pictures, like the
Ethel Waters tour-de-force *The Member of the Wedding* (1952), and another drama of internal conflict,

Fred Zinnemann directs Gary Cooper in High Noon.

> "My mentor was the great director, Fred Zinnemann, whom I used to show all my films to until he died. He said something to me that I always try to keep in my head every time I decide on what film to do next. He told me that making a film was a great privilege, and you should never waste it."
>
> —ALAN PARKER

The Nun's Story (1959). A fact-based reminiscence of quiet power that revealed leading lady Audrey Hepburn to be more than just a pretty face, *The Nun's Story* was only attempted by Zinnemann after he spent a full year researching the Catholic Church.

Based on Robert Bolt's play about sixteenth-century statesman Sir Thomas More, *A Man for All Seasons* (1966) was another movie about a man standing alone on principle, "a cousin" of *High Noon*, as Zinnemann put it. But he had to convince Columbia to get the sex-and-violence-free movie made when it boasted no salacious selling points. The studio's gamble paid off. Bosley Crowther of the *New York Times* judged *A Man for All Seasons* an "uncommonly brave and literate film," one that scored the Academy Award for Best Picture, plus Oscars for direction, acting, screenplay, cine-

MUST-SEE MOVIES

THE SEARCH (1948)

HIGH NOON (1952)

FROM HERE TO ETERNITY (1953)

OKLAHOMA! (1955)

THE NUN'S STORY (1959)

A MAN FOR ALL SEASONS (1966)

THE DAY OF THE JACKAL (1973)

JULIA (1977)

KEY SCENE TO WATCH

A little over an hour into *High Noon*, Will Kane has failed to round up a posse to help him face the murderous Frank Miller, due to arrive in Hadleyville on the twelve o'clock train. Here, Zinnemann draws out suspense with a montage, starting with Kane making out his will—a close-up of Cooper's morose, weather-beaten face—moving quickly through a series of simultaneous shots in real time: a pendulum swinging; a clock showing 11:58; the deserted town square; the train tracks; the church congregation in prayer; the Miller gang; and various characters, including Kane's old flame, Helen Ramirez (Katy Jurado), and his new bride, Amy (Grace Kelly), both looking at the clock. This tightly constructed assemblage helped editor Elmo Williams earn the Oscar for Best Film Editing.

matography, and costumes. Zinnemann added his statuette to the three Oscars he had already collected for directing and producing—not to mention the twenty-four others his films had won.

After spinning Frederick Forsyth's novel *The Day of the Jackal* into a pulse-pounding espionage thriller in 1973, Zinnemann revisited the Holocaust via historical figures Lillian Hellman (Jane Fonda) and her Nazi-opposing friend, Julia (Vanessa Redgrave in an Oscar-winning portrayal). *Julia* (1977) was an unusual film for the 1970s; in an age of mafiosi, spaceships, and killer sharks, the strong bond between two women fueled the intriguing story. Of her Golden Globe–winning role, Jane Fonda noted, "In every other movie I've ever been in, women are either falling in and out of love with men, or are game-playing. There is no game-playing in *Julia*."

Fred Zinnemann stopped directing in the early 1980s, but continued to uphold the integrity of the film industry until his death in 1997. In 1994, he was honored by President Clinton and given a special award for "outstanding courage, vision, and distinguished service on behalf of artists' rights." In Hollywood movies of the 1980s and '90s, he saw a "dangerous uniformity," he said, and suggested an antidote: "The only defense is to remember the standards of our forefathers and the kinds of pictures they made."

Fred Zinnemann, Montgomery Clift, and Donna Reed shoot From Here to Eternity.

INTERNATIONAL INFLUENCES

By the late 1950s, the European and Japanese film industries had fully recovered from the setbacks of World War II, and a new breed of auteurs was making avant-garde movies that gave Hollywood a run for its money.

With his fifty-year output of powerful, beautifully made, and impactful motion pictures, **Akira Kurosawa** gave many Americans their first glimpse of Japanese culture and influenced filmmakers across the globe. From the psychological enigma of *Rashomon* (1950) to the character-driven epic *Seven Samurai* (1954) to the groundbreaking *Yojimbo* (1961), Kurosawa's films inspired Sergio Leone, George Lucas, and Quentin Tarantino to create some of their most indelible works.

A towering figure in world cinema and an idol in his native Sweden, **Ingmar Bergman** reshaped the medium in the second half of the twentieth century with his profound, often mystical films. In 1957, he unleashed a double dose of brilliance with *The Seventh Seal* and *Wild Strawberries*; from there, his work waxed darker and more penetrating with the Oscar-winning *The Virgin Spring* (1960), the surreal *Persona* (1966), and the harrowingly beautiful *Cries and Whispers* (1972).

From the ashes of Italian neorealism sprang the fantastical films of **Federico Fellini**, who in the late-1950s surpassed Roberto Rossellini as Italy's most celebrated cinema export. After gaining international acclaim with two Oscar-winners—the heartbreaking road saga *La Strada* (1954) and the touching *Nights of Cabiria* (1957)—Fellini changed the game with loosely structured, image-driven masterpieces such as *La Dolce Vita* (1960) and *8½* (1963), cultivating a unique, dreamlike style now known the world over as Fellini-esque.

Toshiro Mifune and Machiko Kyō in Rashomon

Chapter Five

THE REVOLUTION BEGINS

A s the 1960s dawned, groundbreaking European auteurs were challenging Hollywood with innovative movies that were both artistic and profitable. International films thrived in America, and impacted cinema everywhere. But if there was more art, there was less commerce; scores of theaters closed down as Hollywood produced fewer films each year—especially those in black and white, which was virtually obsolete by the end of the decade as color became the norm.

Early '60s Hollywood was, in many ways, a continuation of the late '50s, with big screens and lengthy, costly epics dominating. But a shift occurred in the second half of the decade. Seemingly overnight, the manufactured illusion of the glamorous Golden Age felt flat and artificial to many, especially the young. Audiences were ready for the naturalism, experimentalism, and excitement that reflected the cultural revolution of the Swinging Sixties.

Taboos were being shattered left and right, boundaries broken. The Production Code was relaxed in the mid-'50s, increasingly overlooked in the early '60s, and finally abolished in 1968, to be replaced by the current ratings system. In 1970, John Schlesinger's *Midnight Cowboy* (1969) made history as the first (and only) X-rated movie to earn an Oscar for Best Picture. Amid the tumult, Hollywood's silent-reared masters were retiring in droves, while younger, hipper directors picked up the slack.

Mike Nichols directs Dustin Hoffman in The Graduate, *1967.*

BLAKE EDWARDS

Years active: 1958–1993

T RIPLE-THREAT WRITER/PRODUCER/DIRECTOR BLAKE Edwards's name is practically synonymous with comedy, in particular the zany Pink Panther series starring versatile master-wit Peter Sellers as the inept Inspector Clouseau. But Edwards worked in a variety of genres,

even delivering some effectively disturbing drama and heartfelt romance.

He grew up in the movie capital of Los Angeles and broke into acting in the 1940s, only to find he preferred giving direction to taking it. Soon he was scripting B-movies, directing TV episodes, and even creating his own series, *Peter Gunn*, jazzily scored by a young musician named Henry Mancini. "That began a beautiful relationship," Edwards later said of their longstanding professional collaboration that yielded a slew of Grammys and three Academy Awards.

Watching Laurel and Hardy movies sharpened Edwards's comic instincts, and being mentored by screwball sage Leo McCarey didn't hurt.

When he advanced to feature filmmaking, Edwards refined a form of sophisticated slapstick in which physical gags functioned alongside droll dialogue to develop characters and advance the plot. In *The Perfect Furlough* (1958), Janet Leigh's serious-minded army psychologist is pushed into a vat of wine—a stunt Jean-Luc Godard deemed "a gag worthy of Buster Keaton"—and instead of being humiliated, she switches her stained uniform for a strategically pinned bedsheet and is the belle of that evening's ball.

By 1961, Edwards was entrusted with an Audrey Hepburn picture, "a big opportunity for me," he noted, "an indication that people believed in me." The irreverent young filmmaker brought

a bounce to Truman Capote's bittersweet *Break-fast at Tiffany's*, a piquant comic flair that made the romantic dramedy a latter-day classic, though critics at the time weren't sure what to make of it. "It's awfully ingratiating, but *what* is it?" *Photoplay* asked. "An old-style wacky romance? A wistful case history? A comic fantasy? Oh well, Audrey's a delight to watch." With her highlighted French twist and her foot-long cigarette holder, party-girl Holly Golightly reflected a new Hepburn, one ready to swing in '60s style—or softly strum a ballad on her balcony. When she sang Mancini's Oscar-winning "Moon River," a mythical movie was born; the perfect music, the

chicest Givenchy gowns, and the charm of its star all but eclipsed the director.

Edwards was up to his genre-bending tricks again in *Days of Wine and Roses* (1962), a panorama that starts as lighthearted romance, dives deep into emotional drama, and ends as a dire cautionary tale against alcoholism. One typically Edwardian scene straddles the line between comedy and tragedy: abstaining alcoholics Joe (Jack Lemmon) and Kirsten (Lee Remick) sneak bottles of rum into their bedroom, falling off the wagon and into hysterics when

Blake Edwards directs The Man Who Loved Women, *1983.*

Remick tosses pillows under Lemmon's feet as he walks across the floor. Lemmon and Edwards were real-life alcoholics when they made the film, but both would eventually quit drinking. For Edwards, alcohol was self-medication for his lifelong bouts of depression. Making funny movies proved more therapeutic.

Hopping from heavy drama into farce, Edwards sparked a phenomenal franchise with *The Pink Panther* (1963) and *A Shot in the Dark* (1964), the double-shot that kicked off a string of sequels, launched a catchy Mancini theme, and inspired a cartoon spin-off. Originally a supporting role, the character of Clouseau moved to center stage when Edwards's genius for slapstick met Sellers's inspired silliness. Sellers also clowned his way through

1968's *The Party*, an improvisational exercise in ineffable absurdity, and now a cult classic.

With his $12 million chef d'oeuvre *The Great Race* (1965), Edwards expanded an old-fashioned comedy into a 160-minute epic, with two outlandish characters for his pal Jack Lemmon to play: the villainous Professor Fate and the pampered Prince Hapnick. Breathing new life into silent-movie tropes, Edwards boldly staged the cinema's biggest-ever pie fight, requiring four thousand pies and covering Lemmon, Natalie Wood, Keenan Wynn, and Peter Falk in fruit and cream from head to toe. "Some people are wonderful directors, but they're not picture-makers," Lemmon later observed. "They can direct an individual scene and it'll be a real pearl. But when they string the scenes together, the effect isn't worth much." With Edwards, though, "you get a strand of pearls that's just beautiful." Undervalued on its release, *The Great Race*

Lee Remick, Charles Bickford, and Debbie Megowan in Days of Wine and Roses

"I love Blake Edwards movies, the *Pink Panther* movies. With this movie [*Punch Drunk Love*], I was just trying hard to do what he did, trying to learn from that. It's very simple stuff: long takes, and a lot happening within the frame."

—PAUL THOMAS ANDERSON

has come to be regarded as a priceless treasure trove of tomfoolery.

When Edwards met *Mary Poppins* (1964) star Julie Andrews, a true Hollywood love story played out, though the happy couple suffered a disappointment with their first film together, the musical misfire *Darling Lili* (1970). With Andrews by his side for forty-one years (until his death in 2010), Edwards produced nearly as many flops as hits, but always rebounded, constantly reinventing himself with fresh material. The Dudley Moore–Bo Derek sexcapade *10* (1979) was a smash, and the film-industry satire *SOB* (1981) was a movie Hollywood hated, though its vicious humor has aged well. *Victor/Victoria* (1982) stands among Edwards's finest, most fully realized films, a mature-minded sex farce laced with insights into male-female relations, gender roles, and the power of performance. Andrews won a Golden Globe for her dynamic lead as a woman playing a man playing a woman.

For over three decades, Blake Edwards entertained audiences with his consummate dramatic skills and comedic brilliance. As Sam Wasson, author of *A Splurch in the Kisser: The Films of Blake Edwards*, said, "I position him along the line of Hollywood's greatest directors of comedy, beginning with [Charlie] Chaplin and continuing with [Ernst] Lubitsch, [Preston] Sturges, and [Billy] Wilder."

Peter Sellers and Capucine in The Pink Panther

215

MUST-SEE MOVIES

OPERATION PETTICOAT (1959)

BREAKFAST AT TIFFANY'S (1961)

EXPERIMENT IN TERROR (1962)

DAYS OF WINE AND ROSES (1962)

THE PINK PANTHER (1963)

A SHOT IN THE DARK (1964)

THE GREAT RACE (1965)

THE PARTY (1968)

VICTOR/VICTORIA (1982)

KEY SCENE TO WATCH

Holly Golightly's cocktail party in *Breakfast at Tiffany's* was only briefly indicated in George Axelrod's screenplay, so Edwards had to improvise the scene from scratch, staging assorted comic episodes: Holly's cigarette sets a woman's hat on fire; a drunk woman howls in laughter and tears seeing herself in the mirror; a man sits on Paul (George Peppard), mistaking him for a chair, while Cat (played by award-winning feline actor Orangey) roams freely among the guests. "Paramount panicked because I took eight days to shoot the party scene, and insisted on actors instead of extras," Edwards later recalled. But the time and effort paid off in a memorably funny and eccentric soiree sequence.

Blake Edwards directs Audrey Hepburn and George Peppard in Breakfast at Tiffany's *as a New York City crowd looks on.*

STANLEY KRAMER

Years active: 1955–1979

I T HAS BEEN SAID THAT STANLEY KRAMER DIDN'T MAKE movies; he made statements. A forward-thinking filmmaker sometimes called "Hollywood's conscience," the gutsy director/producer drove American movies toward social consciousness with his cutting-edge screen commentaries on

racism, nuclear weapons, the Holocaust, and other fraught issues facing humanity.

In the 1950s, the movie colony was not the politically liberal place it is today. Back when Hollywood was overwhelmingly conservative, Kramer advanced an antiestablishment mentality that would become dominant by the early '70s. "When I started in film I was nineteen," he recalled. "I didn't listen to anybody." With more attitude than money or experience, Kramer scraped together an independent production company to attack the subjects most mainstream studios avoided. "I found out early in my life that nobody really objected to 'message' films. They object to messages which didn't make money, which was something very

different," he observed, and set out to craft socially aware pictures that also sold tickets.

After making Kirk Douglas a star in 1949's *Champion* (a film Kramer talked a retired Miami dry-goods manufacturer into financing), he produced Mark Robson's *Home of the Brave* (1949), a blistering exposé of the treatment Black soldiers received in World War II. His first directorial effort was *Not as a Stranger* (1955), featuring Robert Mitchum as an aspiring surgeon who evolves from heartless to human. But Kramer was just getting warmed up. In 1958, he served his most powerful statement yet to a segregated America: *The Defiant Ones*, a lesson in racial tolerance disguised as a chase film about two chained convicts on the lam, one Black (Sidney

Poitier), one White (Tony Curtis). The visual metaphor of Black and White forced to cooperate or die was fortified with explosive dialogue by Harold Jacob Smith and blacklisted writer Nedrick Young. (Curtis: "I'm just calling a spade a spade, I didn't make up no names!" Poitier: "No, you breathe it in when you're born and you spit it out from then on!") As a head-on assault of bigotry, nothing like it had been seen before.

The film was nominated for nine Oscars, winning for its original screenplay and for Sam Leavitt's richly shaded photography. With *The Defiant Ones*, Kramer proved himself capable of not only delivering a message, but getting the best from performers; Curtis and Poitier were lavished with more

Stanley Kramer directs Tony Curtis and Sidney Poitier in The Defiant Ones.

THE REVOLUTION BEGINS

> "Stanley Kramer was quite a remarkable personality, and a wonderful filmmaker who had a vision of himself, a vision of our country, and a vision of the industry. And it was a personal choice of his to articulate himself as an artist. So Hollywood was lucky to have him in its midst."

—SIDNEY POITIER

praise than either had yet received, *Variety* declaring both "virtually flawless." *The Defiant Ones* made Poitier the first African American to net a Best Actor nomination and the first to win a British Academy Award, sending him into superstardom and eventually into a second career as a director/producer. Released the same year that Poitier made his iconic starring turn in Norman Jewison's *In the Heat of the Night*, *Guess Who's Coming to Dinner* (1967) teamed Poitier with the director's other favorite actor, Spencer Tracy, in a lighthearted yet thought-provoking look at interracial marriage. *Dinner* was a family reunion of sorts, with Katharine Hepburn and her niece, Katharine Houghton, appearing in what would be Tracy's final film before his death.

"Spence" (as Kramer called his friend) gave one of the most powerful performances in his esteemed career as a lawyer arguing for reason over religious fundamentalism in *Inherit the Wind* (1960), though Kramer was disappointed by the film's lack of box office power. Another courtroom drama with Tracy—this one about German judges tried for their involvement in Nazi crimes against humanity—

Judgment at Nuremburg (1961) fared better, earning both critical laurels and money. Because the nearly three-hour-long film was filled with actors forced to remain stationary (either in the witness stand or behind the bench), Kramer used a mobile camera so the story would flow, employing zooms and 360-degree spins; the entire courtroom set was even built on rollers to facilitate camera maneuvers.

In 1963, Kramer shelved all messages and morality to make the cockamamie caper *It's a Mad, Mad, Mad, Mad World*, again headed by Spence. "Everyone who's ever been funny is in it," the trailer promised, and the supporting cast was indeed an accumulation of comedy greats: Milton Berle, Buddy Hackett, Ethel Merman, Jonathan Winters—the Three Stooges even showed up. After trying out a few titles (it was briefly called *One Damn Thing After Another*), Kramer and screenwriters William and Tania Rose settled on *It's a Mad World*. But they couldn't seem to stop themselves from adding more *Mad*s as the epic (and the $9 million budget) grew bigger and more bonkers. Shot in Ultra Panavision, the movie was huge on every level, an unexpected laugh-riot from the "message man," as Kramer put it. "Comedy is a dangerous mission," he once said, "something which, in timing and perspective, is totally different" from the dramas he was used to. The film's success demonstrated Kramer's versatility and levity.

For his relentless pursuit of social progress via entertainment, Stanley Kramer became the inaugural recipient of the NAACP Vanguard Award in 1998. Following his 2001 death, the Produc-

ers Guild of America created the Stanley Kramer Award, given annually to films that "illuminate provocative social issues." Although *The Defiant Ones*, *Inherit the Wind*, and *Guess Who's Coming to Dinner* have been rebooted in recent years, no remake quite captures the revolutionary spirit of the originals with Kramer at the helm.

Spencer Tracy and Ethel Merman in It's a Mad, Mad, Mad, Mad World

MUST-SEE MOVIES

THE DEFIANT ONES (1958)

ON THE BEACH (1959)

INHERIT THE WIND (1960)

JUDGMENT AT NUREMBURG (1961)

IT'S A MAD, MAD, MAD, MAD WORLD (1963)

SHIP OF FOOLS (1965)

GUESS WHO'S COMING TO DINNER (1967)

Judy Garland prepares to take the stand in Judgment at Nuremberg.

KEY SCENE TO WATCH

The second time she takes the stand as reluctant witness Irene Hoffman in *Judgment at Nuremberg*, Judy Garland rips up the screen with her emotionally complex characterization. Although she's only on camera for four minutes defending her forbidden friendship with a Jew, her reactions range from demure to volatile, as she finally shouts "Stop it!" to her interrogator (Maximilian Schell). "There's nobody in the entertainment world today, actor or singer, who can run the complete range of emotions, from utter pathos to power . . . the way she can," her director said. Because of performances like Garland's, *Nuremberg* was Kramer's favorite of all his films.

STANLEY KUBRICK

Years active: 1951–1999

IN A CAREER SPANNING NEARLY HALF A CENTURY, Stanley Kubrick directed only thirteen feature films. Because he spent years preparing and executing his projects with meticulous artistry, his is a filmography of quality over quantity. From the ironic tragedy of *Paths of Glory* (1957) to the

doom-laden humor of *Lolita* (1962); the quiet magnitude of *2001: A Space Odyssey* (1968) to the grotesque terror of *The Shining* (1980), every Kubrick movie was a major event.

As the Bronx, New York, native transitioned from teenaged *Look* magazine photographer to indie auteur to Hollywood wunderkind, his still photography skills (and the work of his celluloid heroes, Ingmar Bergman and Federico Fellini) informed his striking compositions. Picture bikini-clad, sun-hatted Lolita (Sue Lyon) lounging in the backyard; the card game played beneath a blazing chandelier in *Barry Lyndon* (1975); the *Shining* twins positioned center-frame against a wallpapered corridor. Practically every frame of a Kubrick film could stand

on its own like a picture in a gallery.

After impressing MGM head Dore Schary with his first major feature, 1956's stark racetrack heist *The Killing* (a prototype for Quentin Tarantino's *Reservoir Dogs* [1992]), Kubrick was given a healthy budget and a star (Kirk Douglas) for *Paths of Glory*, the World War I drama that plays more like a pitch-black battlefield satire. When Douglas replaced Anthony Mann with Kubrick on the ancient Roman epic *Spartacus* (1960), it was the young director's chance to show his prowess on a grand scale. He crafted a classic of "sheer pictorial poetry that is sweeping and savage, intimate and lusty, tender and bittersweet," as *Variety* observed.

Barely skirting the censors, Kubrick took sug-

gestive humor to new heights in *Lolita*, Vladimir Nabokov's twisted tale of an ill-fated professor and the pubescent girl who steals his heart. He then upped the ante by mercilessly satirizing the US president and nuclear war in *Dr. Strangelove* (1964), with Peter Sellers improvising his way through three distinctive characters. Originally planned as a tense drama about accidental nuclear annihilation, *Dr. Strangelove or: How I Learned to Stop Worrying and Love the Bomb* became what Kubrick called "a

nightmare comedy" in the planning stage. "Ideas kept coming to me which I would discard because they were so ludicrous. I kept saying to myself: 'I can't do this. People will laugh.'" So, he embraced the absurdity, crafting a wildly irreverent Cold War spoof that "age has not withered," according to *Guardian* critic Peter Bradshaw in 2019.

Stanley Kubrick shoots the dismantling of the HAL 9000 in 2001 with a handheld camera, 1966.

"Stanley Kubrick was a film milestone for me. To choose one, I think probably *2001: A Space Odyssey*. That preempted all the *Star Wars* and things, and I remember when he made it, the studios were all very nervous: 'God, what's he doing, it doesn't make sense.' So I liked that. That certainly set off things in me."

—NICOLAS ROEG

Moving to England in 1961, Kubrick grew more reclusive with success, his films becoming darker and more intense. Though never a part of the Tinseltown scene, he was granted an unfathomable amount of creative freedom by the Hollywood establishment. What visionaries like Orson Welles had struggled to gain in the 1940s, Kubrick finally attained in the freer '60s and '70s: the power to artistically control every aspect of his films with little studio interference—even when he went $4 million over budget (and two years behind schedule) on *2001: A Space Odyssey*, his jaw-dropping science-fiction masterpiece.

Throwing himself into the realm of outer space, the obsessive director spent a year researching, even working with NASA to design more realistic spacecraft than any yet seen on-screen. In Kubrick's hands, the germ of an Arthur C. Clarke story became an epic symphony illustrating the wonders—and potential dangers—of the possible future, climaxing in the psychedelic Star Gate sequence, a kaleidoscope of color that MGM pro-

moted to the emerging hippie culture as "the ultimate trip." Raising the stakes yet again, Kubrick delivered a still more terrifying vision of the future in *A Clockwork Orange* (1971), a brutal hellscape of gangs run amok in a lawless London. One of the most iconic shots in cinema is Kubrick's antihero, Alex (Malcolm McDowell), strapped to a theater seat, his eyelids clamped open, forced to "viddy" violent films as part of a "cure" for his evil inclinations. So subversive was *A Clockwork Orange* that it was originally given an X rating and banned in the UK until 2000. "You don't protect your reputation by playing it safe," the filmmaker once said. "Only things meaningful and personally exciting are worth doing."

When Kubrick set his sights on the supernatural, he avoided ghost-story clichés at all costs. With gothic horror expert Diane Johnson as cowriter, he spun the raw ingredients of Stephen King's *The Shining* (isolation, clairvoyance, and past sins) into a haunted hotel conundrum, the specifics of which were left unexplained. "With this type of story,"

MUST-SEE MOVIES

THE KILLING (1956)

PATHS OF GLORY (1957)

SPARTACUS (1960)

LOLITA (1962)

DR. STRANGELOVE (1964)

2001: A SPACE ODYSSEY (1968)

A CLOCKWORK ORANGE (1971)

THE SHINING (1980)

FULL METAL JACKET (1987)

Gary Lockwood and Keir Dullea in 2001:
A Space Odyssey

KEY SCENE TO WATCH

"Open the pod bay doors, HAL," Dave Bowman (Keir Dullea) tells the malfunctioning HAL 9000 in *2001* when he finds himself locked out of the spacecraft *Discovery*. "I'm sorry, Dave. I'm afraid I can't do that," HAL replies, the hypnotic yellow pupil in the center of its red eye never blinking as it takes control of the ship. First toying with the idea of a female voice for the sentient computer, then trying an English man, Kubrick finally settled on American actor Douglas Rain, who had just the right soft monotone to make HAL believable.

STANLEY KUBRICK

Kubrick told a reporter in 1980, "reason doesn't help you. If you try to be verbally analytical, it becomes suddenly ridiculous." As critic Roger Ebert expressed: "There is no way, within the film, to be sure with any confidence exactly what happens, or precisely how, or really why." But the how and why didn't matter as much as the eerie atmosphere and the ever-intensifying suspense Kubrick generated. Gliding through the Overlook's labyrinthine hallways with the then-new Steadicam, he mesmerized audiences into experiencing the same claustrophobic terror Wendy (Shelley Duvall) feels when her husband (Jack Nicholson) turns from blocked writer to axe-wielding maniac. Kubrick captured another agonizing descent into madness—this one happening to Vincent D'Onofrio's bullied army recruit—in his Vietnam statement *Full Metal Jacket* (1987).

"Stanley Kubrick was one of the most audacious filmmakers in history," Steven Spielberg said of his friend and associate in 2019. Although he died shortly after wrapping his final movie, *Eyes Wide Shut* (1999), the maverick's vision lived on in Spielberg's *AI Artificial Intelligence* (2001), a project developed by Kubrick. "He never made the same picture twice," marveled Spielberg. "Every single picture is a different genre, a different period, a different story, a different risk. The only thing that bonded all of his films was the incredible virtuoso that he was with craft." James Cameron, Ridley Scott, and Guillermo del Toro are among dozens of other directors who have been impacted by Kubrick's cinematic genius.

Shelley Duvall in The Shining

DAVID LEAN

Years active: 1942–1984

ENGLISHMAN DAVID LEAN HAD BEEN DIRECTING GREAT films since the 1940s. He surpassed himself with each decade until hitting his stride with two magnificent 1960s spectacles, *Lawrence of Arabia* (1962) and *Doctor Zhivago* (1965), both of them cultural landmarks years in

the making. The pictorial Lean was that rare filmmaker who succeeded as both technical craftsman and artist, who mastered both the intimate and the expansive. "There was a machine-like quality about him," actor Anthony Quinn recalled, "almost as if one of his eyes was a camera."

The South London son of Quakers entered the industry early, working his way up from clapper boy to messenger to editor, and finally codirector of the wartime drama *In Which We Serve* (1942) with playwright Noël Coward. As solo director, Lean handled Coward's *Blithe Spirit* (1945) with a light touch, concocting a saucy supernatural love-triangle "in blushing Technicolor," as advertisements claimed. Before his films grew super-

size, he enhanced a simple, small romance with the dramatic strains of Rachmaninoff, making *Brief Encounter* (1945) one of the most elegant illicit affairs in all of cinema.

For his definitive version of Charles Dickens's *Great Expectations* (1946), Lean and art director John Bryan experimented with different camera lenses to superb effect, making Miss Havisham's house look cavernous and imposing to young Pip, yet small and cramped to Pip the adult (John Mills). When a reporter asked if he thought most viewers noticed what kind of lens he used, Lean retorted, "Well, they don't notice the fourteen coats of paint on a Rolls-Royce, but they're still there." And that's what his films were: the cinematic equivalents of

luxury automobiles, impeccably crafted, exceptionally stylish, and built to last.

Lean partnered with Columbia producer Sam Spiegel to bring Pierre Boulle's *The Bridge on the River Kwai* (1957) to the screen in the full grandeur of Technicolor and CinemaScope. The perfectionistic Lean had an actual bridge built in the jungles of Sri Lanka for this character-driven adventure layered with conflicts between Sessue Hayakawa's honor-bound Japanese colonel, William Holden's scrappy American, and Alec Guinness's Col. Nicholson, with his stiff-upper-lip British resolve.

The action culminates in one of the most gripping finales in movie history. *The Bridge on the River Kwai* was not only the year's top-grossing film, but the winner of Best Picture, Best Director, and five other Oscars.

Lawrence of Arabia was even more ambitious, a nearly four-hour telling of T. E. Lawrence's fascinating journey as the British intelligence officer who led the Arab revolt in World War I. The dynamic leading role made Shakespearean stage actor Peter

David Lean shoots Lawrence of Arabia *in Jordan.*

THE REVOLUTION BEGINS

> "*The Bridge on the River Kwai* is a movie that takes its time in a way that is almost unbelievable. . . . It's kind of an amazing film in terms of the time it takes. It could never be made today. Never. Not with a computer generation, not with a generation that's used to things happening fast. It's a true narrative movie."

—SYDNEY POLLACK

O'Toole a major movie star. From the wide shots of Jordan's golden sands to the luminous close-ups of O'Toole's ice-blue eyes against his sun-bronzed skin, Lean's camera lingers, drinking in the majestic beauty of its surroundings. The director saw the film as "a sort of movie opera," an epic of lifelike realism, and yet larger than life. "Movies are a kind of dream," he observed. "I think they should have an unreal edge to them, and that's what I try to do." Freddie Young earned one of *Lawrence*'s seven Oscars for his Super Panavision 70 photography.

Alec Guinness, William Holden, and Jack Hawkins in The Bridge on the River Kwai

By the time Lean released *Doctor Zhivago* in 1965, his lengthy, prestigious pictures were known in the industry as "Oscar machines." Although some considered Lean a difficult, demanding man to work for, his gift for visual storytelling was unsurpassed. In *Zhivago*, Omar Sharif (a Lean discovery from *Lawrence of Arabia*) and Julie Christie head a mammoth melodrama without a hint of camp, a king-size romance of staggeringly lovely imagery and emotion heightened by the strains of Maurice Jarre's melodic "Lara's Theme."

After his critically unpopular *Ryan's Daughter* (1970), Lean waited fourteen years before stepping on set again; when he did, his efforts yielded another opulent adaptation. Sourced from E. M. Forster's 1924 critique of British colonialism, *A Passage to India* (1984) became a lush period piece featuring Judy Davis as an English tourist on a fateful course with an Indian local played by Victor Banerjee. Once again, Lean balanced the intimate with the exotic like no one else could. Michael Blowen of the *Boston Globe* wrote, "David Lean's *A Passage to India*, a masterful film by a master filmmaker, reminds us of the medium's potential. The casting, script, cinematography, and set design are perfectly orchestrated in an ambitious symphony of drama, symbol, and art."

In 1989, *Lawrence of Arabia* was fully restored and reissued to theaters to universal acclaim, cementing Lean's reputation as a superlative auteur. When he died in 1991, he was busy planning—

what else?—a grand-scale literary adaptation, this one based on Joseph Conrad's *Nostromo*.

Sir Richard Attenborough, the actor/director who made his screen debut in *In Which We Serve*, called his 1982 Oscar-winner *Gandhi* "my tribute to [David Lean] as much as it was to Gandhi. He had a profound impact on my desire to want to make films." Directors as varied as Sergio Leone, Spike Lee, and Hong Kong filmmaker John Woo have cited Lean as a major influence. Since 1977, George Lucas has filled his bottomless Star Wars franchise with homages to *Lawrence of Arabia*. Entertainment that owes a debt to David Lean just keeps coming.

Julie Christie and Omar Sharif in Doctor Zhivago

MUST-SEE MOVIES

BLITHE SPIRIT (1945)

BRIEF ENCOUNTER (1945)

GREAT EXPECTATIONS (1946)

SUMMERTIME (1955)

THE BRIDGE ON THE RIVER KWAI (1957)

LAWRENCE OF ARABIA (1962)

DOCTOR ZHIVAGO (1965)

A PASSAGE TO INDIA (1984)

KEY SCENE TO WATCH

One of the most stunning passages in *Lawrence of Arabia* begins with Lawrence blowing out a match just before it burns him, followed by a shot of the sun rising over a breathtaking desert horizon. As Maurice Jarre's emotionally overpowering score swells, Lawrence and his Bedouin guide (Zia Mohyeddin) appear, crossing the vast sand dunes on camelback. Sequences like this helped Anne V. Coates snare an Oscar for the poetic precision of her editing.

Peter O'Toole stars in Lawrence of Arabia.

MIKE NICHOLS

Years active: 1966–2007

L IKE SO MANY OF HIS HOLLYWOOD FOREBEARS, Mike Nichols immigrated to America to escape Nazi Germany. Unlike most of his predecessors, he was only seven. Born in Berlin to a Russian family, Mikhail Igor Peschkowsky landed in New York City in 1939. In trying to assimilate into the culture and learn the language, Nichols developed "the defining characteristic of his talent," screenwriter/director Douglas McGrath has speculated, "which is his acute and very precise understanding of human nature." His wit and perception drew Nichols into performing.

In 1958, he and his comedic kindred spirit, writer/director Elaine May, formed the Nichols and May improvisational comedy duo. From there, he nailed his first directing assignment, winning a Tony for Neil Simon's *Barefoot in the Park*, a Broadway comedy that led to a string of successful plays. The *Los Angeles Times* dubbed Nichols "the Whiz Kid" in 1966, when Elizabeth Taylor and Richard Burton plucked him from the stage to helm the film

Mike Nichols directs Richard Burton and Elizabeth Taylor in Who's Afraid of Virginia Woolf?

232

of Edward Albee's caustic dramedy *Who's Afraid of Virginia Woolf?* The power couple disappeared into boozy, bickering George and Martha, aging marrieds who excel in the art of insults. "Look, sweetheart, I can drink you under any goddamned table you want," Taylor snarls at her celebrated husband. Between the pitch-black humor and the salty dialogue, *Virginia Woolf* was the final nail in the Hollywood Production Code's coffin. It raked in profits, British Academy of Film and Television Arts (BAFTA) Awards, and Oscars, most notably for Haskell Wexler's stripped-down cinematography.

His delightfully skewed outlook gave Nichols the requisite skill set for drama, comedy, and everything in between. "I find it hard to think of comedy and tragedy separately," he told a reporter in 1967. "There are laughs all the way through *Hamlet*, and *Virginia Woolf* brings down the house. Is *Virginia Woolf* a comedy? Life is the same. Life is pretty funny, and yet people die." He drew upon these same tragicomic instincts for *The Graduate* (1967), his coming-of-age classic that made a star out of the

Nichols on the set of Catch-22, *1970*

233

> "If you're a writer, you really want Mike Nichols to direct your screenplay. Because you know that every shot and every costume and every piece of furniture and every shoe and everything you see is going to tell your story, and never give it away."
>
> —ELAINE MAY

hitherto unknown Dustin Hoffman and a hit out of Simon and Garfunkel's "Mrs. Robinson." More than a movie, it was a defining moment in '60s pop culture.

Hoffman's Benjamin is a college grad who returns home only to be used as a status symbol by his wealthy family, and used again by the older woman who seduces him (Anne Bancroft). "The picture is really about being drowned—in objects," Nichols said. With this in mind, he and cameraman Robert Surtees told half the story visually, framing Ben submerged in water, trapped behind furniture, and, of course, caught in the arch of Mrs. Robinson's stockinged leg in an iconic image. Nichols not only became the first director to earn a million dollars for a single movie, but was rewarded with an Academy Award for Best Director, a signal that a new kind of cinema had arrived: youth-oriented, more irreverent, and less obvious. *New York Times* critic Bosley Crowther raved that *The Graduate* was "not only the best film of the year, but also one of the best seriocomic social satires we've had from Hollywood since Preston Sturges was making them."

Once again, the in-demand filmmaker's finger was on the pulse of social politics as he encapsulated the absurdity of war in *Catch-22* (1970) and took a cold, hard look at the sexual revolution with 1971's *Carnal Knowledge*. Never one to shy away from hot-button issues, Nichols tackled nuclear power in *Silkwood* (1983), turning the true story of activist Karen Silkwood, played by Meryl Streep, into an engrossing drama. Nichols and Streep struck gold again in *Postcards from the Edge* (1990), based on Carrie Fisher's semifictionalized memoir of a drug-addled young adulthood tainted by her movie-star mother.

Always highly regarded in Hollywood, Nichols had the clout to assemble a dream cast for his definitive '80s Cinderella story, *Working Girl* (1988): Melanie Griffith, Harrison Ford, and Sigourney Weaver, all at the top of their game. With soaring aerial shots of the Statue of Liberty and Staten Island, Nichols lovingly showcased his New York, the New York of the American Dream, where immigrants and underdogs can rise to the top with hard work—and a little white lie or two, such as the one Griffith's secretary tells to take her boss's place.

THE REVOLUTION BEGINS

MUST-SEE MOVIES

WHO'S AFRAID OF VIRGINIA WOOLF? (1966)

THE GRADUATE (1967)

CATCH-22 (1970)

CARNAL KNOWLEDGE (1971)

SILKWOOD (1983)

BILOXI BLUES (1988)

WORKING GIRL (1988)

THE BIRDCAGE (1996)

Dustin Hoffman is seduced by Anne Bancroft in The Graduate.

KEY SCENE TO WATCH

Nichols's favorite scene in *The Graduate* was the ambiguous ending. Benjamin has just rescued his girlfriend Elaine (Katharine Ross) from the altar, where her parents expected her to marry another man. The couple flees the church, catching a bus and sitting in the back. After a momentary eruption of glee, their smiles fade, leaving Ben and Elaine looking lost and uneasy. With this perfect parting shot, Nichols visually expressed his doubts that Ben was any better off in the end than he was in the beginning. "He fights his way free, but he's still in the same world," the director said of the film's finale.

Nichols's long career hit another high point when he tapped his favorite accomplice Elaine May to coscript an adaptation of the French farce *La Cage aux Folles* (1978). Twenty-five years later, *The Birdcage* (1996) remains equal parts hilarious and ingratiating, a sincere plea for gay acceptance chock-full of that razor-sharp Nichols-May humor. "Whatever I am, he made me!" drag performer Albert (Nathan Lane) shrieks in a fit of hysteria. "I was adorable once, young and full of hope. And now look at me! I'm this short, fat, insecure, middle-aged *thing*!" Unmoved, Armand (Robin Williams) snaps back, "I made you short?"

Nichols remained relevant to the end of his life, guiding Tom Hanks through *Charlie Wilson's War* (2007) and copping his eighth (yes, eighth) Tony for directing Philip Seymour Hoffman in Arthur Miller's *Death of a Salesman* in 2012. As Hanks observed, Mike Nichols "went on and on, from the '50s to well after the year 2000. Who transcends decades like that?"

Robin Williams and Nathan Lane in Miami Beach for The Birdcage

ROMAN POLANSKI

Years active: 1962–present

I ALWAYS WANTED TO BE A FILM DIRECTOR. THAT WAS my prime interest, and I don't even remember the beginnings of it all," Roman Polanski stated in 2009, recalling the harrowing childhood that lured him into the fantasy land of cinema. One of the industry's most compelling and polariz-

ing figures, Polanski has lived a life laden with tragedy, controversy, and scandal. Yet he's still thriving, more than fifty years after first gaining fame as a filmmaker who specialized in paranoia and unsettling undercurrents of dread.

After both of his parents were sent to German concentration camps during the Holocaust, Polanski spent his childhood running from the constant threat of violence or death if he were captured. He was only seven when he peered through the Polish ghetto walls to watch newsreels projected to those on the outside. Right then, movies became an addictive form of escape. "As for *The Pianist*, I can tell you I always wanted to make the picture about those things and that period," he told the

Hollywood Reporter in 2015. Winning an Oscar for directing the haunting true story of a Polish war refugee (played by Adrian Brody) was a late-career high point for the artist who started at the National Film School in Lodz, Poland.

His debut feature *Knife in the Water* (1962) was the first Polish film to be nominated for an Academy Award. A spare, economical triangle of tension that builds between three characters on a sailboat, *Knife in the Water* set the stage for Philip Noyce's *Dead Calm* (1989), a similar scenario played for horror. Polanski would not tackle the horror genre until heading to England to craft the disturbing *Repulsion* (1965), a story he conceived and cowrote. As a skinned rabbit rots in the kitchen and the

apartment walls threaten to crumble around her, repressed manicurist Carol (Catherine Deneuve) sinks further into a psychotic abyss, becoming a danger to every man who crosses her path. Polanski delicately suggests reasons why Carol breaks down but never explains anything, leaving room for audience interpretation. Mood, character, and images have always interested him more than exposition.

Polanski aimed his "Gothic mind" and "really grotesque sense of humor" (in the words of pro-

ducer Gene Gotowski) at *The Fearless Vampire Killers* (1967), a macabre mockery of Hammer horror movies costarring himself as a vampire hunter and Sharon Tate as the innkeeper's daughter. While the freewheeling fairy tale didn't quite hit the mark, Polanski later revealed that it was his happiest film because he met Tate, who became his wife in 1968.

Roman Polanski shoots Frantic *in France, 1987*

THE REVOLUTION BEGINS

"It's not only the cast that is all coming together to do some of their best work forever, but also you have this incredibly cohesive world that is created for these actors. The propping in this movie, that shaving kit . . . the business cards . . . the silver ashtray . . . all of these visual cues. It's all so effortless and doesn't draw attention to itself in that kind of sweaty, horrible, period-movie way. It just is. And I think that's what makes [*Chinatown*] so great."

—DAVID FINCHER

When Paramount Pictures head Robert Evans brought Polanski to Hollywood, it was to direct Ira Levin's novel of modern-day deviltry, *Rosemary's Baby* (1968). With his laser-focus on detail—from the significant silver bauble expectant mother Rosemary (Mia Farrow) wears around her neck to the claw marks on her back—Polanski plants clue upon clue that something sinister is happening right beneath the rosy surface. Often using long or medium shots, he cuts to close-ups of Farrow's face in key moments, revealing the faintest traces of fear in her wide eyes and hesitant smiles. He micro-managed every aspect of shooting, even penning the script and operating a handheld camera for the dream sequences and Rosemary's dazed walk into oncoming traffic (a stunt he and Farrow performed on a real Manhattan street). Having been reared on classic Hollywood, Polanski relished filling minor roles with a gallery of Golden Age actors, including Ralph Bellamy, Patsy Kelly, and Elisha Cook Jr.

Like Hitchcock's *Psycho* (1960) and William Friedkin's *The Exorcist* (1973), *Rosemary's Baby* stands as one of the all-time greatest big-screen scares. But in Polanski's chiller, no murderous maniacs appear, no graphic demonic possessions occur. It is almost purely psychological, "the greatest horror film without any horror in it," said production designer Richard Sylbert. As a movie critic, Charles Champlin judged the film "a gem," but as a human being, he considered *Rosemary's Baby* "a most desperately sick and obscene motion picture whose ultimate horror is that it was made at all." Nevertheless, it remains a certified classic that inspired Jordan Peele's 2017 spine-tingler *Get Out*.

When a pregnant Tate was murdered by members of Charles Manson's cult in 1969, the traumatized director left Los Angeles to live and work in Europe, returning in 1973 to helm one last Hollywood film. Based on Robert Towne's Oscar-winning screenplay, *Chinatown* (1974) is a vintage

1937 LA neo-noir steeped in the rich detail and atmosphere characteristic of the director. As Jack Nicholson's detective, former Chinatown cop Jake Gittes, becomes entangled in a puzzling web of intrigue spun by Faye Dunaway's wealthy widow, he winds up in familiar territory but way out of his depth. "Forget it, Jake," his partner (Joe Mantell) ultimately advises. "It's Chinatown." As time goes by, *Chinatown*'s reputation grows; it is now believed by many to be one of the finest films ever made.

Polanski has lived in France since 1978, when he was faced with the threat of prison for unlawful sex with a thirteen-year-old girl. While widely condemned for his actions, the veteran has continued to produce works of merit. The exquisitely tragic *Tess* (1979) was in memory of Tate, who had suggested he make a movie of Thomas Hardy's *Tess of the d'Urbervilles*, and 2010's *The Ghost Writer* proved Polanski hasn't lost his knack for suspense. "I would like to be judged for my work," he once said, "and not for my life. If there is any possibility of changing your destiny, it may be only in your creative life, certainly not in your life, period."

Roman Polanski directs Faye Dunaway in Chinatown.

MUST-SEE MOVIES

KNIFE IN THE WATER (1962)

REPULSION (1965)

ROSEMARY'S BABY (1968)

CHINATOWN (1974)

TESS (1979)

FRANTIC (1988)

THE PIANIST (2002)

THE GHOST WRITER (2010)

Mia Farrow in Rosemary's Baby

KEY SCENE TO WATCH

In the end, Rosemary finally delivers her baby and discovers that the satanic plot against her is even more horrific than she imagined. When she peeks inside the basinet, Krzysztof Komeda's score erupts in a trombone wail that sounds like both a scream and a laugh. Surreal comic tones enhance the nightmarish scene. Is it really happening, or has Rosemary slipped into a postpartum hallucination? Polanski keeps the audience guessing, never showing us the demonic offspring who has, as Roman Castevet (Sidney Blackmer) says, "his father's eyes."

NEW WAVE NOTABLES

A band of renegade film critics turned filmmakers emerged in late-1950s France. With its emphasis on youth, low budgets, and realistic mise-en-scène, the *Nouvelle Vague*, or French New Wave, movement bucked France's tradition of glossy, refined films, impacting cinema across the globe in the '60s.

The prolific **Claude Chabrol** kicked off the movement with his slightly Hitchcockian drama *Le Beau Serge* in 1958, becoming the first *Cahiers du cinéma* critic to succeed as a filmmaker. He followed up *Serge* with *Les Cousins* (1958) and *Les Bonnes Femmes* (1960). A consummate craftsman, Chabrol progressed into adapting literary works after his acclaimed *Les Biches* (1968), and kept making films until his death in 2010.

Jean-Luc Godard is perhaps the most revolutionary of the New Wave directors—and the one that Quentin Tarantino has borrowed most liberally from. His stunning debut *Breathless* (1960) deliberately broke all the rules of filmmaking with its jump cuts and jagged edges. Godard cast his wife, Anna Karina, in a string of wildly diverse films, including the tragic *Vivre sa Vie* (1962), the heist film *Band à Part* (1964), and the sci-fi oddity *Alphaville* (1965). Today, Godard's ever-evolving style continues to enthrall.

Alain Resnais turned narrative structure on its head with the nonlinear romance *Hiroshima Mon Amour* (1959), scripted by Marguerite Duras, who would embark on her own successful directorial career in the late '60s. Resnais's *Last Year at Marienbad* (1960) scattered the ashes of traditional filmmaking even further with its bafflingly enigmatic dialogue and story, whereas 1963's *Muriel* was a captivating rumination on the nature of memory.

Journalist/writer/filmmaker **Éric Rohmer** was a multitalented auteur who broke through with his Oscar-nominated *My Night at Maud's* (1969), a moral dilemma wrapped in the guise of sexy, smart entertainment. A man is filled with desire to caress a woman's knee in the much-acclaimed *Claire's Knee* (1970), though the richly drawn story is about so much more. The sublimely summery *Pauline at the Beach* scored a Boston Society of Film Critics Award for Best Screenplay in 1983.

The most commercially successful New Wave director, **François Truffaut** earned a Best Director award at the Cannes Film Festival for his poignant debut *The 400 Blows* (1959). His free-spirited love triangle *Jules and Jim* (1961) influenced the world, making lead actress Jeanne

Moreau the queen of the New Wave, while the much-copied pseudodocumentary *Day for Night* (1973) snared Truffaut an Oscar.

A pioneer of the "Left Bank" branch of the New Wave, **Agnès Varda** started as a photographer, documentarian, and wife of director Jacques Demy. Her engrossing drama chronicling two hours in a pop singer's life, *Cleo from 5 to 7* (1962), still stands as a masterpiece. Shortly before her death in 2019, she received an Oscar nomination for her vibrant, humanist documentary *Faces Places* (2017). As critic Roger Ebert observed in 2012, "Varda is sometimes referred to as the godmother of the French New Wave. . . . Nothing could be more unfair. Varda is its very soul."

Jean-Luc Godard directs Brigitte Bardot in Contempt, *1963.*

Chapter Six

A WHOLE NEW HOLLYWOOD

ennis Hopper's biker odyssey *Easy Rider* rock-and-rolled into theaters in 1969, heralding the arrival of the countercul-ture: the hippies, the radicals, the rebels. Bergman, Fellini, and the French New Wave had decon-structed the conventions and revised the rules, mak-ing American movies more abstract. With no more Production Code to follow, gritty films rife with vio-lence, profanity, and nudity became the new nor-mal. Seventies cinema was for grown-ups.

This freedom was born of collapse. By 1970, Hollywood, California, was in decline as the epi-center of filmmaking; the old studio system was not only dead, it was decomposing. Once-thriving Golden Age lots stood empty and dilapidated. The moving-picture dream was threatening to end, and it was up to new blood to save the day.

Enter the film-school graduates. If *Bonnie and Clyde* (1967) director Arthur Penn was the move-ment's godfather, such auteurs as Francis Ford Coppola and Martin Scorsese best represented its image: youthful, bearded, brash—and insistent on total creative control. So-called New Hollywood was an exclusive club of typically White, male, upper-middle-class kids who could afford to study filmmaking in college. But a few who didn't fit the mold crept in, bringing a minority perspective to the '70s screen.

Director William Friedkin (far left) visits Francis Ford Coppola on the set of The Godfather Part II, *1974.*

WOODY ALLEN

Years active: 1966–present

ALLEN KONIGSBERG OF BROOKLYN WAS ONLY SEVenteen when he began writing jokes, selling them as Heywood Allen, and pulling in more money than his parents. Heywood was eventually shortened to "Woody," a comedian turned screenwriter whose

lust-and-marriage farce *What's New, Pussycat?* (1965) put him on Hollywood's radar just in time for the cultural shift toward more experimental fare. "Nuttiness triumphant," a phrase taken from a *Look* magazine review, was used to promote *Take the Money and Run* in 1969. Allen cowrote, directed, and starred in the sight-gag-heavy pseudodocumentary, a genre he says he "finally perfected" when he filmed the innovative *Forrest Gump* (1994) blueprint *Zelig* in 1983.

The first effort yielded by the triple-threat's five-picture deal with United Artists was *Bananas* (1971), the absurd tale of Fielding Mellish (a name that says it all), who becomes president of a Latin American country through a crackpot coup.

Solidifying Allen's stature was *Sleeper* (1973), a broad science fiction satire cowritten with Marshall Brickman. The kooky yet cerebral *Sleeper* marked a turning point in Allen's work; a mature, romance-driven narrative was emerging behind the slapstick bits, thanks in part to his kinship with Diane Keaton. The two first struck a rapport in Allen's *Casablanca*-inspired *Play It Again, Sam* (1972), a movie-lover's tribute to Bogart and Bergman (Ingrid) that sparked another iconic screen duo. Penelope Gilliatt of the *New Yorker* declared Allen and Keaton "an unbeatable new team . . . working as if each of them were a less mock-assertive Groucho Marx with a duplicate of him to play against."

The raw materials were converging to make

magic: Allen, Keaton, Brickman, and cinematographer Gordon Willis, who had suffused Francis Ford Coppola's *The Godfather* (1972) with sublime shadows and out-of-the-box framing. Each contributed their best work to *Annie Hall* (1977), an offbeat love story detailing the funny yet melancholy relationship between neurotic Alvy (Allen) and insecure Annie (Keaton). "I could never, ever write from a woman's point of view until I met Keaton," Allen has remarked of his bittersweet opus that presents male and female viewpoints with an equal balance, reflective of the women's lib era. Allen used a grab bag of techniques to meld humor with heartache: breaking the fourth wall; subtitles; Disney-type animation; abrupt flashbacks; split screen; broken continuity. This self-aware storytelling surprised critics and beguiled audiences, leading to the film's collecting four of the top five Oscars in 1978, including Best Director. After the bustling Manhattan energy of *Annie Hall*, Allen rarely filmed anywhere besides his familiar New York City.

Allen and cinematographer Remi Adefarasin on the set of Match Point, *2005*

To open *Manhattan* (1979), Willis shot the city in a velvety monochrome widescreen, a montage set to George Gershwin's "Rhapsody in Blue," establishing a mythic backdrop to the tale of Isaac (Allen) and his three loves: teen Tracy (Mariel Hemingway), culture maven Mary (Keaton), and the Big Apple. These relationships are never as clearly black-and-white as the imagery surrounding them. More subtle technique is employed than in *Annie Hall*, Allen moving another step closer to breezy perfectionism. His compositions are painterly; his camera stays steady while characters walk and talk in and out of frame, a very Manhattan thing to do. "Mr. Allen's progress,"

Vincent Canby of the *New York Times* reported, "is proceeding so rapidly that we who watch him have to pause occasionally to catch our breath."

Woody Allen continued to progress, one film a year, for decades. When Mia Farrow appeared as Tina Vitale in *Broadway Danny Rose* (1984), she filled Keaton's shoes as the director's leading lady, personally and professionally. Farrow did some of her best work as an abused wife who finds a too-good-to-be-true screen-idol savior in *The Purple Rose of*

Mia Farrow, Barbara Hershey, and Dianne Wiest in Hannah and Her Sisters

"I wore what I wanted to wear, or, rather, I stole what I wanted to wear from cool-looking women on the streets of New York. They were the real costume designers of *Annie Hall*. Well, that's not entirely true. Woody was. Every idea, every choice, every decision, came from the mind of Woody Allen."

—DIANE KEATON

Cairo (1985); with her title role in the Best Original Screenplay–winning tale of two troubled yet amusing years in the lives of *Hannah and Her Sisters* (1986); as the cigarette-girl-turned-gossip-queen in 1987's nostalgic *Radio Days*; and the embodiment of love unrequited in the fatally philosophical *Crimes and Misdemeanors* (1989).

The fruitful relationship was torn apart in 1992, when Farrow discovered that Allen was having an intimate relationship with her adopted daughter, twenty-one-year-old Soon-Yi Previn, whom he later married. While the former power couple's quarrels and custody battles made headlines, their seven-year-old adopted daughter Dylan accused Allen of sexual abuse. Investigations and courtroom trials followed; although Allen was never found guilty of the charges of sexual abuse, a New York Supreme Court judge denied Allen custody of his children with Farrow.

Allen's reputation has been tarnished by the scandals, though he continues to work in an industry divided for and against him, still churning out a movie a year—some more successful than others. In 2012, the auteur proved his twenty-first-century relevance by snaring an Oscar for his solo screenplay *Midnight in Paris* (2011). In 1995, he earned seven nominations for his Great White Way–meets–gangland urban legend *Bullets over Broadway* (1994), a darkly ridiculous backstage lark with a story that poses the question: Can one separate the art from the artist?

In his fifty-plus features, Allen has refined an inimitable style, a talkative tone of quick native–New Yorker wit, woven with somber threads reminiscent of his favorite filmmaker, Ingmar Bergman. "It's an odd influence," the comically inclined director has said of his longtime hero. "If you're influenced by Ingmar Bergman—who is, even among dramatic filmmakers, particularly poetic, heavy thematically, heavy in technique—it makes for an unusual end product. And it did for me, for better or for worse."

MUST-SEE MOVIES

PLAY IT AGAIN, SAM (1972)

SLEEPER (1973)

ANNIE HALL (1977)

ZELIG (1983)

THE PURPLE ROSE OF CAIRO (1985)

HANNAH AND HER SISTERS (1986)

CRIMES AND MISDEMEANORS (1989)

BULLETS OVER BROADWAY (1994)

MIDNIGHT IN PARIS (2011)

Diane Keaton and Woody Allen in Annie Hall

KEY SCENE TO WATCH

Compare two side-by-side sequences from *Annie Hall*. In split screen, we see the Singers and the Halls seated at holiday meals. The Singer gathering is large and noisy; the Halls sit in near silence, methodically slicing their cuts of Easter ham. Without raising her eyes from her plate, Mrs. Hall asks Mrs. Singer a question, the ensuing brief exchange crossing the divide of time and space. Later, dual therapy sessions are contrasted. Alvy and Annie's therapists both ask: "How often do you sleep together?" Alvy is gloomy, answering, "Hardly ever. Maybe three times a week." Annie's irritated reply: "Constantly. I'd say three times a week."

ROBERT ALTMAN

Years active: 1957–2004

TO ME, I'VE JUST MADE ONE, LONG FILM," ROBERT Altman said of his career upon accepting a Lifetime Achievement Oscar in 2006. "I know some of you have liked some of the sections, and others, you . . . anyway, it's all right." At eighty-one, the writer/producer/

director was still a renegade who tore through the Hollywood clichés with his trademark overlapping dialogue, long takes, and seemingly disjointed style that belied a method to the madness. Through the ups and downs, he stuck to his personal vision, proudly stating, "I've never had to direct a film I didn't choose or develop."

The former documentarian caused a stir when M*A*S*H was reeled out to the nation in 1970, wildly dividing critics and audiences. The film's field hospital was populated with new faces (forming something of an unofficial Bob Altman repertory company) to ground the improvisational comic slang of Elliott Gould and Donald Sutherland. As critic David Ansen noted, "It may be hard

for someone who wasn't around in 1970 to understand how revolutionary the impudent, off-the-cuff M*A*S*H looked at the time, with its dark, disenchanted antiwar gallows humor." Although the setting was early '50s South Korea, the Vietnam War was the implied target. Hollywood liberals showed their approval by nominating Altman for a Best Director Academy Award, while Cannes crowned the antiestablishment dramedy with the Palme d'Or.

Altman followed the out-of-nowhere smash that was M*A*S*H with *Brewster McCloud* (1970), an American Fellini fantasy, complete with a circus and parade. Bud Cort takes the title role, be-winged in the heights of the Houston Astrodome, heading

251

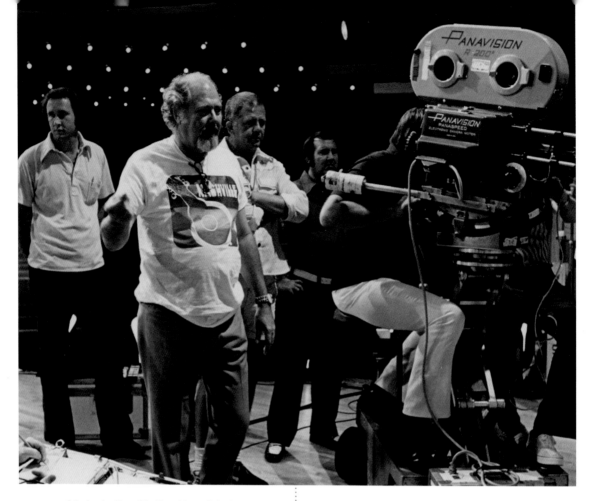

an ensemble including Shelley Duvall in her movie debut. Putting aside the fantastical, Altman crafted an alternative western led by McCabe (Warren Beatty) and Mrs. Miller (Julie Christie), two business rivals in a 1902 frontier town who partner to run a whorehouse. Cinematographer Vilmos Zsigmond shot Altman's bustling scenes and faultlessly dressed sets as if they were old faded snapshots, an atmosphere underscored by the haunting music of Leonard Cohen. *McCabe and Mrs. Miller* (1971) remains a favorite with critics who have hailed the de-glammed celebrity costars; the two don't star in the movie as much as inhabit its territory.

The Long Goodbye (1973) refashioned Raymond Chandler's Golden Age gumshoe Philip Marlowe as Elliott Gould, privately eyeing his way through contemporary Los Angeles. A comedy about addicted gamblers, *California Split* (1974) starred Gould and George Segal, while Keith Carradine and Shelley Duvall robbed banks through Missouri and Kansas, à la Bonnie and Clyde, in *Thieves Like Us* (1974).

Altman sent coscreenwriter Joan Tewkesbury to Tennessee to pick up some local color for *Nash-*

Robert Altman and crew on the set of Nashville, *1975*

A WHOLE NEW HOLLYWOOD

> "I really was thinking a lot about *Nashville* when I wrote *Boogie Nights*. I was blatantly either ripping it off or totally being influenced.... It's in my DNA. I grew up watching those [Altman] movies and it's just informed me and informed how I want to tell stories."
>
> —PAUL THOMAS ANDERSON

ville (1975), a country music masquerade featuring Karen Black as a version of Tammy Wynette, Keith Carradine as a Kris Kristofferson type, and Ronee Blakley as a riff on Loretta Lynn. Busy with dialogue overlaps, music, zoom effects, and deliberately imperfect camerawork, the film wrote its own rules as its stories converged at an outdoor political rally on the steps of Nashville's columned Parthenon, where a kind of Greek tragedy plays out. The *New Yorker*'s Pauline Kael called *Nashville* "a radical, evo-lutionary leap" in the history of American cinema. The Academy agreed, granting it five nominations.

From an actual dream he had—mixed with a dash of Ingmar Bergman's *Persona* (1966)—Altman created a dreamlike scenario titled *3 Women* (1977), a desert hallucination of three ladies (Sissy Spacek, Shelley Duvall, Janice Rule) who intersect and exchange personas. Molly Haskell called the feverish movie "pretentious," but also "gentle, goofy, mesmerizing." Without relying on a screenplay, only

MUST-SEE MOVIES

*M*A*S*H* (1970)

McCABE AND MRS. MILLER (1971)

THE LONG GOODBYE (1973)

CALIFORNIA SPLIT (1974)

NASHVILLE (1975)

VINCENT & THEO (1990)

THE PLAYER (1992)

SHORT CUTS (1993)

GOSFORD PARK (2001)

KEY SCENE TO WATCH

At a *Nashville* club, dimly lit and packed with fans, Keith Carradine (as folk singer Tom Frank) performs his self-penned Oscar-winning ballad "I'm Easy." The woman Tom is involved with, and all the others he has seduced since he blew into town, are there: trio partner Mary, Opal from the BBC, LA lady Joan, and dutiful mother Linnea. The camera spies on them in medium close-up, each believing she is his focus in the crowd. Carradine recalled feeling uneasy during the shoot, playing "an abject narcissist." Altman dismissed his hesitation, telling him to go for it. "The end result," Carradine said, "is this actor who doesn't like the character he's playing. What the audience gets is a guy who doesn't like himself. So smart."

improvised rehearsals, Altman concocted "a masterpiece," according to critic Roger Ebert.

On the difference between 1970s and 1980s filmmakers, Ebert once said, "In the '70s, the best directors were trying to make the great American film; in the '80s, they were trying to make the great American hit. The career of one director in particular dramatizes that, and his name is Robert Altman." Though he continued to make thoughtful, effective films, Altman maintained a low profile in the '80s, when highly commercial blockbusters eclipsed his freewheeling, understated style. The spectacular success of his back-to-back satirical glimpses inside Los Angeles, *The Player* in 1992 and *Short Cuts* in 1993, almost seemed like a comeback, though Altman had never gone away.

In 2002, his sharp, witty English manor-house murder mystery *Gosford Park* (2001) racked up a total of sixty-one award nominations, making it one of the director's most acclaimed works. Something of a companion piece to *Nashville*, *A Prairie Home Companion* (2006) was the cherry that topped the career of Robert Altman, a cinema maverick who colored outside the lines to produce his own kind of art.

The ensemble cast of **Gosford Park**

HAL ASHBY

Years active 1970–1988

S HAGGY, LONG-HAIRED HIGH-SCHOOL DROPOUT HAL Ashby was an unlikely candidate to become an A-list director. Starting as an assistant editor, Ashby studied his craft until he could remember every take and cut. After father figure Norman Jewison shepherded him into an Acad-

emy Award for Best Editing of Jewison's *In the Heat of the Night* (1967), Ashby was poised to make his mark as one of the premier filmmakers in a turbulent era.

Producer Jewison handed Ashby his first directing job on 1970's *The Landlord*, a prescient comedy with a bit to say about gentrification, civil rights, and class divisions. Although it came and went without much fanfare, *The Landlord* demonstrated Ashby's sensitive humanitarian instincts as well as his gift for satirizing society.

A quintessential Ashby film, the sleeper *Harold and Maude* (1971) rose from the ashes of its initial marketplace failure to become a cult classic. Heaped with dark humor and mock-serious irony,

the fable rolls out on the wheels of a black Cadillac hearse, sheltered rich-boy Harold's (Bud Cort) ride of choice. At a funeral, he meets the eccentric eighty-year-old Maude (Ruth Gordon), and mutual affection flowers. Along the way, the audience is treated to Harold's pranks on his arch mother, employing rope and knives to stage suicides. Mrs. Chasen (Vivian Pickles) is not amused, offhandedly admonishing her son, "I suppose you think that's very funny, Harold." Enlivened by the sing-along tunes of Cat Stevens, the movie is like no other; gentle and surprisingly lovely. "There are so many issues addressed in it," Cort has observed, "the right to love, the right to choose whom to love."

After *Harold and Maude* played to near-empty

houses, a dispirited Ashby was sent *The Last Detail*, Robert Towne's adaptation about a court-martialed navy private being escorted to the brig. The piece spoke to the antiauthoritarianism vibrating in the early '70s air, and in Ashby's head. "He had a sense of truth, and what was a real moment," Towne said of Ashby. "He didn't like to watch moments that were not real." A star-making lead for Jack Nicholson (who later called the film "my best role"), *The Last Detail* (1973) captured the zeit-geist of its age: true-to-life, unfiltered, swiftly paced, and obscene. *Time* critic Richard Schickel admired Ashby's handling of the camera "with a simplicity reminiscent of the way American directors treated lower-depth material in the '30s."

Towne and Warren Beatty provided Ashby with his next script, inspired by the rakish ways of Hollywood hairstylist Jay Sebring (though Towne

Hal Ashby directs Harold and Maude.

A WHOLE NEW HOLLYWOOD

"I watched *Harold and Maude* with Jason Segel and I just cried . . . but it's also really, really funny, so I thought, 'This Hal Ashby guy is onto something.' To me, it was amazing to see someone that was able to comedically do anything I would ever hope to do, and at the same time made me cry profusely."

—SETH ROGEN

later insisted that the source was Gene Shacove). Set on the presidential election eve in 1968, *Shampoo* (1975) gave Beatty, Julie Christie, Goldie Hawn, and Lee Grant a delicious retro romp to sink their teeth into. Beatty was born to play George Roundy,

tooling around the foothills on his motorcycle, hair dryer holstered, the wind giving him the perfect blow-out. More formidable than expected at

Bud Cort and Ruth Gordon in Harold and Maude

the box office, *Shampoo* took in nearly $100 million worldwide, easily making it Ashby's biggest hit.

He tailored *Coming Home* (1978) to "make a statement," he said before its release. "I hope every one of my movies tells something about America." This one illustrated the toll taken on America's Vietnam soldiers, a story prompted by Jane Fonda, who recruited the formerly blacklisted Waldo Salt for a script about a disabled vet (Jon Voight) and the woman he loves (Fonda). The famously anti-war Ashby centered the narrative on improvisation and intimacy, and fueled the action with a stellar soundtrack bursting with Beatles and Rolling Stones cuts, "as though a radio were switched on throughout the movie," he said. Another Vietnam drama, Michael Cimino's *The Deer Hunter* (1978), muscled *Coming Home* out of Best Picture, but Fonda and Voight both took home acting Oscars.

After comic legend Peter Sellers saw *Harold and Maude*, he decided Ashby should direct him as the hero of a 1970 Jerzy Kozinski novel. In Hal's hands, *Being There* (1979) became a softly satirical fable of well-dressed simpleton Chance the gardener's transformation into Chauncey Gardner, genius economic consultant in Washington, DC. All Chauncey wants is to be fed, tend a garden, and watch TV; all other people want from him is everything. "The fact that it works, and it's inventive and challenging and fresh for two hours is a real triumph," said Roger Ebert, who attributed the film's success to Ashby's delicate touch with tone

and mood. Today, *Being There* retains its charm as one of the National Film Registry's significant selections.

Hal Ashby's cinematic heroes were outliers, damaged dreamers, truth-tellers, and so was he. Although he lived his entire adult life laboring among the Hollywood big shots and industry suits, he was never one of them. He always stood apart, making his voice heard in as few words as possible.

Julie Christie and Warren Beatty in Shampoo

A WHOLE NEW HOLLYWOOD

MUST-SEE MOVIES

THE LANDLORD (1970)

HAROLD AND MAUDE (1971)

THE LAST DETAIL (1973)

SHAMPOO (1975)

BOUND FOR GLORY (1976)

COMING HOME (1978)

BEING THERE (1979)

Peter Sellers and Shirley MacLaine in Being There

KEY SCENE TO WATCH

At a black-tie Washington event in *Being There*, Chauncey is offered a book deal by a publisher (Richard McKenzie). "I can't write," he says, biting into an apple. "Of course not, who can nowadays?" replies the publisher with a knowing laugh. "I can't read," Chauncey responds, his mouth full of apple. "Of course you can't! No one has the time! We glance at things, we watch television. . . ." With simple, amusing scenes like this, Ashby balances social commentary with sincere appreciation of Chauncey's naive, childlike innocence. Sellers was voted Best Actor by the New York Film Critics Circle for this final film before his premature death in 1980.

PETER BOGDANOVICH

Years active: 1968–present

H OW MANY UP-AND-COMING DIRECTORS GET THE chance to learn straight from Alfred Hitchcock, John Ford, Howard Hawks, and Orson Welles? Because he started as a movie critic and historian, Peter Bogdanovich exhaustively interviewed a choice selec-

tion of Hollywood's living legends before stepping behind the camera himself. The film fan–turned–filmmaker tipped his hat to the medium's glory days in the screwball *What's Up, Doc?* (1972), the black-and-white *Paper Moon* (1973), and the silent-era homage *Nickelodeon* (1976).

A cinema savant from a young age, the native New Yorker educated himself on his favorite subject: the movies. In 1966, Bogdanovich and wife, aspiring production designer Polly Platt, traveled to the left coast and met producer Roger Corman, who was always on the lookout for new talent. From his Corman apprenticeship emerged the cheaply made but suspenseful *Targets*, a well-received thriller from 1968.

Another fateful encounter: When actor Sal Mineo handed Bogdanovich and Platt a copy of Larry McMurtry's nostalgic novel and suggested they film it, *The Last Picture Show* (1971) was born. The novice filmmaker rustled in some newcomers—Jeff Bridges, Cybill Shepherd, Timothy Bottoms—and some seasoned players—Ellen Burstyn, Ben Johnson, Cloris Leachman—to populate the fictional burg of Anarene, Texas, and dramatize a slice of small-town life spanning from October 1951 to November 1952. On a thin budget of scarcely over $1 million, production designer Platt and cinematographer Robert Surtees conjured a black-and-white picture postcard of desolation and bygone Americana, from the opening pan of the

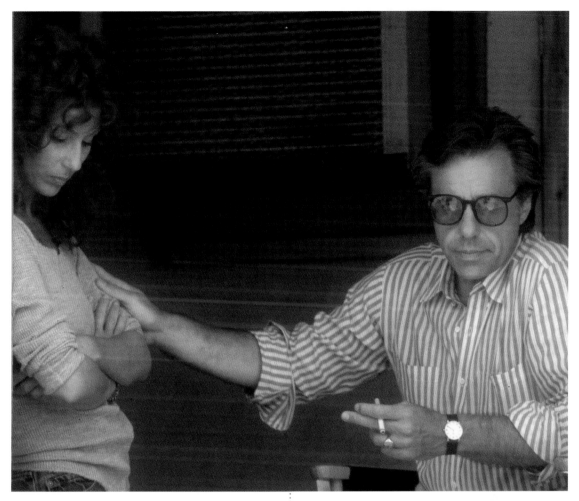

dusty Royal Theatre to the final movie screened in town: Howard Hawks's *Red River* (1948).

Bogdanovich pulled deeply affecting performances from his cast, conjuring a wistful tone steeped in Texas-dry humor and sentiment, with a dose of last-chance desperation. Eight Oscar nominations, with four wins, followed the film's profitable run. David Denby of the *Atlantic* hailed it as a great American movie, writing: "*The Last Picture Show* is clear, perfectly controlled, and beautifully wrought. . . . From his idol Howard Hawks, Bogdanovich has learned the value of a plain style; like Hawks, he keeps the camera at eye level and allows the scenes to play in medium depth." Unfurling at a slow, confident pace, Bogdanovich's classic-inspired creation became an instant classic in its own right. "*The Last Picture Show* is just one of the most beautifully photographed and timeless works

Cher and Peter Bogdanovich on the set of Mask, *1984*

PETER BOGDANOVICH

> "When I was a kid, I'd never seen a screwball comedy. So for me, [*What's Up, Doc?*] was just this mind-blowing, new type of comedy. . . . I went bananas for it."
>
> —PAUL FEIG

of art that still inspires me," director Mark Pellington stated in 2013.

And then for something completely different, he devised a madcap ode to Hawks's *Bringing Up Baby* (1938), the fast-paced romantic farce *What's Up, Doc?* The sharp punchlines and pratfall throwbacks made for a surprise smash starring Barbra Streisand, on a comic high, and Ryan O'Neal, disarmingly blank and bespectacled. Immortalizing the name "Eunice," Madeline Kahn is hilariously besieged in her movie debut. Bogdanovich managed to sustain, with a zing, the comic machinations involving four matching suitcases in a San Francisco hotel, at a house party, and through the city streets in an epic chase, with a witty script and unrestrained physicality.

If Bogdanovich started by emulating his heroes, he came fully into his own with *Paper Moon*, another monochromatic masterpiece, this one a road picture striking a tragicomic chord. Father and daughter Ryan and Tatum O'Neal play off each other brilliantly as squabbling hucksters chugging through the Depression-era Midwest. "It was hard work," the director recalled of shooting on location with a

child. "I just wanted to get it over with, and I didn't think it would be that big a success." Bogdanovich brought back his discovery Kahn to play hooker Trixie Delight, directing her to an Oscar nod for Best Supporting Actress—an award that ten-year-old Tatum won, becoming the youngest recipient in history. Her acceptance speech was short and sweet: "All I really want to thank is my director, Peter Bogdanovich, and my father."

Breaking up his marriage to Platt was the director's affair with Cybill Shepherd, the model turned actress he built his next two movies around: the costume drama *Daisy Miller* (1974) and a musical experiment employing the Cole Porter songbook, *At Long Last Love* (1975). Both failed to find an audience, and some began to wonder whether—like one of his mentors, Welles—the young Bogdanovich had peaked too soon.

After reuniting the O'Neals (adding Burt Reynolds and John Ritter to the mix) in *Nickelodeon*, a story loosely based on director Leo McCarey's early days, Bogdanovich suffered a personal tragedy; his girlfriend Dorothy Stratten's shocking and brutal 1980 murder slowed the director's progress. Rebounding from the poor critical reception of *They All Laughed* (1981), costarring Stratten and Audrey Hepburn in the final feature for both actresses, Bogdanovich returned to full form with 1985's *Mask*. Directing simply, even self-effacingly, he allowed the lead performers—Cher, Eric Stoltz, and Stoltz's makeup "mask" of extreme congenital disfigurement—to do the heavy lifting and elevate the screenplay above mere sentimentality. In the ensuing years, the veteran has come out of undeclared retirement to direct occasionally, as he did in 1990, with the *Picture Show* sequel *Texasville*, and the 1920s-Hollywood urban legend *The Cat's Meow* (2001).

In 2019, movie fan/director Wes Anderson interviewed his hero, as Bogdanovich himself once did with the old masters. "I'm always surprised by every single picture," he revealed. "Finally, when it's up there, you say, 'Oh, *that's* what it's going to look like.'" Still burning with an insatiable curiosity and passion for movies, Peter Bogdanovich has refashioned himself as a contemporary fixture, a podcaster and commentator sought for his insider insight on historic Hollywood.

Peter Bogdanovich directs Barbra Streisand and Ryan O'Neal in What's Up, Doc?

MUST-SEE MOVIES

THE LAST PICTURE SHOW
(1971)

WHAT'S UP, DOC? (1972)

PAPER MOON (1973)

NICKELODEON (1976)

THEY ALL LAUGHED (1981)

MASK (1985)

NOISES OFF (1992)

Cybill Shepherd in her first film,
The Last Picture Show

KEY SCENE TO WATCH

One of many heartbreaking moments in *The Last Picture Show* happens when teenage Sonny (Bottoms) dumps Ruth (Leachman), the married middle-aged woman he's been sleeping with. Wounded, she unleashes her anger, breaking a coffeepot and screaming, "Why am I always apologizing to you, you little bastard? You're the one that oughta be sorry!" Bogdanovich wouldn't let Leachman rehearse the explosive scene before shooting, to keep the emotion real. "It was the first time she had ever done it, and you can feel that in the way she's breathing; she gets out of breath, and it's wonderfully touching," the director observed. Cloris Leachman was rewarded with an Oscar for her work.

MEL BROOKS

Years active: 1967–1995

T HE INGENIOUS COMIC FORCE BEHIND SOME OF the best-loved parody films of all time, Mel Brooks took the seventies by storm with his outlandish humor. With favorites such as the monster mockery *Young Frankenstein* and the wild western send-up *Blazing Saddles*

(both from 1974), Brooks poked a stickpin in some of the conventions (and pretentions) of Hollywood filmmaking and let the air out.

Brooklyn's Melvin Kaminsky was exposed to motion pictures at a young age. Although his widowed mother struggled financially, she took her son to Broadway shows and movies, where he absorbed musicals, comedies, and westerns. "I loved the movies because they saved my life," Brooks later wrote. "I was so grateful to cinema for opening up worlds that were not open to me as a poor Jewish kid." After serving in World War II at age eighteen, he scripted one-liners for Sid Caesar's TV series *Your Show of Shows*. The success of his 1960s secret-agent sitcom *Get Smart* enabled the freshly renamed

Mel Brooks to write and direct a major feature film—and *The Producers* (1968) was born.

Financed independently, the subversive Broadway farce lampooned the Third Reich with its show-stopping musical *Springtime for Hitler*, featuring goose-stepping Nazi soldiers extolling the virtues of the Führer in song. "I wanted to put down Nazism, but I didn't want to get on a soapbox," Brooks has said of his intentions. By exposing the ludicrousness of Hitler's ideology, *The Producers* sent an antiauthoritarian message buried inside an astoundingly original comedy. Although some critics felt it crossed lines of decency, Brooks's showbiz satire earned him an Oscar for Best Original Screenplay. In 2001, he adapted *The Producers*

265

into a hit Broadway musical that raked in twelve Tony Awards.

Set in a lawless (and deliberately anachronistic) Old West of 1874, *Blazing Saddles* served as an irreverent homage to the big-screen westerns of yesteryear, with the bonus of skewering racism. Placing a Black sheriff (played by Cleavon Little) in the all-White frontier town of Rock

Mel Brooks in High Anxiety

Ridge presented opportunities galore for laughter to triumph over prejudice. As Brooks's writing team—which included rising comedian Richard Pryor—assembled to hammer out the story, he implored them via a hand-lettered sign: PLEASE DO NOT WRITE A POLITE SCRIPT. Brooks felt that without use of the "the N-word," as he said, "You've got no movie." Pryor and star Little agreed, marshaling the term's use as a way to strip it of its power. Brooks has never avoided offensive jokes, famously stating, "Good taste is the enemy of comedy."

Cleavon Little as Sheriff Bart in Blazing Saddles

The director rounded out his ensemble cast with *Producers* costar Gene Wilder as the washed-up Waco Kid (a role Brooks initially offered to John Wayne), Madeline Kahn as Marlene Dietrich–inspired saloon siren Lili von Shtupp, horse opera regular Slim Pickens, plus a stallion with a gift for pratfalls, and a herd of cowboys scarfing indigestible beans around a campfire—one of the film's most iconic scenes. The ending is sheer chaos, as the characters crash through a Warner Bros. soundstage wall, then convene for a final showdown at the premiere of *Blazing Saddles*. "I broke the rules and I broke the walls. It was just silly. I loved it,"

recalled the director of his surprise crowd-pleaser that grossed $120 million worldwide, and remains one of the most audacious movies ever produced by a mainstream studio.

While filming *Saddles*, Wilder suggested Brooks helm a *Frankenstein* (1931) spoof he had conceived called *Young Frankenstein*. Starring Wilder as Dr. Frederick "Fronk-en-shteen," inheritor of his father's creepy Transylvania castle, and Peter Boyle as his man-made monster with an abnormal brain, the black-and-white comedy was a salute to Golden Age Hollywood horror. As Brooks pointed out, "We set out to make a beautiful period picture with all of the craftsmanship of James Whale's 1930s films," complete with *Frankenstein* set designer Kenneth Strickfaden's original laboratory equipment from 1931, expressionist set design, inky shadows, and rarely revived iris-outs, wipes, and fades to black. Brooks even engaged makeup pioneer William Tuttle to create the creature's look.

Young Frankenstein not only riffed on Universal horror but classic Hollywood romances; take the scene in which Frederick and his fiancée, Elizabeth (Madeline Kahn), say good-bye in a smoke-swirled train station. "How can I say in a few minutes what it's taken me a lifetime to understand?" she sighs. "Won't you try?" he asks. "All right," Elizabeth says with heartfelt sincerity, "You've got it, mister." Brooks's gag-heavy dialogue has a way of building expectations, then undercutting them with infec-

tious goofiness. "Every time he opens that mouth, words tumble out in a way that we never would have imagined them," longtime admirer Billy Crystal observed of Brooks in 2014.

In 1976, Twentieth Century-Fox released the first silent film since Charlie Chaplin's *Modern Times* in 1936. Brooks called it *Silent Movie*, a motion picture about making a motion picture, with all dialogue printed on title cards. Casting himself in the lead as director Mel Funn, he bellows on-set: "Lights! Camera! Action! No Sound!" The clever concoction was another winner for Brooks. "*Silent Movie* is full of laughs and other satisfactions," wrote Charles Champlin of the *Los Angeles Times*, noting that "the most dazzling of surprises in a surprise-rich movie" was the cameo of Mrs. Mel Brooks, also known as actress Anne Bancroft.

Brooks next aimed his lampoonery at Alfred Hitchcock with *High Anxiety* (1977), a comic take on psychological suspense that earned the director a Golden Globe nomination for Best Actor. From his *Star Wars* (1977) spoof *Spaceballs* (1987) to the perfectly titled *Robin Hood: Men in Tights* (1993), Mel Brooks has continued to take no-holds-barred swipes at virtually every Hollywood genre. Today, his varied skill set has made him a member of that rare circle of EGOTs: artists who have won Emmy, Grammy, Oscar, and Tony awards. As Carl Reiner said of his friend and colleague, "He is gifted with a genius brain and a brilliantly uncensored tongue. For Mel Brooks, comedy is joy."

MUST-SEE MOVIES

THE PRODUCERS (1968)

BLAZING SADDLES (1974)

YOUNG FRANKENSTEIN (1974)

SILENT MOVIE (1976)

HIGH ANXIETY (1977)

ROBIN HOOD: MEN IN TIGHTS (1993)

Mel Brooks on the set of Young Frankenstein *with Marty Feldman, Gene Wilder, Teri Garr, and Peter Boyle*

KEY SCENE TO WATCH

After he tames and befriends the monster in *Young Frankenstein*, Dr. Frankenstein presents his creation to the public in what is advertised as "a startling new experiment in reanimation," a nod to Kong's New York City theater debut in *King Kong* (1933). Brooks sets up a standard display of the monster's motor skills—and then suddenly delivers the unexpected: the doctor and his creature break into a jazzy song-and-dance routine to Irving Berlin's "Puttin' on the Ritz," complete with top hats, canes, tap shoes, and the monster warbling the chorus right on cue. Originally concerned that the number was too over the top even for him, the director initially considered cutting it, later to admit it was his favorite scene. "Of all my films," Brooks said of *Young Frankenstein* in 2016, "I am proudest of this one."

FRANCIS FORD COPPOLA

Years active: 1962–2015

YOU'RE A BIG BOY NOW, FROM 1966, WAS ORIGINALLY Francis Ford Coppola's thesis project for his master's degree in film at UCLA. The movie was shot for only $800,000 and was snapped up by Warner Bros. distribution. Coppola himself discounted its importance,

but critic Andrew Sarris didn't; taking into consideration two other efforts—*Dementia 13* (1963) and *The Rain People* (1969)—he wrote that Coppola was "probably the first reasonably talented and sensibly adaptable directorial talent to emerge from a university curriculum in filmmaking."

Born in Detroit and named for Henry Ford, Coppola grew up in Woodside, Queens, where a childhood bout with polio allowed him the time to watch and study movies. Soon after helming the anachronistically peppy musical *Finian's Rainbow* (1969), Coppola won his first Oscar at age thirty-one for scripting *Patton* (1970). When Peter Yates, Sergio Leone, Constantin Costa-Gavras, and Peter Bogdanovich declined to direct a screenplay titled

Mafia, Paramount's Robert Evans approached Coppola, an Italian American whom he felt could impart authenticity to the movie. The young director resisted, believing the story sensationalistic and melodramatic. George Lucas, his friend and partner in his indie endeavor, American Zoetrope, convinced him to accept the job. They needed the money.

Coppola remodeled Mario Puzo's story into one of Mafia-American capitalism, a family tale of heritage, betrayal, and life-for-life violence. "I wrote the *Godfather* script," Coppola has reminded us. "I did the adaptation. I credit Mario completely with creating the characters and the story." In other words, he elevated the material to art. Cinema-

tographer Gordon Willis and production designer
Dean Tavoularis gave the film an operatic look,
sepia-toned and mythic, whether Coppola's camera
records a grandiose family wedding, or withdraws
from a sinister clan conference. Indoor scenes are
low-lit, with a hand-tinted quality, like a 1940s family portrait. That portrait, accompanied by Nino
Rota's darkly romantic score, is shattered at inter-

vals by rapid-fire editing. Every element was a cog
in Coppola's overall vision, the result a triumph.
The Godfather (1972) was ultimately declared a contemporary masterpiece, winning three of eleven
Oscars: Best Adapted Screenplay, Best Picture,

Francis Ford Coppola on location in the Philippines shooting
Apocalypse Now, *1977*

271

> "He's truly the godfather of a generation that changed the course of motion picture history. He is an innovator, an artist, an icon, a rebel, and most importantly to me, a friend and a brother."

—GEORGE LUCAS

and Best Actor, even though Marlon Brando—as the titular godfather, Don Vito Corleone himself—had little screen time.

The Godfather II (1974) was accomplished, from green-light to premiere, at warp speed—just over two and a half years—coming in at the biblical length of almost three and a half hours. At first, "the idea of a sequel seemed horrible to me," Coppola admitted, "like a tacky spin-off." But he persuaded himself to think of it as a "companion piece," addressing the back story of Vito Corleone while continuing the larger saga. With its soft-focus flashbacks and richly detailed aesthetic, Coppola would refer to the picture as "a $13 million art film."

A young virtuoso named Robert De Niro emerged as the obvious choice to play Vito in his rise to Mafia don, and became a star doing it. Al Pacino again embodied the reluctant Michael, and Diane Keaton returned as his ever-more-estranged wife, Kay. Many of the same artists from Part I worked behind the scenes on Part II: Willis, with his depth-of-field photography in Sicily and at Ellis Island; Tavoularis, with his astonishing delineation of Little Italy and Havana; Theadora

Van Runkle and her glorious costuming of two distinct time periods. Critic Judith Crist wrote: "Coppola has provided us with perhaps the most lavish modern-dress spectacular on film." He nailed three Oscars at the 1975 ceremony, including Best Picture, a category in which he competed against himself. Also nominated was his documentary-style experiment *The Conversation* (1974), made between the two *Godfather*s. Raising issues of privacy as technology was becoming easier to deploy and misuse, the film starred Gene Hackman as a sound surveillance expert.

After the blockbuster success of *The Godfather II*, the filmmaker felt confident enough to tackle what would become an Everest-size cautionary tale: Joseph Conrad's *Heart of Darkness*, reset in wartime Vietnam. With cast, crew, cameras, military vehicles, aircraft, and his wife, documentarian Eleanor, in tow, Coppola decamped to Manila to make *Apocalypse Now* (1979). The production quickly ranged out of hand. "We were in the jungle," Coppola later recalled, "there were too many of us, we had access to too much money, too much equipment, and little by little, we went insane." Lead Martin Sheen suffered a serious heart attack,

A WHOLE NEW HOLLYWOOD

MUST-SEE MOVIES

THE GODFATHER (1972)

THE CONVERSATION (1974)

THE GODFATHER PART II (1974)

APOCALYPSE NOW (1979)

THE OUTSIDERS (1983)

THE COTTON CLUB (1984)

THE GODFATHER PART III (1990)

BRAM STOKER'S DRACULA (1992)

Marlon Brando and Talia Shire share a wedding dance in The Godfather.

KEY SCENE TO WATCH

After writing the first draft of *The Godfather*, Mario Puzo said to Coppola, "There's something missing from the ending. I don't quite know what." The director responded, "That's easy. We'll combine the executions with the christening." With skillful editing, the traditional church ritual is intercut with the preparations for a string of carefully appointed assassinations ordered by Don Michael Corleone; a montage linking sudden death to new life. This sequence correlates to *The Godfather III* (1990), when *Cavalleria rusticana* is performed in the grand opera house in Palermo, Sicily, as contract murders take place through the city.

Brando did his Method-best to cause delays and dissension, and a typhoon destroyed the sets. The estimated fourteen-week shoot dragged on for a year. But if *Apocalypse Now* was Coppola's bête noire, it was also his greatest victory over adverse filmmaking conditions.

The fourteen-helicopter assault on a Vietcong village to full-blast Wagner is an example of Coppola's excess, and his genius. Bombastic and brutal, with a killer rock soundtrack and carnage galore, the war spectacle is packed with iconography: Robert Duvall's regiment commander kneeling on the beach as he states with sincerity, "I love the smell of napalm in the morning"; Jerry Ziesmer casually ordering "Terminate with extreme prejudice" while grabbing a cigarette; Sheen's war-painted Capt. Willard emerging from the water as a buffalo is slaughtered. In 1979, the film tied for the Palme d'Or with Volker Schlöndorff's *The Tin Drum* (1979). Eight Oscar nominations followed in early 1980, welcome amends for a director's survival after nearly three years of bad press. *Variety* concluded, "Coppola here reaffirms his stature as a top filmmaker. *Apocalypse Now* takes realistic cinema to a new extreme—he virtually creates WW III onscreen."

An attractive cast of future stars—a pre-Brat Pack—made up the ensemble of *The Outsiders* (1983), adapted by Kathleen Rowell from S. E. Hinton's young-adult novel, and filmed in naturalistic, accessible style by Coppola. Based on a photo-memoir of the same title, *The Cotton Club* premiered in late 1984; lengthy and over budget (costing $58 million), it was a meticulous rendering of the influential '30s Harlem nightspot as a smoky, sexy hothouse of jazz. The film might have been a significant breakthrough in Black lives represented onscreen, yet it failed to gain traction when grosses totaled just $28 million.

Bram Stoker's Dracula (1992) was Coppola's ticket to reinvention, a genre picture of period baroque

Lonette McKee and Gregory Hines in The Cotton Club

horror meant for blockbuster status. The iconoclastic director got his superhit—and profits for American Zoetrope—with the opening weekend gross of a record-breaking $30 million. Cinematographer Michael Ballhaus pointed to F. W. Murnau's *Nosferatu* (1922) as Coppola's inspiration, and *Bram Stoker's Dracula* as "his last great must-see movie." For his contributions to the art of filmmaking, Francis Ford Coppola received the Irving G. Thalberg Memorial Award from the Academy of Motion Picture Arts and Sciences in 2011. The talented Coppola dynasty continues with his Oscar-winning offspring, writer/directors Sofia and Roman, and his nephew, actor Nicolas Cage.

Francis Ford Coppola directs Al Pacino in The Godfather Part II.

BRIAN DE PALMA

Years active: 1963–present

WHEN EIGHTEEN-YEAR-OLD BRIAN DE PALMA first saw Alfred Hitchcock's *Vertigo* (1958), he was mesmerized. "There was something about the way the story was told," he later recalled, "and the cinematic language used in it that connected to me, even though, at that point, I was studying to be an engineer." The psychological thriller ultimately altered the course of De Palma's life. After Columbia University, the New Jersey native swapped his physics major for theater at Sarah Lawrence College, where he was one of the first male students. Films by documentarians Albert and Davis Maysles, Jean-Luc Godard, and of course, Hitchcock, inspired his own indie feature, *The Wedding Party* (shot in 1963, but not released until 1969), starring his twenty-year-old discovery, Robert De Niro, mistakenly credited onscreen as "Robert Denero."

The more sophisticated *Sisters* (1972) marked the writer-director's first stab at suspense. Featuring Margot Kidder as surgically separated twins Danielle and Dominique, *Sisters* employs split-screening, alternating points of view, and the eerie music of frequent Hitchcock collaborator Bernard Herrmann. Rather than fashioning carbon copies of Hitchcock thrillers, De Palma used Hitch as a springboard to develop his own visually dynamic, heavily stylized, and often graphic stamp. The theme of doppelgängers arose again in *Obsession* (1976), with Genevieve Bujold playing both a deceased wife and her look-alike, in the midst of some Machiavellian manipulations and dizzying camerawork. The multilayered script by Paul Schrader and the hazy cinematography of Vilmos Zsigmond merged with De Palma's talents to yield a sleeper success.

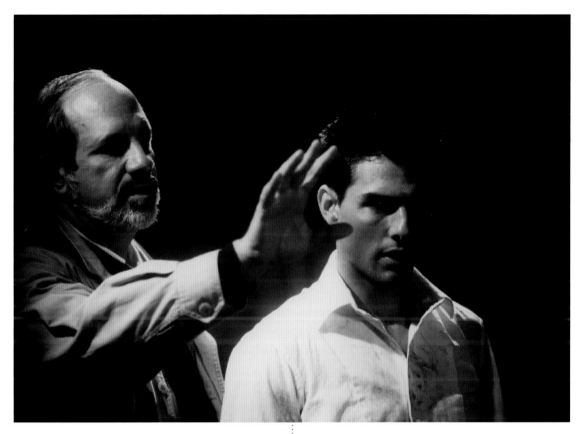

If *Obsession* put him on the map, *Carrie* (1976) made De Palma a big-name filmmaker. The slowly building high school horrorfest follows Stephen King's narrative—albeit with De Palma's shock ending—about not only psychic power over objects, but the bullying that leads to its manifestation. From massive casting sessions (held in tandem with George Lucas's *Star Wars* [1977]) emerged Sissy Spacek, with her slight figure and wide-eyed fragility, as Carrie White, a blood-soaked Cinderella of revenge. Piper Laurie, Amy Irving, Betty Buckley, and Nancy Allen fleshed out a movie about women, "a fairy tale," De Palma suggests, "about what hap-

pens when you push the ugly duckling too far; she does some pretty nasty things." Making the most of his minimal budget and compressed schedule, De Palma crafted "an absolutely spellbinding horror movie" (in the words of Roger Ebert), a box office smash, and one of few in its genre to be honored with Academy Award nominations. The hitherto unfamiliar term *telekinesis* soon became part of the national vocabulary as *Carrie* came to be "a modern classic," Spacek has said, "and a rite of passage."

Brian De Palma directs Tom Cruise in Mission Impossible, *1996.*

B R I A N   D E   P A L M A

> "Brian De Palma is one of the finest directors of his generation. As much as his films were the violent set-pieces, as much as they were the suspense set-pieces, as much as they were the cinematic set-pieces . . . there was a social satire going on through his entire career . . . he's actually skewering the culture at large."
>
> —QUENTIN TARANTINO

After revisiting supernatural phenomena with *The Fury* (1978), De Palma wrote and directed a seductive mix of slashing and style titled *Dressed to Kill* (1980). Perfectly cast Angie Dickinson and a handsome stranger (Ken Baker) shadow each other through an art museum in one of the film's highlights, a ten-minute sequence with no words spoken, only the lush, low-level soundtrack by Pino Donaggio and the click-clacking of Dickinson's high heels. Later, the sensual spell is broken in an elevator, as a fearsome female figure makes lethal use of a straight razor in "the best murder scene I've ever done," in De Palma's words. In the *Los Angeles Times*, Sheila Benson spoke for many when she proclaimed: "The brilliance of *Dressed to Kill* is apparent within seconds of its opening gliding shot; it is a sustained work of terror—elegant, sensual, erotic, bloody, a directorial tour de force."

Although *Blow Out* (1981) received mixed reviews, its striking blend of audio and visual artistry has made the mystery revered among contemporary film aficionados. Howard Hawks's blunt and violent—but not bloody—pre-Code *Scarface* (1932) was the model Oliver Stone used to pen an update concerning Florida's Cuban immigrants and the drug trade. All the blood dismissed from the original found its way into De Palma's furious and explosive $66 million remake. Boasting an iconic central

Angie Dickinson in Dressed to Kill

MUST-SEE MOVIES

SISTERS (1972)

PHANTOM OF THE PARADISE (1974)

OBSESSION (1976)

CARRIE (1976)

DRESSED TO KILL (1980)

BLOW OUT (1981)

SCARFACE (1983)

THE UNTOUCHABLES (1987)

MISSION: IMPOSSIBLE (1996)

KEY SCENE TO WATCH

Carrie White has done her worst. Her telekinetic rage has overpowered her sweet nature when cruelly pranked on prom night, unleashing a torrent of hellfire. Then, De Palma arranges a second climax: a household crucifixion and a demolition of the White house and its inhabitants, including Carrie. But still De Palma is not through. He has Sue (Amy Irving) come to place flowers at the site; in a flash, a bloody hand thrusts through the rubble to grab her. Stephen King recalls seeing *Carrie* for the first time with an audience in 1977. The hand sent them all "to the roof," he said, and realized that De Palma had accomplished "something new": a double-shock ending. King told himself, "We have a monster hit on our hands."

Sissy Spacek as Carrie

performance by Al Pacino, a synthesized score by Giorgio Moroder, and a palette of tacky Miami pastels, De Palma's 1983 *Scarface* has machine-gunned its way into latter-day-classic status.

Another gangland drama, this one on the right side of the law, earned four Academy Award nods. "*The Untouchables* is by far the most complete and successful film Mr. De Palma has made," wrote Janet Maslin in the *New York Times*. "It is his most coherent work, as well as his most emotionally accessible." Adapted by David Mamet from accounts of Eliot Ness and his squad's crusade to bring down Al Capone in 1930s Chicago, *The Untouchables* (1987) made Kevin Costner (as Ness) a star, and won Sean Connery his only Oscar as seasoned cop

Jimmy Malone. Among the film's most memorable scenes is the climactic gunfight De Palma staged on the steps of Union Square, a direct homage to the Odessa Steps sequence in Sergei Eisenstein's landmark silent *Battleship Potemkin* (1925), complete with baby carriage and all. The period piece was one of the top-grossing movies of the year.

After the success of his harrowing Vietnam morality play *Casualties of War* (1989), an ever-more-mature De Palma was poised for greatness, when a misstep set him back—though the expensive flop *The Bonfire of the Vanities* (1990) was not the first failure for the disenchanted director. "They basically want you to duplicate the same thing over and over again," he has said of the Hollywood system, "but you need to make hits in order to make movies. So I would go in and make a hit, be able to make a couple of weird movies, then have to start over again." Brian De Palma's career has followed this fitful pattern for decades. While his films are just as often lambasted as lauded by reviewers, young directors—Noah Baumbach and Jake Paltrow, for example, who made the 2015 documentary *De Palma*—continue to find inspiration in De Palma's richly varied body of work. From Hitchcock mimic to creative iconoclast in his own right, he continues to make challenging and exhilarating films on his own terms.

Kevin Costner in De Palma's climatic shootout scene in The Untouchables

GEORGE LUCAS

Years active: 1971–present

ALTHOUGH GEORGE LUCAS HAS ONLY DIRECTED A handful of movies—proving more prolific as a producer and special-effects pioneer than a director—his cultural impact has been immense. The *Star Wars* universe sprang from his imagination, as did the premise for the Indiana Jones series (Steven Spielberg and screenwriter Lawrence Kasdan helped fill in the details). Both franchises have entertained worldwide audiences of all ages for generations, becoming among the most successful motion pictures ever.

As a graduate student as USC, Lucas garnered buzz with his experimental sci-fi short *Electronic Labyrinth THX-1138: 4EB* (1967). Friend and business partner Francis Ford Coppola wrangled studio distribution for the feature-length version, *THX-1138*, released in 1971. Though it failed to find an audience, the starkly designed fable about a dystopian man (Robert Duvall) who rebels against his soulless society has become a cult classic; the film's innovative sound engineering also spawned Lucas's audio system THX.

Pivoting from chilly pessimism about the future to warm optimism about the past, Lucas delivered a slice of bygone teenage life with *American Graffiti* (1973). Like Martin Scorsese's *Mean Streets* (released in the same year), *Graffiti* was a personal film, a reminiscence of Lucas's early '60s youth spent cruising the boulevard in hot rods. "It was the way I grew up, and I wanted to make a picture about it," he has said. Petaluma, California, stood in for his hometown of Modesto, the film populated by a cast of unknowns who wouldn't be unknown for long: Ron Howard, Harrison Ford, Richard Dreyfuss, and twelve-year-old Mackenzie Phillips.

281

American Graffiti was a word-of-mouth smash made for only $700,000, $80,000 of which paid for the rock-and-roll oldies that Wolfman Jack broadcasts from a local radio station. "It took fourteen months to get the various rights we needed," Lucas admitted, "but it was worth the effort." Whether Dell Shannon's catchy "Runaway" or the bluesy "Ain't That a Shame" by Fats Domino, music is integral to the film's nostalgic atmosphere.

Based on Graffiti's success, Twentieth Century-Fox said yes to Lucas's ambitious dream project:

a space saga he described in 1973 as "a combination of 2001, the Bond films, and Lawrence of Arabia." He aimed the story at kids, seeking to remedy the fact that, as he saw it, "a whole generation was growing up without fairy tales." So, he created a myth of his own—part future, part past (Star Wars is set "a long time ago"), all positive good-beats-evil energy (in the form of the Force)—with the noble goal of "getting children to believe there is more to

George Lucas on the set of American Graffiti

life than garbage and killing and all that real stuff." With this simple aim, *Star Wars* (1977) was born, and Lucas revolutionized the film industry.

The writer-director and his team's determination to depict a realistic intergalactic world led to the founding of the special-effects company Industrial Light and Magic. The effects were like nothing yet seen: young Luke Skywalker (loosely based on Lucas himself at eighteen, played by Mark Hamill) gazes at a seamless double sunset on the planet Tatooine, and practices wielding

Mark Hamill, Carrie Fisher, Peter Mayhew, and Harrison Ford in a 1977 publicity photo for Star Wars

"That first *Star Wars*, that George Lucas directed, came out in 1977 when I was seven years old. It made a huge impression on me, in terms of the scope of it and the idea that you could create an entirely different experience for the audience . . . a whole different galaxy."

—CHRISTOPHER NOLAN

his lightsaber on a droid that hovers in midair— no strings attached. From the humanlike androids R2-D2 and C-3PO to the explosion of the Death Star, the pre-CGI graphics were mind-blowing in their day, making the epic a pop culture sensation and winner of seven Academy Awards. When *Time* magazine declared *Star Wars* "the year's best movie," *Flash Gordon*–style outer-space adventures were suddenly cool again.

Staying on as producer and cowriter, Lucas handed the reins to Irvin Kirshner for the sequel *The Empire Strikes Back* (1980) and to Richard Marquand for the third in the trilogy, *Return of the Jedi* (1983). After record-breaking numbers of fans lined up for tickets, *Jedi* made *New York Times* headlines when it earned a whopping $41 million in a mere six days, cementing Lucas's status as one of the wealthiest men in the entertainment industry. Conceiving the story for Spielberg's beloved adven-

ture *Raiders of the Lost Ark* (1981) and its sequels have generated additional capital and clout. The Star Wars and Indiana Jones franchises aside, *American Graffiti* alone is one of the most profitable movies in Hollywood history in terms of cost ($700,000) over revenue ($177 million).

By 1997—the film's twenty-year anniversary— it was estimated that the average American had seen *Star Wars* seven times. Such enduring popularity drew Lucas out of his comfortable retirement to write and direct a prequel, an origin story of the Skywalker family titled *Star Wars: Episode I— The Phantom Menace* (1999). Its success with fans resulted in Lucas helming two more entries in the saga, *Attack of the Clones* (2002) and *Revenge of the Sith* (2005). Though Disney acquired the Star Wars rights in 2012, Lucas continues to serve as creative consultant as the blockbuster franchise rolls on.

MUST-SEE MOVIES

THX-1138 (1971)

AMERICAN GRAFFITI (1973)

STAR WARS (1977)

KEY SCENE TO WATCH

The conversation between Luke and Obi-Wan "Ben" Kenobi (Alec Guinness) in the former Jedi's home is integral to *Star Wars*, and to the back story of the entire series. Here, Luke not only learns about Darth Vader and sees Princess Leia's (Carrie Fisher) message projected from R2-D2 ("Help me, Obi-Wan Kenobi. You're my only hope"), but is told about the Force by Ben: "It's an energy field created by all living things." The nifty visual tricks of the lightsaber and Leia's hologram message help us forget we're listening to exposition.

George Lucas directs Star Wars, *1976*

SIDNEY LUMET

Years active: 1957–2007

H E WAS A PRODUCT OF THE NEW YORK THEATER world who brought the hyperrealism and intensity of the city to movie screens everywhere. Although he started in the 1950s, prolific Sidney Lumet sculpted the spirit of the '70s with his era-defining

classics, such as *Serpico* (1973), *Dog Day Afternoon* (1975), and the remarkable *Network* (1976). A genuine love for movies propelled him. In his 1995 book *Making Movies*, Lumet called directing "the best job in the world."

Acting on and off Broadway since age four, Lumet graduated to directing TV dramas for *Playhouse 90* and other live anthology programs. When he migrated to Hollywood, he related to actors as one of them, tuned to their wavelength and ready to collaborate. Ali MacGraw spoke for many when she referred to Lumet as "every actor's dream" after starring in his comedy *Just Tell Me What You Want* (1980). "He conspires with you to help him with whatever he has in mind," said Ossie Davis,

who appeared in Lumet's World War II prison drama *The Hill* (1965).

Right out of the gate, the director blew the public away with his first feature, *12 Angry Men* (1957), a one-room wonder shot in twenty days, with twelve actors, for only $343,000. One by one, upstanding Henry Fonda (as Davis, juror 8) challenges his fellow jurors' hasty, apathetic, and sometimes racist assumptions that a young man has committed murder. A movie set inside a small, stifling room can be a recipe for boredom, but Lumet had the ingenuity to keep the action flowing while accentuating the claustrophobia with lenses and lighting that give the impression of walls closing in. In 2008, the American Film Institute ranked

12 Angry Men the second best courtroom drama of all time, just behind Robert Mulligan and Alan J. Pakula's *To Kill a Mockingbird* (1962).

Lumet incorporated theater-style rehearsals into his filmmaking process, fine-tuning the actors for four weeks before shooting *Long Day's Journey into Night* (1962), starring Katharine Hepburn in an emotional turn that earned her a Best Actress award at Cannes. *Fail Safe* (1964) reunited Lumet with Henry Fonda—this time playing the president of the United States—in a nuclear war nail-biter based on the same source novel as Stanley Kubrick's *Dr. Strangelove* (1964), but without the laughs. Although Lumet's films show tremendous breadth and variety, most have a distinct energy, a certain Manhattan vitality that crackles through *Dog Day Afternoon* like an electric current. The 1975

Sidney Lumet shoots Long Day's Journey Into Night, *1962.*

heist-gone-wrong drama was so ahead of its time that it still feels ultramodern, more than forty-five years later.

Opening with a summer-in-the-city montage to Elton John's soulful "Amoreena," *Dog Day Afternoon* proceeds with no musical score, just the needle-drop that kicks off the true story of a man who holds up a Brooklyn bank to fund a sex reassignment surgery for his transgender wife, Leon (played by Chris Sarandon). Victor Kemper's streetwise cinematography lends the feel of an honest-to-god crisis unfolding in real time, presaging the rise of reality TV, twenty-four-hour news channels, and YouTube celebrities. Lumet filled minor roles with skilled actors, so that Al Pacino could improvise with bank employee–hostages and they could improvise right back. Pacino performs like a ticking

time bomb that might explode at any second—yet his sad-eyed Sonny is sympathetic, an inept bank robber without the criminal mind required to pull it off. Pacino won four acting awards, while Frank Pierson's screenplay scored an Oscar.

Pacino and Lumet had first collaborated on *Serpico*, another fact-based account, this one of the lone cop who refuses to take bribe money in a precinct rife with casual corruption. Where is the line between justice and injustice drawn? Where is our morally loose society headed? These are questions Lumet's work frequently raised. A prophetic, provocative satire about a TV anchor who threatens to kill himself on the air, *Network* applies just as easily to life in the 2020s as in 1976. "There is

Al Pacino and Penelope Allen in Dog Day Afternoon

MUST-SEE MOVIES

12 ANGRY MEN (1957)

LONG DAY'S JOURNEY INTO NIGHT (1962)

THE PAWNBROKER (1964)

SERPICO (1973)

DOG DAY AFTERNOON (1975)

NETWORK (1976)

THE WIZ (1978)

THE VERDICT (1982)

BEFORE THE DEVIL KNOWS YOU'RE DEAD (2007)

Peter Finch in Network

KEY SCENE TO WATCH

Peter Finch's rant as the fed-up newsman Howard Beale is delivered straight to a live television camera in *Network*. "You've got to get mad!" he tells his audience. "You've got to say, 'I'm a human being, god damn it, my life has value!'" Listing the evils of the modern world—depression, inflation, rampant crime, air that's unfit to breathe—he instructs the American television-viewing public to stand up, open their windows, and yell, "I'm as mad as hell and I'm not going to take this anymore!" It became a catchphrase for a generation raised on TV. In 2005, the Writers Guild of America voted Paddy Chayefsky's *Network* screenplay one of the ten greatest in film history.

"One of my favorite directors is Sidney Lumet. He's this very versatile filmmaker who worked in the way that I want to work: consistently, he challenged himself with different genres, and until he was an old man. He kept going, and made great stuff."

—AVA DuVERNAY

no America," the exec who runs the news channel (Ned Beatty) says. "There is no democracy. There is only IBM . . . AT&T, and Exxon." By confronting corporate media control, *Network* "restored to the screen a point of view and quantities of anger and eloquence it has rarely known ever," the *Los Angeles Times* proclaimed. Oscars for its script and lead actress (Faye Dunaway) were among four the film collected.

Lumet shifted William F. Brown's Kansas-set *Wizard of Oz* musical to his beloved New York City to modernize it, urbanize it, and make it flashier, expanding *The Wiz* (1978) into a spectacle of monumental scope. He turned Astoria Studios in Queens into a dazzling cityscape reminiscent of classic Busby Berkeley numbers, and had the show's original music funked up by Quincy Jones. With a cast boasting Diana Ross as Dorothy and Michael Jackson as the Scarecrow, *The Wiz* overflowed with star power. "Michael may be the purest talent I've ever seen," Lumet told a reporter on the set in 1977. "He's incapable of a false moment."

The 1980s and '90s ushered in the age of the popcorn blockbuster, the guaranteed moneymaker; insightful, thought-provoking films became a tougher sell. "People don't want to work at a movie anymore," Lumet observed in 1997. "I like doing movies that make you work. I want you to come away asking yourself questions. 'Where are my compromises? What have I done in my life?' Frankly, many of my earlier movies would have trouble getting made today." *The Verdict* (1982), starring Paul Newman, and *The Morning After* (1986), featuring Jane Fonda, were two powerful dramas Lumet managed to slip through the system.

Sidney Lumet continued to direct relevant, insightful films for the rest of his life, receiving more than fifty Academy Award nominations for his body of work. *Night Falls on Manhattan* (1997) echoed his *Serpico* theme of corrupt cops and bent politicians. His last film was one of his best: the complex heist drama *Before the Devil Knows You're Dead* (2007), featuring an ensemble led by Albert Finney, Philip Seymour Hoffman, and Ethan Hawke.

ELAINE MAY

Years active: 1971–1987

ALTHOUGH SHE ONLY MADE FOUR FILMS, ACTRESS/ writer/director Elaine May warrants a place in movie history as one of very few women directing in the male-dominated Hollywood of the 1970s. Burt Reynolds, Clint Eastwood, Sylvester Stallone—

always directed by men—were the screen gods in this macho era. Golden Age movies catered to both sexes equally, but when the studio system crumbled, gone also was the obligation to appeal to a female demographic. May's sketch-comedy mind was funny enough to earn a foot in the boys' club door.

Born to Yiddish vaudeville actors, the naturally witty and independent-spirited May studied acting with Maria Ouspenskaya before cofounding Chicago's Compass Players in 1955. From there, she and Mike Nichols joined forces as a comedy duo. When the popular team split in 1961 to navigate the industry separately, May, with a daughter to raise, took her sweet time perfecting a screenplay,

hoping for a chance to helm it herself, as Nichols was doing in Hollywood.

In 1969, Paramount snatched up her original dark-comedy script, *A New Leaf.* When she requested director approval, the studio told her, "You can't pick a director, but you can direct it." Her directorial debut was championed by lead actor Walter Matthau, though he faltered when it came to taking her direction, jokingly calling her "Mrs. Hitler," among other names. "On the first day, when we began, it was a very tough movie for me," admitted the untrained May. "I knew absolutely nothing. I barely knew what a camera looked like."

She learned on the spot, crafting a hilariously cynical romance between spoiled layabout Henry

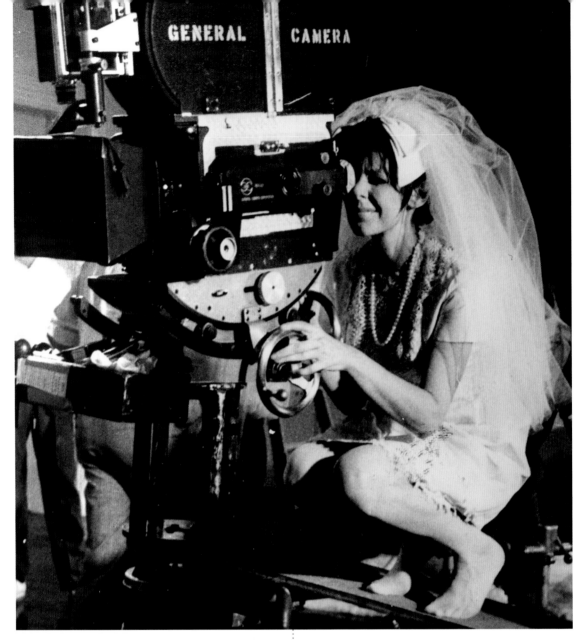

(Matthau) and awkward heiress/botanist Henrietta (May) in a lethal mismatch. Once complete, *A New Leaf* (1971) was delayed for two years as Paramount head of production Robert Evans had May's nearly three-hour cut pared to 102 minutes. A legal conflict ensued, the case landing in the New York State Supreme Court. When the studio cut was shown to the judge, producer Howard Koch recounted, "He screamed and laughed, then declared, 'It's the funniest picture in years. You guys win.'" May lost her case, but her film won box office and critical approval, Charles Champlin deeming it "a bliss-

Elaine May directs A New Leaf.

> "Luckily, there have been several courageous women [directors] in the world . . . and Elaine May has had probably as turbulent a time in pictures as any of them. Yet she's managed to leave the same distinctive, savagely satirical stamp on four very different works."
>
> —PETER BOGDANOVICH

fully funny movie, [its] level of successful invention marvelously high." Today, the half-forgotten *A New Leaf* remains a cult gem, and a landmark: the first time a woman wrote, directed, and starred in a major Hollywood feature.

Twentieth Century-Fox entrusted May with the Neil Simon adaptation *The Heartbreak Kid* (1972), which places Jewish newlyweds Lila and Lenny (Jeannie Berlin, May's daughter, in an inspired performance, and Charles Grodin) on a honeymoon trip to Miami. She is needy and annoying; he is self-involved and soon-to-be faithless, when he spots blond dream-girl Kelly (Cybill

Shepherd) at the hotel pool. The director kept her camera close and her edits in check, letting the comic bits play out uninterrupted. A disgruntled Simon abandoned the project, believing May was too irreverent with his carefully constructed lines, but her results spoke for themselves. "Humor flows effortlessly," the *Hollywood Reporter* raved, "from the rhythmic dialogue; explosions of laughter appear, as if by magic." Some critics attributed the movie's success to Neil Simon's material, but the *New Yorker*'s Pauline Kael detected May's increasingly refined touch, noting that *The Heartbreak Kid* was "in a different league from her first wobbly movie."

MUST-SEE MOVIES

A NEW LEAF (1971)

THE HEARTBREAK KID (1972)

MIKEY AND NICKY (1976)

KEY SCENE TO WATCH

A New Leaf presents Henrietta Lowell as a bumbler, a bumper, a spiller—even on her honeymoon. Watch as, for more than two minutes, May does battle with a nightgown of Grecian style, contorting cluelessly to set it straight after unwittingly wedging her head through the armhole. Matthau's Henry Graham speaks a line that sums up the woman he's intent on taking for all she's got: "She has to be vacuumed every time she eats."

"It's very hard to talk to a dead person. We have nothing in common." So says Nicky (John Cassavetes) in May's self-scripted gangster tragicomedy, *Mikey and Nicky* (1976). The premise, the dialogue, the acting were solid, but once again, May and Paramount locked horns. Shooting miles of footage with three cameras whirring at once from different angles, she doubled the modest budget. May built her one-night-long buddy flick on the chemistry between friends Cassavetes and Peter Falk (Mikey). The two are on the lam, dodging a hit man (Ned Beatty), their wordplay sharp yet improvisational. A climactic moment—Nicky versus Mikey in a street brawl that May captured with her three cameras—has been compared to a dance, as the best friends startle each other by coming to blows. Another lawsuit over the final edit kept Elaine out of action for ten years, until she wrote and directed the much-disparaged *Ishtar* (1987), another buddy movie, for two big stars.

May had made such significant contributions to the scripts for Warren Beatty's *Reds* (1981) and Sydney Pollack's *Tootsie* (1982), starring Dustin

Charles Grodin and Cybill Shepherd in The Heartbreak Kid

Hoffman, that Beatty thanked her when he won a Best Director Oscar, while Hoffman singled her out as "the one who made *Tootsie* work."

A veiled satire on Ronald Reagan's Middle East conflict, *Ishtar* brought Beatty and Hoffman together as two has-been entertainers embroiled in a political skirmish in Morocco. Columbia dumped it on the world with no publicity, and savage reviews resulted in a box office bomb. "If all of the people who hate *Ishtar* had seen it," May quipped in 2006, "I would be a rich woman today."

Elaine May might have been a more prolific filmmaker had she bowed and scraped to the male bigwigs, but she never did. Instead, she did her own thing, transitioning to a successful career penning scripts, doctoring the writing of others, and occa-sionally acting. Such diverse colleagues and fans as Sherry Lansing, Amy Heckerling, Polly Platt, and Natasha Lyonne have applauded her efforts and found inspiration in her work.

In 2013, President Obama awarded May a National Medal of Arts, and the Writers Guild of America honored her with a lifetime achievement award in 2016. She won her first Tony in 2019 for her role on Broadway in *The Waverly Gallery*. According-ing to longtime friend Marlo Thomas, "It's no acci-dent that Elaine was name-checked several times on the first season of *The Marvelous Mrs. Maisel*. That's the kind of historical and cultural impact she's had."

Peter Falk and John Cassavetes in Mikey and Nicky

MARTIN SCORSESE

Years active: 1967–present

H IS WORK HAS BEEN INFORMED BY A LIFETIME OF absorbing classic movies. While enamored of studio-era Hollywood, Martin Scorsese has cultivated an anti-studio style of his own: street-tough yet lyrical, a heightened realism rooted in the 1970s. "The over-

riding, compelling impulse" to make movies, he said in 2012, was born of the Italian neorealist films he saw as a child in New York. The naturalism and immediacy of Roberto Rossellini and Vittorio De Sica "cast a shadow over me, and my family, who were Sicilian American."

Often bedridden as an asthmatic child, Marty fixated on the moving image. He put his NYU master's in film to good use in his first major feature, *Mean Streets* (1973), an unvarnished look back at his own life in Little Italy, shot for a slim $300,000. With young unknowns Harvey Keitel and Robert De Niro starring, Scorsese employed a handheld camera for a documentary flavor, layered with Ronettes hits, slangy dialogue, and hyped-up editing reflective of

his own fast-talking disposition. Critic Pauline Kael hailed Scorsese as "a true original" and the picture "a triumph of personal filmmaking." His low-budget benchmark has proven influential to many in the industry, including *The Sopranos* star James Gandolfini, who once confided that he "saw *Mean Streets* ten times in a row" in his youth.

When Ellen Burstyn sought "somebody new and young and exciting" to direct her in *Alice Doesn't Live Here Anymore* (1974), Francis Coppola recommended Scorsese. "What do you know about women?" Burstyn asked. "Nothing," Scorsese answered. "But I'd like to learn." Although he's been accused of focusing almost exclusively on the male psyche and leaving his ancillary female characters

unexplored, Scorsese expanded upon Robert Getch-ell's script about a young, newly widowed mother in Tucson, adding stylized flashbacks and dynamic camera moves to create a captivating, authentic, and woman-centered romantic dramedy. It broadened his résumé and boosted Burstyn to an Oscar.

The grim urban character study *Taxi Driver* (1976) was so hard for Scorsese to get financed that he considered shooting it on a video cam-era, he recalled, "to just get it made." Fortunately, he was able to do 35 mm justice to the script he'd been handed by friend Brian De Palma. De Niro,

another close friend, took on an all-consuming anti-hero role—losing 25 pounds, cultivating a Midwest-ern accent, even obtaining a license and driving an actual cab—to portray Travis Bickle, a Vietnam vet with no sane way to channel his rage. Jodie Foster, at twelve, is the child prostitute, while Cybill Shep-herd plays a Hitchcock-cool, unattainable blonde, both linked in Travis's mind to assassinations he has primed himself to carry out. Accompanied by

Martin Scorsese directs Leonardo DiCaprio and Matt Damon in The Departed.

"My mother was responsible for me being a great fan of Martin Scorsese; she took me to see *Mean Streets*. . . . That film really had an impact on me. That was the first time I saw Robert De Niro and Harvey [Keitel]."

—SPIKE LEE

Bernard Herrmann's restless score (completed by Herrmann mere hours before his death), Bickle cruises the nightshift in his Checker cab that screenwriter Paul Schrader has equated to a metal box, an airless coffin awaiting its final fare. Schrader has also likened his protagonist to a modern-day version of John Wayne's caustic cowboy Ethan Edwards in John Ford's *The Searchers* (1956), a film that heavily influenced Scorsese as well.

"One of the things about *Taxi Driver* that is so amazing," Quentin Tarantino once noted, "is that it truly puts you in the point of view of this man. If you've ever been lonely and lived in a ghetto area, it's easy to feel Travis Bickle's kind of feelings." Scorsese challenges audiences to empathize with a dangerous loner, drawing us into his unhinged mind using slow motion, hypnotic tracking shots, and editing that mirrors Bickle's ruminations. When the Motion Picture Association of America board threatened *Taxi Driver* with an X rating, Scorsese secured an R by desaturating the color of the climactic slaughter scene, draining the blood of its lurid red tones. The indie effort received the Palme d'Or at Cannes and heaps of critical praise. "Scorsese," wrote Charles Michener in *Film Comment*, "is a fantasist who supercharges the clichés of *Taxi Driver* into the surreal figments of a nightmare that is at once comic, romantic, and terrifying."

His first megabucks feature, *New York, New York* (1977) was a bold, brassy, and costly experiment; "a film noir musical," Scorsese called it, "a valentine to Hollywood." Inspired by his encyclopedic memory of old movies and the troubled off-screen life of Doris Day, Scorsese's 1940s hybrid piece was burdened with a chaotic shoot, an overblown budget, and a near-impossible editing job of merging original story with improvisation. Fueled by the once-in-a-lifetime romantic pairing of Robert De Niro and Liza Minnelli, *New York, New York* is a gorgeous, often fascinating folly, but its lack of popularity sent its creator into a deep depression exacerbated by drug addiction.

After De Niro helped Scorsese get back on track, the actor convinced his pal to helm a memoir of 1940s–'50s prizefighter Jake LaMotta. Filmed in high-contrast black-and-white, *Raging Bull* (1980)

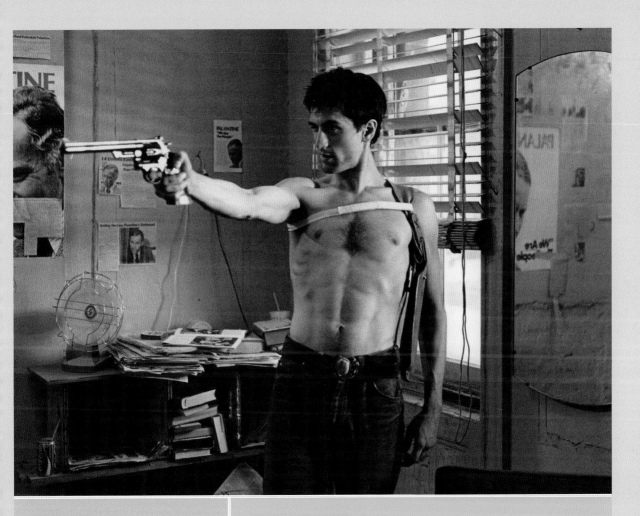

MUST-SEE MOVIES

MEAN STREETS (1973)

ALICE DOESN'T LIVE HERE ANYMORE (1974)

TAXI DRIVER (1976)

RAGING BULL (1980)

GOODFELLAS (1990)

THE AGE OF INNOCENCE (1993)

CASINO (1995)

THE AVIATOR (2004)

THE DEPARTED (2006)

KEY SCENE TO WATCH

An unscripted, almost throwaway scene that made it into *Taxi Driver* has become the film's most iconic highlight. Standing before the mirror in his shabby apartment, Travis practices his tough-guy persona, quick-drawing his handgun and repeatedly asking his reflection, "You talkin' to me?" Schrader had written no dialogue for this scene, but Scorsese asked De Niro, "Could you say something to yourself in the mirror?" On the last day of shooting, the director spent a few minutes filming this experiment as De Niro improvised the line, "like a jazz riff," Scorsese recalled.

Robert De Niro as Travis Bickle in Taxi Driver

was enhanced by carefully staged fight scenes—shot inside the ring with a hand held camera—giving the sweat and the blows some close-up emotion. Editor Thelma Schoonmaker established herself as Scorsese's best collaborator next to De Niro; both won Academy Awards. *Raging Bull* received mixed notices upon release, but its reputation began to grow almost immediately, and in 1990, the modern-day classic was singled out for preservation by the National Film Registry in its first year of eligibility.

Another greatest-film contender is *Goodfellas* (1990), a darkly witty slice of gangland nostalgia. Refining his masterful approach to the level of perfection, Scorsese employed New Wave–esque techniques (uninflected narration, abrupt scene reversals, freeze frames) to mark the turning points in Henry Hill's (Ray Liotta) mob career. A very dif-

ferent period piece was the grand yet intimate nineteenth-century social comment *The Age of Innocence* (1993), released to wide acclaim just as Scorsese was plotting *Casino* (1995), his second collaboration with writer Nicholas Pileggi, his eighth with De Niro. Laced with obscenity and punctuated with violence, the saga begins with an auto explosion, and careens through the flashy excess of '70s Las Vegas in its most notorious era. Nabbing a Golden Globe as De Niro's alcoholic mess of a wife, Sharon Stone nearly steals the show from her heavyweight costars De Niro and Joe Pesci.

Martin Scorsese received his first Oscar in 2007. Starring Leonardo DiCaprio (his current favorite leading man), *The Departed* (2006) finally won him the gold after five previous Best Director nominations. In addition to producing new films of exceptional quality—such as the enchanting *Hugo* (2011), a fictionalized account of real-life silent-film pioneer Georges Méliès's later years, shot in 3-D—Scorsese remains committed to preserving and restoring the movies of the past. In 2018, he received the inaugural Robert Osborne Award from Turner Classic Movies for his work in film preservation. "The miracle of cinema," he said upon accepting the honor, "is that it gives us that common image—that common idea of who we are or who we've been, and who we're becoming—in time and motion, shot by shot."

Sharon Stone rolls the dice in Casino.

STEVEN SPIELBERG

Years active: 1971–present

T HROUGH THE MANY PHASES OF STEVEN SPIEL-berg's long and phenomenally successful career, the writer/director/producer has crisscrossed a wide variety of genres. Between the adrenaline rush of *Jaws* (1975), the socially conscious humanity of *The Color*

Purple (1985), the futuristic speculation of *Minority Report* (2002), and dozens of other favorites, Spielberg has proved himself an entertainer above all else. No matter what story he tells, his keen ability to tap into the popular mind-set has brought laughter, tears, and wonder to millions.

They were dubbed the "movie brats": the first generation of filmmakers to have formally studied their craft in prestigious universities. Francis Ford Coppola (UCLA), Martin Scorsese (NYU), George Lucas (USC), and Brian De Palma (Columbia) were flush with youth, ambition, and maybe a little arrogance, when they took Hollywood by storm in

Akosua Busia and Desreta Jackson in The Color Purple

the early '70s. Spielberg, freshly under contract at Universal and younger than the youngest of them, earned inclusion in that fraternity, even though he had dropped out of Cal State Long Beach after a rejection letter from USC.

Born into an Orthodox Jewish household in Cincinnati but raised in Phoenix, Spielberg had mild dyslexia that made school challenging, but prompted an avid interest in movies. "If I have any

kind of secret to my craft," he said in 2003, "it's that I've watched a lot of old pictures from the 1930s, '40s, and '50s; films by Howard Hawks, Preston Sturges, and Alfred Hitchcock." By high school, he was shooting professional-quality films of his own. At twenty-four, he came across Richard Matheson's

Steven Spielberg directs Harrison Ford and Karen Allen in Raiders of the Lost Ark.

> "We have finally seen *Close Encounters*. It is a very good film, and I regret that it was not made in France. This type of popular science would be most appropriate for the compatriots of Jules Verne and Méliès. You are excellent in it because you're not quite real. There is more than a grain of eccentricity in this adventure. The filmmaker is a poet."

—JEAN RENOIR, WRITING TO FRANÇOIS TRUFFAUT

"very Hitchcocky and suspenseful" script that pitted a businessman (played by Dennis Weaver) in his Plymouth Valiant sedan against the unseen, maniacal driver of a menacing Peterbilt tanker truck. Spielberg shot *Duel* (1971) in three weeks on the parched backroads of the Mojave Desert, revving up a high-speed chase with minimal dialogue and maximum action. The *Los Angeles Times* called the TV movie "the most hair-raising fictional work on television this year—and one of the most impressive."

The precocious director next tackled another road movie, this one more upbeat, and made for the big screen. *The Sugarland Express* (1974) stars Goldie Hawn as ex-con Lou Jean Poplin, hell-bent on retaining custody of her baby by leading an epic slow chase across Texas. Already, Spielberg was marrying pulse-pounding excitement with heartwarming family dynamics, two themes that have permeated his filmography. Even in his wild, wet, and toothy disaster thriller *Jaws*, he centered the Brody family (led by Roy Scheider's police chief) at the story's heart.

Because Spielberg insisted on an authentic seaside setting, Martha's Vineyard hosted the crew and cast, with its three protagonists—Scheider, Richard Dreyfuss, Robert Shaw—and villain "Bruce," the temperamental animatronic shark, which, along with the weather and the unpredictable currents, caused huge delays and cost overruns. With his job on the line, Spielberg cleverly strategized, shooting Bruce in glimpses: a tail breaking the surface, a fin skimming the shore. "What's scary about the movie is the unseen," he noted later. Plus, there was John Williams's foreboding score "grinding away at you," the composer explained, "as a shark would do, instinctual, relentless, unstoppable." The movie earned an Oscar for Williams, one for editor Verna Fields, and one for sound editing. When *Jaws* opened in the summer of '75 to long-lined excitement, Hollywood's template for the seasonal box office blockbuster was set, and Steven Spielberg became the hottest director in town.

Before his shark picture grossed $100 million, he found it hard to finance his dream project about the UFO phenomenon. But the success of *Jaws* made *Close Encounters of the Third Kind* (1977) possible, its enigmatic title referring to ufologist J. Allen Hynek's third level of alien interaction: actual contact. Since childhood, Spielberg had harbored "a real deep-rooted belief that we had been visited," he said, and that childlike awe informed his self-scripted story about outer-space pioneers, told without CGI, but with precise imagination. Casting relatable everyman Dreyfuss and stage-trained Melinda Dillon in the leads, Spielberg discovered four-year-old Alabama native Cary Guffey to play the young alien abductee, and reserved a special role for one of his heroes, director François Truffaut, as a French scientist. With director of photography Vilmos Zsigmond, he staged the most touching UFO landing yet seen: children in vapory alien costume were back-lit and defocused as they descended from their spacecraft and welcomed passengers onboard. Vincent Canby of the *New York Times* called *Close Encounters* "the best—the most elaborate—1950s science-fiction movie ever made."

Funneling his fascination with aliens into a more intimate narrative, Spielberg beamed *E.T. The Extra-Terrestrial* (1982) into an $800 million worldwide box office bonanza. This time, the

E.T. says good-bye to Elliott (Henry Thomas) in E.T. The Extra-Terrestrial.

MUST-SEE MOVIES

JAWS (1975)

CLOSE ENCOUNTERS OF THE THIRD KIND (1977)

RAIDERS OF THE LOST ARK (1981)

E. T. THE EXTRA-TERRESTRIAL (1982)

THE COLOR PURPLE (1985)

SCHINDLER'S LIST (1993)

SAVING PRIVATE RYAN (1998)

LINCOLN (2012)

THE POST (2017)

KEY SCENE TO WATCH

The attack on a crowded beach is one of the most skillfully choreographed and suspenseful scenes in *Jaws*. Suspecting a killer shark in the waters off Amity Island, Brody tensely watches swimmers, on high alert for signs of danger. Deftly establishing the key players—a man playing catch with his dog, a little boy on a float, and the boy's mother—Spielberg sets the stage for a grisly tragedy to play out, as a stunned Brody sees his worst fears realized in a famous dolly-and-zoom shot reminiscent of Alfred Hitchcock's *Vertigo* (1958). When the view switches from land to ocean, Spielberg and cinematographer Bill Butler keep the camera at water level, forcing the audience to experience the terror alongside the victims.

Steven Spielberg and "Bruce" on the set of Jaws

visitor is a 3-foot-tall wrinkled shuffler with a glowing heart, designed by Carlo Rambaldi, accidentally left behind on Earth by his space exploration team. Melissa Mathison's fable of childhood, suburbia, divorce, government control, and a love connection between different species remains a worldwide favorite, buoyed by its catchphrase, spoken by seven-year-old Drew Barrymore: "E.T. phone home." To the '80s, Spielberg brought the all-ages movie, entertainment for kids and adults alike, an almost unheard-of concept in the saucy '70s. With story by George Lucas—a throwback adventure reminiscent of 1940s Saturday matinee serials—Spielberg took a cue from *Star Wars* and

packed *Raiders of the Lost Ark* (1981) with all the fun essentials: attractive yet unlikely hero, good-sport girlfriend, villains to hiss, action to cheer, and leading man Harrison Ford.

Putting aside aliens and adventure, he surprised many by filming *The Color Purple* (1985), adapted from Alice Walker's novel about the intertwined lives of Black women in the Deep South. Spielberg received some backlash for presuming, as a White director, to know the subject and its themes. He later admitted to an overly cautious approach, a softening of the hard edges and

Ralph Fiennes and Liam Neeson in Schindler's List

A WHOLE NEW HOLLYWOOD

controversial elements of the material. Despite its shortcomings, Walker herself praised the finished product, which received eleven Academy Award nominations—including one for Quincy Jones's spirited score and one for Whoopi Goldberg's heartfelt lead performance.

Jurassic Park author Michael Crichton once called Spielberg "arguably the most influential artist of the twentieth century," adding, "and arguably the least understood." Behind the mass-appeal-master has always lurked a man of deep social conscience. When his ten-year struggle to make *Schindler's List* (1993) finally yielded a powerful black-and-white Holocaust epic, filmgoers were stunned. With tremendous sensitivity and clear-eyed commitment, he worked in documentary style, with a handheld camera supervised by Janusz Kaminski. In this film, the only spot of color—the recurring little girl in a red coat—is an embodiment of hope, of life. *Schindler's List* made stars of Liam Neeson and Ralph

Fiennes, and an Oscar-winner of Spielberg for Best Picture and Best Director. Confronting World War II from a different angle was *Saving Private Ryan* (1998), one of the filmmaker's five collaborations with Tom Hanks, boasting three times the budget of *Schindler's List* and a relentless depiction of battlefield barbarism.

A Steven Spielberg production is almost always an event. His skills and artistry have grown year after year, from *Catch Me If You Can* (2002) to *Munich* (2005), from *Lincoln* (2012) to his update of *West Side Story* (2021). "Sometimes we take Spielberg for granted because he's the most successful director in the history of movies," Roger Ebert stated in 2002, but "he's a great director . . . a brilliant visionary." Spielberg has created a body of cinematic work like few others—in its quality, its volume, and its ability to still surprise us, after fifty years.

Tom Hanks and Matt Damon in Saving Private Ryan

THE OUTSIDERS

Independent cinema flourished in the 1970s. Although the major Hollywood studios still held the bulk of money and power, hungry young writer/director/producers were able to scrape together films on micro budgets, and distribute them to drive-ins or art houses. Working outside of the mainstream, these filmmakers had creative control and freedom to experiment.

With his unpredictable cinéma vérité style, New York actor turned auteur **John Cassavetes** influenced many a modern-day filmmaker, including Ridley Scott. He shattered romantic clichés in the Oscar-nominated *Faces* (1968), thrust viewers into a family grappling with mental health in *A Woman Under the Influence* (1974), and gave his wife, actress Gena Rowlands, a scintillating lead in *Gloria* (1980). Making money was never the goal, but striving for "some kind of personal truth," he said. Working under this ethos, Cassavetes was about as anti-Hollywood as it got.

As a director, **Roger Corman** is the godfather of independent film, a veteran purveyor of low-budget cult classics from the 1950s through the 1980s, including *The Little Shop of Horrors* (1960), *The Wild Angels* (1966), and *Bloody Mama* (1970). As a producer and mentor, he has launched the careers of A-list stars, and some of the greatest filmmakers in modern times, from Martin Scorsese to Ron Howard, Francis Ford Coppola to Jonathan Demme. "He was my life-blood," recalled Corman regular Jack Nicholson in 2011, "to whatever I thought I was going to be as a person."

Referred to as "the Howard Hawks of exploitation filmmaking" by fan Quentin Tarantino, Los Angeles native **Jack Hill** mastered almost every grade-B subgenre: horror (*Spider Baby* [1968]), women in prison (*The Big Doll House* [1971]), blaxploitation (*Foxy Brown* [1974]), and sexploitation (*The Swinging Cheerleaders* [1974]). After making the unknown Pam Grier into a low-budget luminary, Hill delivered his outrageous feminism-fueled girl-gang masterpiece, *Switchblade Sisters* (1975).

In 1970, stage and screen actress, theater director, and Elia Kazan's wife, **Barbara Loden** used her own money to write, direct, and star in *Wanda*. A hypnotic drama with a documentary feel, the Venice Film Festival prize-winner *Wanda* raises questions about oppression as it details a small-town woman's unfulfilled life. Although Loden left several other projects uncompleted when she died in 1980, her one groundbreaking film paved the way for indie women, such as Claudia Weill, Penelope Spheeris, and Julie Dash.

Directing movies was just one of **Gordon Parks**'s many talents. The novelist, *Life* magazine photographer, and musician adapted his own book *The Learning Tree* in 1969, making him Hollywood's first successful Black filmmaker since the days of Oscar Micheaux. With the groundbreaking *Shaft* (1971) and *Shaft's Big Score* (1972), he kicked the blaxploitation genre into gear, while his son, **Gordon Parks Jr.**, carried on the family tradition with the successful *Super Fly* (1972), a crime drama bolstered by its groovy Curtis Mayfield soundtrack.

After his 1967 adaptation of his own novel *The Story of a Three-Day Pass* earned **Melvin Van Peebles** raves at the 1968 San Francisco Film Festival, the Chicago native dipped a toe into the Hollywood studio system with the race-themed comedy *Watermelon Man* (1970). Turning down a Columbia contract, Van Peebles opted instead to write, produce, direct, edit, and compose the score for *Sweet Sweetback's Baadasssss Song* (1971), a landmark of Black cinema and the highest-grossing independent film of 1971.

Richard Roundtree in Gordon Parks's Shaft

BIBLIOGRAPHY

BOOKS

Anderson, Mary Ann, and Ida Lupino. *Ida Lupino: Beyond the Camera*. Albany, Ga.: BearManor, 2018.

Basinger, Jeanine. *A Woman's View*. New York: Alfred A. Knopf, 1995.

Bergan, Ronald. *The United Artists Story*. New York: Crown, 1986.

Biskind, Peter. *Easy Riders, Raging Bulls: How the Sex-Drugs-and-Rock 'n' Roll Generation Saved Hollywood*. New York: Simon & Schuster, 1998.

Bogdanovich, Peter. *Who the Devil Made It*. New York: Alfred A. Knopf, 1997.

Bogle, Donald. *Hollywood Black: The Stars, the Films, the Filmmakers*. Philadelphia: Running Press, 2019.

Bosworth, Patricia. *Jane Fonda: The Private Life of a Public Woman*. New York: Houghton Mifflin Harcourt, 2011.

Bowman, Manoah. *Fellini: The Sixties*. Philadelphia: Running Press, 2015.

Bowser, Pearl, Jane Gaines, and Charles Musser, eds. *Oscar Micheaux and His Circle: African American Filmmaking and Race Cinema of the Silent Era*. Bloomington, Ind.: Indiana University Press, 2016.

Brooks, Mel, with Rebecca Keegan. *Young Frankenstein: The Story of the Making of the Film*. New York: Black Dog & Leventhal, 2016.

Bubbeo, Daniel. *The Women of Warner Brothers: The Lives and Careers of Fifteen Leading Ladies*. Jefferson, N.C.: McFarland, 2002.

Callow, Simon. *Orson Welles: The Road to Xanadu*. New York: Penguin Books, 1995.

Capra, Frank. *The Name Above the Title*. New York: Macmillan, 1971.

Carver, Raymond. *Short Cuts*. New York: Knopf Doubleday, 2015.

Chaplin, Charlie. *My Autobiography*. Brooklyn, N.Y.: Melville House Publishing, 2012.

Crowe, Cameron. *Conversations with Wilder*. New York: Alfred A. Knopf, 1999.

Curtis, James. *Between Flops: A Biography of Preston Sturges*. New York: Limelight Editions, 1984.

Dawson, Nick. *Being Hal Ashby: Life of a Hollywood Rebel*. Lexington: University Press of Kentucky, 2009.

Dick, Bernard F. *That Was Entertainment: The Golden Age of the Hollywood Musical*. Jackson, Miss.: University Press of Mississippi, 2018.

Edwards, Blake. *Blake Edwards: Interviews*. Edited by Gabriella Oldham. Jackson, Miss.: University Press of Mississippi, 2018.

Evanier, David. *Woody: The Biography*. New York: St. Martin's Press, 2015.

Evans, Robert. *The Kid Stays in the Picture*. New York: Hyperion, 1994.

Eyman, Scott. *Empire of Dreams: The Epic Life of Cecil B. DeMille*. New York: Simon & Schuster, 2010.

———. *The Speed of Sound: Hollywood and the Talkie Revolution, 1926–1930*. New York: Simon & Schuster, 1997.

Fishgall, Gary. *Gregory Peck: A Biography*. New York: Scribner, 2002.

Girgus, Sam B. *The Films of Woody Allen*. Cambridge, UK: Cambridge University Press, 2002.

Halliday, Jon. *Sirk on Sirk*. London: Martin Secker & Warburg, 1971.

Henderson, Robert M. *D. W. Griffith: The Years at Biograph*. New York: Farrar, Straus and Giroux, 1970.

Hirschhorn, Clive. *The Warner Bros. Story*. New York: Crown Publishers, 1979.

Jarman, Claude Jr. *My Life and the Final Days of Hollywood*. Murrells Inlet, S.C.: Covenant Books, 2018.

Jorgensen, Jay, and Manoah Bowman. *Grace Kelly: Hollywood Dream Girl*. New York: HarperCollins, 2017.

Kazan, Elia. *A Life*. New York: Alfred A. Knopf, 1988.

Kellow, Brian. *Pauline Kael: A Life in the Dark*. New York: Viking, 2011.

Knight, Arthur. *The Liveliest Art: A Panoramic History of the Movies*. Signet Classics, 1979.

Koury, Phil A. *Yes, Mr. DeMille*. New York: G.P. Putnam's Sons, 1959.

Lambert, Gavin. *On Cukor*. New York: Capricorn Books, 1972.

Lopate, Phillip, ed. *American Movie Critics: An Anthology from the Silents Until Now*. New York: The Library of America, 2006.

Lower, Cheryl Bray, and R. Barton Palmer. *Joseph L. Mankiewicz: Critical Essays with an Annotated Bibliography and a Filmography*. Jefferson, N.C.: McFarland, 2001.

Lumet, Sidney. *Making Movies*. New York: Random House, 1995.

Mast, Gerald. *Howard Hawks: Storyteller*. New York: Oxford University Press, 1982.

McBride, Joseph. *Hawks on Hawks*. Berkeley and Los Angeles: University of California Press, 1982.

McGilligan, Patrick. *Fritz Lang: The Nature of the Beast*. Minneapolis: University of Minnesota Press, 2013.

———. *Oscar Micheaux: The Great and Only*. New York: Harper Collins, 2009.

Miller, Gabriel. *William Wyler: The Life and Films of Hollywood's Most Celebrated Director*. Lexington: University Press of Kentucky, 2013.

Milne, Tom. *Rouben Mamoulian*. Bloomington, Ind.: Indiana University Press, 1969.

Mitchell, Deborah C. *Diane Keaton: Artist and Icon*. Jefferson, N.C.: McFarland & Company, 2001.

Palmer, R. Barton, and Murray Pomerance, eds. *The Many Cinemas of Michael Curtiz*. Austin: University of Texas Press, 2018.

Phillips, Gene. *Some Like It Wilder: The Life and Controversial Films of Billy Wilder*. Lexington: University Press of Kentucky, 2010.

Rode, Alan K. *Michael Curtiz: A Life in Film*. Lexington: University Press of Kentucky, 2017.

Schickel, Richard. *Conversations with Scorsese*. New York: Alfred A. Knopf, 2011.

———. *Steven Spielberg: A Retrospective*. New York: Sterling Publishing Co., 2012.

———. *The Stars*. New York: Bonanza Books, 1962.

Schumacher, Michael. *Francis Ford Coppola: A Filmmaker's Life*. New York: Crown Publishers, 1999.

Sikov, Ed. *On Sunset Boulevard: The Life and Times of Billy Wilder*. Jackson, Miss.: University Press of Mississippi, 2017.

Smith, Robert B. *Idyllwild and the High San Jacintos*. San Francisco: Arcadia, 2009.

Spoto, Donald. *The Art of Alfred Hitchcock: Fifty Years of His Motion Pictures*. New York: Doubleday, 1992.

Sragow, Michael. *Victor Fleming: American Movie Master*. New York: Pantheon, 2008.

Stern, Sydney Ladensohn. *The Brothers Mankiewicz: Hope, Heartbreak, and Hollywood Classics*. Jackson, Miss.: University Press of Mississippi, 2019.

Sturges, Preston. *Preston Sturges by Preston Sturges: His Life in His Words*. Edited by Sandy Sturges. New York: Simon & Schuster, 1990.

Taylor, Philip M. *Steven Spielberg: The Man, His Movies, and Their Meaning*. New York: Continuum, 1992.

Tonguette, Peter. *Picturing Peter Bogdanovich: My Conversations with the New Hollywood Director*. Lexington: University Press of Kentucky, 2020.

Tracy, Tony, and Roddy Flynn, eds., *John Huston: Essays on a Restless Director*. Jefferson, N.C.: McFarland and Company, 2010.

Truffaut, François. *The Films in My Life*. Translated by Leonard Mayhew. New York: Diversion, 1978.

Vance, Jeffrey. *Chaplin: Genius of the Cinema*. New York: Harry N. Abrams, 2003.

Von Sternberg, Josef. *Fun in a Chinese Laundry*. New York: Macmillan, 1965.

Wasson, Sam. *A Splurch in the Kisser: The Movies of Blake Edwards*. Middletown, Conn.: Wesleyan University Press, 2009.

———. *Paul on Mazursky*. Middletown, Conn.: Wesleyan University Press, 2012.

ARTICLES

Bart, Peter. "Lupino, the Dynamo." *Los Angeles Times*, March 7, 1965.

Beach, Barbara. "As in Life." *Motion Picture*, March 1921.

Carr, Harry. "Charlie Again Is Champion." *Los Angeles Times*, February 13, 1921.

———. "The Tree That Grew Alone: An Impression of the Unique Genius of Erich von Stroheim." *Los Angeles Times*, December 31, 1922.

Champlin, Charles. "Critic at Large: LeRoy Went to Heart of Matter." *Los Angeles Times*, September 15, 1987.

———. "The Fine, Flaky Flow of 'Silent Movie.'" *Los Angeles Times*, June 27, 1976.

———. "Movies: All Wise, Always." *Los Angeles Times*, February 15, 1998.

———. "Picking the Top 10 Motion Pictures in a Lean Year." *Los Angeles Times*, January 2, 1977.

———. "'Rosemary's Baby' on Crest Screen." *Los Angeles Times*, June 14, 1968.

Corliss, Richard. "Can Even a Cranky Guy Fall for *The Sound of Music*?" *Time*, March 2, 2015.

Cowie, Peter. "Ingmar Bergman Bids Farewell to Movies." *New York Times*, October 10, 1982.

Crowther, Bosley. "'Casablanca,' with Humphrey Bogart and Ingrid Bergman, at Hollywood." *New York Times*, November 27, 1942.

———. "'The Lady Eve,' a Sparkling Romantic Comedy, with Barbara Stanwyck and Henry Fonda, at the Paramount." *New York Times*, February 26, 1941.

Denby, David. "Movies: Visions of the End." *Atlantic*, December 1971.

Denton, Beryl. "Through Death Valley with von Stroheim." *Motion Picture*, January 1925.

Dowling, Marky. "The Screen's Only Woman Director." *Movie Classic*, December 1936.

Falk, Ray. "Japan's 'Rashomon' Rings the Bell: Venice Festival Prize-Winner Boosts Morale of Nipponese Industry." *New York Times*, October 21, 1951.

"Go Out to a Movie: *Breakfast at Tiffany's*." *Photoplay*, November 1961.

Gregory, Adele. "First Wit of the Films." *Screenland*, March 1935.

Haber, Joyce. "Mike Nichols—Sanely Askew." *Los Angeles Times*, December 10, 1967.

Hall, Mordaunt. "Mr. Lubitsch in Old Heidelberg." *New York Times*, September 25, 1927.

———. "The Screen: A Superlative War Picture." *New York Times*, November 20, 1925.

"'The Hitch-Hiker' Exciting Suspense Meller." *Film Bulletin*, February 9, 1953.

"Jean Harlow Gives Brilliant Performance in Mercilessly Frank 'Bombshell.'" *Los Angeles Times*, October 29, 1933.

Johnson, Sheila. "Filmmakers on Film: Claude Chabrol." *Telegraph*, January 24, 2004.

Kehr, Dave. "A Subverter of Clichés About '50s Conformity." *Los Angeles Times*, July 11, 1999.

Kennedy, Harlan. "I'm a Picture Chap." *Film Comment*, January/February 1985.

Kingsley, Grace. "D. W. Griffith Plays Picture Methods." *Los Angeles Times*, December 19, 1926.

"Largest Camera Crane Built." *Los Angeles Times*, February 17, 1940.

Lusk, Norbert. "The Screen in Review." *Picture-Play*, July 1927.

"Magnificent Film Spectacle Holds Thousands Entranced." *Los Angeles Times*, October 18, 1916.

Maslin, Janet. "Film View; De Palma Breaks the Mold." *New York Times*, June 21, 1987.

McLellan, Dennis. "Obituaries: Blake Edwards 1922–2010; Director Was Master of Cinematic Comedy." *Los Angeles Times*, December 17, 2010.

Meisel, Myron. "Ray: Directing from the Corners of His Soul." *Los Angeles Times*, July 1, 1979.

Michener, Charles. "Taxi Driver." *Film Comment*, March/April 1976.

Nugent, Frank S. "The Screen: Among the Best Is 'Make Way for Tomorrow' at the Criterion—the Central Has 'That I May Live.'" *New York Times*, May 10, 1937.

Oliver, Myrna. "Billy Wilder / 1906–2002; Movie-Maker Left 'Indelible Stamp.'" *Los Angeles Times*, March 29, 2002.

———. "Oscar-Winning Director George Stevens, 70, Dies." *Los Angeles Times*, March 10, 1975.

"Otto Preminger, 80, Dies." *New York Times*, April 24, 1986.

Panero, James. "Andrew Wyeth Forever." *The New Criterion*, March 2017.

Portman, Jamie. "Lumet Still a Luminary." *Kingston Whig-Standard*, May 16, 1997.

Powers, James. "Cleopatra." *Hollywood Reporter*, June 13, 1963.

———. "The Trial." *Hollywood Reporter*, April 25, 1963.

"Quiet! When These Folks Speak, Great Stars Listen." *Photoplay*, October 1932.

Rawitch, Robert. "Director John Ford Dies at 78." *Los Angeles Times*, September 1, 1973.

"Reviews." *Box-Office*. August 28, 1948.

Schallert, Edwin. "'Little Foxes' Reckoned Great in Art and Acting." *Los Angeles Times*, August 12, 1941.

———. "'Magnificent Obsession' Has Inspirational Values." *Los Angeles Times*, July 22, 1954.

———. "'Wizard of Oz' Epochal as Fantasy." *Los Angeles Times*, August 10, 1939.

Scheuer, Philip K. "Accentuate the Personal, Minnelli's Theme for Pictures with Punch." *Los Angeles Times*, October 14, 1945.

———. "A Director's Own Place in the Sun." *Los Angeles Times*, November 4, 1979.

———. "Fellini's '8 ½' Again Reveals Film Genius." *Los Angeles Times*, July 11, 1963.

———. "Lubitsch Looks at His 'Oscar.'" *Los Angeles Times*, April 6, 1947.

———. "Masina Sparkles in Fellini Cinema." *Los Angeles Times*, January 18, 1958.

———. "Minnelli Film Work Reveals Him as a Poet." *Los Angeles Times*, November 30, 1952.

———. "Nichols: The Whiz Kid Whizzes Onward." *Los Angeles Times*, February 5, 1967.

———. "Stevens Sees Tragedy as Hopeful Theme." *Los Angeles Times*, July 29, 1951.

———. "'Written on the Wind' Strong Sex Drama." *Los Angeles Times*, December 26, 1956.

Schumach, Murray. "Hollywood Trial: 'Nuremberg' Tests Set as Well as Players." *New York Times*, April 30, 1961.

Scorsese, Martin. "The Lives They Lived: Ida Lupino; Behind the Camera, a Feminist." *New York Times*, December 31, 1995.

Sharpe, Howard. "The Star Creators of Hollywood: W. S. Van Dyke." *Photoplay*, December 1936.

"Shoes." *Moving Picture Weekly*, July 7, 1917.

"Stories Run Parallel: Remarkable Feat in Photoplay Construction Is Achieved in Big Griffith Spectacle 'Intolerance,' Which Is to Open Here Next Week." *Los Angeles Times*, October 8, 1916.

"Sunrise—A Song of Two Humans." *Variety*, December 31, 1926.

Taylor, Clarke. "Brian De Palma Boxed in by Shadows." *Los Angeles Times*, September 19, 1976.

Thomas, Kevin. "30th Anniversary Showing of Original 'Anne Frank' at Bing." *Los Angeles Times*, December 18, 1989.

Tully, Jim. "The Highest Paid Director." *The New Movie*, November 1931.

Turan, Kenneth. "The Best of the Worst Humanity Has to Offer." *Los Angeles Times*, September 10, 2006.

"Van Dyke, the Trouble-Shooter." *New York Times*, August 14, 1938.

Warga, Wayne. "Graffiti's George Lucas Sees Handwriting on the Studio Wall." *Los Angeles Times*, August 12, 1973.

ONLINE ARTICLES

Bailey, Jason. "Celebrate Quentin Tarantino's Birthday with 16 of His Favorite Films." *Flavorwire*. March 27, 2013. Accessed March 1, 2020. https://www.flavorwire.com/380185/celebrate-quentin-tarantinos-50th-birthday-with-16-of-his-favorite-films.

Crowe, Cameron. "Billy and Me: Why I Love *The Apartment*." *The Guardian*. December 2, 1999. Accessed September 30, 2020. https://www.theguardian.com/film/1999/dec/03/culture.features.

Ebert, Roger. "Isolated Madness." *Rogerebert.com*. June 18, 2006. Accessed October 27, 2020. https://www.rogerebert.com/reviews/great-movie-the-shining-1980.

———. "A Streetcar Named Desire." *Rogerebert.com*. November 12, 1993. Accessed August 15, 2020. https://www.rogerebert.com/reviews/a-streetcar-named-desire-1993.

———. "Urban Renewal on a Very Large Scale." *Rogerebert.com*. June 2, 2010. Accessed April 7, 2020. https://www.rogerebert.com/reviews/great-movie-metropolis-2010-restoration-1927.

Greenberg, James. "A Life in Pictures." *Dga.org*. Winter 2009. Accessed October 31, 2020. https://www.dga.org/Craft/DGAQ/All-Articles/0804-Winter-2008-09/Interview-Roman-Polanski.aspx.

Haskell, Molly. "*Fanny and Alexander*: The Other Side." *Criterion. com*. November 18, 2018. Accessed September 30, 2020. https://www.criterion.com/current/posts/6014-fanny-and-alexander-the-other-side.

Hoberman, J. "In Mikey and Nicky, Elaine May Nails a Pair of Desperate Characters." *New York Times*. July 2, 2019. Accessed July 27, 2020. https://www.nytimes.com/2019/07/02/movies/elaine-may-mikey-and-nicky-html.

James, Caryn. "Lois Weber: The Trailblazing Director Who Shocked the World." *BBC*. March 20, 2019. Accessed March 27, 2020. https://www.bbc.com/culture/article/20190318-lois-weber-the-trailblazing-director-who-shocked-the-world.

K magazine. "The Godfather's Godmother: FFC on Female Filmmakers." *The Luxury Channel*. January 2016. Accessed June 20, 2020. https://theluxurychannel.com/magazine/the-godfathers-godmother-francis-ford-coppola-on-female-film-makers/.

Krebs, Albin. "Fritz Lang, Film Director Noted for 'M,' Dead at 85." *New York Times*. August 3, 1976. Accessed April 10, 2020. https://archive.nytimes.com/www.nytimes.com/books/97/07/20/reviews/lang-obit.html.

Landler, Edward. "Down Went 'McGinty.'" *Cinemontage*. August 1, 2015. Accessed August 7, 2020. https://cinemontage.org/down-went-mcginty.

Lincoln, Kevin. "Bill Condon on *Beauty and the Beast*, His Musical Influences, and Lindsay Lohan's Plan for *The Little Mermaid*." *Vulture*. March 15, 2017. Accessed July 29, 2020. https://www.vulture.com/2017/03/bill-condon-on-directing-beauty-and-the-beast.html.

Perè, Olivier. "Jean Douchet Talks about Vincente Minnelli." *Locarnofestival.ch*. August 8, 2011. Accessed August 22, 2020. https://www.locarnofestival.ch/en/pardo/pardo-live/today-at-festival/2011/Jean-Douchet-talks-about-Vincente-Minnelli-?.

Schasny, Josh. "25 New Hollywood Era Films that Projected the Hopes and Fears of the Times." *Taste of Cinema*. March 4, 2016. Accessed June 18, 2020. http://www.tasteofcinema.com/2016/25-new-hollywood-era-films-that-projected-the-hopes-and-fears-of-the-times/.

Siegel, Robert. "For Filmmaker Brian De Palma, It All Started with Alfred Hitchcock." *NPR*. July 1, 2016. Accessed November 11, 2020. https://www.npr.org/2016/07/01/484381681/for-filmmaker-brian-de-palma-it-all-started-with-alfred-hitchcock.

Stein, Ruthe. "How Ida Lupino Broke into Man's World of Directing." *San Francisco Chronicle*. November 11, 2015. Accessed July 14, 2020. https://www.sfchronicle.com/movies/article/How-Ida-Lupino-broke-into-man-s-world-of-6625925.php.

Stevens, Jenny. "*All About Eve* Is a Perfect Feminist Film—How Did the Play Get It So Wrong?" *The Guardian*. February 19, 2019. https://www.theguardian.com/film/2019/feb/19/all-about-eve-perfect-feminist-film-play-the-favourite.

"Tippi Hedren on Filming *The Birds*." *Vogue*. December 4, 2016. Accessed September 1, 2020. https://www.vogue.co.uk/article/tippi-hedren-memoir-the-birds-extract.

Zoladz, Lindsay. "True Confessions of a Female Director." *The Ringer*. February 16, 2017. Accessed August 25, 2020. https://www.theringer.com/2017/2/16/16042696/amy-heckerling-fast-times-at-ridgemont-high-clueless-female-directors-ee9568144c24.

AUDIO/VIDEO

American Film Institute. "Billy Crystal Salutes Mel Brooks at the 2014 Emmy-Winning AFI Life Achievement Award Show." *YouTube* video, 2:41. July 18, 2014. https://www.youtube.com/watch?v=f5hD3sdcpGw.

———. "Sidney Poitier on *The Defiant Ones*." Video, 1:26. July 16, 2020. https://www.afi.com/news/afi-movie-club-the-defiant-ones/.

American Masters. "Directed by William Wyler." Directed by Aviva Slesin. PBS, 1986.

anaheimu. "Akira Kurosawa 100th Anniversary Memorial Tribute." *YouTube* video, 2:45. June 13, 2013. https://www.youtube.com/watch?v=ErelcWcNelQ .

BAFTA Guru. "Martin Scorsese's Advice to Beginners—'You Can Do Anything, Make Your Own Industry.'" *YouTube* video, 4:19. May 4, 2012. https://www.youtube.com/watch?v=H0C1jh5NuwQ.

Basinger, Jeanine. "Commentary." *The Philadelphia Story*, DVD. Directed by George Cukor. The Criterion Collection, 2017.

Becoming John Ford. Directed by Nick Redman. Century City, Calif.: Twentieth Century Fox, 2007. DVD.

BFI. "Carol Morley on Federico Fellini's *Nights of Cabiria*." *YouTube* video, 14:03. January 21, 2020. https://www.youtube.com/watch?v=atSWR5XYHA4.

Bogdanovich, Peter. "Tomorrow, Yesterday and Today." *Make Way for Tomorrow*, DVD. Directed by Leo McCarey. The Criterion Collection, 2010.

Capra, Frank Jr. "A Personal Remembrance." *It's a Wonderful Life*, DVD. Directed by Frank Capra. Hollywood, Calif.: Paramount Home Entertainment, 2006.

Erich von Stroheim: The Man You Loved to Hate. Directed by Patrick Montgomery. London: BBC, 1979.

Eyes on Cinema. "An Interview w/Alfred Hitchcock on Filmmaking, Suspense, Nightmares & More!" *YouTube* video, 21:20. https://www.youtube.com/watch?v=DGA6rCOyTh4.

———. "Otto Preminger Reflects His Thoughts on Being a Filmmaker." *YouTube* video, 7:37. May 27, 2016. https://www.youtube.com/watch?v=wfm5OwtgI8U.

———. "Paul Thomas Anderson about the Influence of Blake Edwards & Peter Sellers on 'Punch-Drunk Love.'" *YouTube* video, 29:55 November 13, 2014. https://www.youtube.com/watch?v=udhJNPEvF_w.

———. "Rare 103-Minute Documentary on Director Joseph L. Mankiewicz: 'All About Mankiewicz' (1983)." *YouTube* video, 1:42:24. https://www.youtube.com/watch?v=0aTNbVyl2Gc.

———. "Rare Marlon Brando Interview on *Guys & Dolls* w/Joseph L. Mankiewicz, Samuel Goldwyn & More!" *YouTube* video, 29:55. https://www.youtube.com/watch?v=y7y5FRMU1Tw.

———. "Stanley Kubrick Talks about *The Shining* in 11-Minute 1980 Interview." *YouTube* video, 11:35. October 26, 2015. https://www.youtube.com/watch?v=keo5HQcC0po.

Eyman, Scott. "Commentary." *Trouble in Paradise*, DVD. Directed by Ernst Lubitsch. The Criterion Collection, 2003.

Fincher, David, and Robert Towne. "Commentary." Blu-Ray. Directed by Roman Polanski. Hollywood, Calif.: Paramount Home Entertainment, 2012.

franco rossville. "Sidney Lumet Talks about Diana Ross and M. Jackson on *The Wiz* Movie." *YouTube* video, 14:37. https://www.youtube.com/watch?v=gm5XNTJXiio.

George Stevens: A Filmmaker's Journey. Directed by George Stevens Jr. 1985. Burbank, Calif.: Warner Home Media, 2004. DVD.

GQ. "Spike Lee Breaks Down His Film Heroes." *YouTube* video, 12:18. August 17, 2018. https://www.youtube.com/watch?v=NfRMe-gnP6s.

Hanson, Curtis. "*In a Lonely Place*: Revisited." Disc 1. *In a Lonely Place*, DVD. Directed by Nicholas Ray. The Criterion Collection, 2016.

Kitses, Jim. "Commentary." Disc 1. *Stagecoach*, DVD. Directed by John Ford. The Criterion Collection, 2009.

lachambraverte. "Fritz Lang Interview 1968." *YouTube* video, 27:30. 2019. https://www.youtube.com/watch?v=BYk0qzqqjmQ.

Last Android. "Terry Gilliam on Fellini's *8½*." *YouTube* video, 6:10. https://www.youtube.com/watch?v=WCDX1j0jMZA.

Magician: The Astonishing Life and Work of Orson Welles. Directed by Chuck Workman. Cohen Media Group, 2014. DVD.

"The Making of *Lawrence of Arabia*." Disc 2. *Lawrence of Arabia*, special 50th anniversary edition DVD. Directed by David Lean. Culver City, Calif.: Columbia Tristar Home Entertainment, 2012.

"The Making of Psycho." *Psycho*, collector's edition DVD. Directed by Alfred Hitchcock. Universal City, Calif.: Universal Home Entertainment, 1999.

McGee, Scott. "Jim Jarmusch on Nicholas Ray for FilmStruck." *YouTube* video, 18:38. November 13, 2018. https://www.youtube.com/watch?v=legrr0uGCVc.

The Men Who Made the Movies: King Vidor. Directed by Richard Schickel. Museum of Modern Art, 1973.

The Movies. "The Sixties." CNN, 2019.

The Narrative Art. "Quentin Tarantino on Hitchcock and Brian De Palma." *YouTube* video, 2:55. August 25, 2016. https://www.youtube.com/watch?v=B2zys_rkjwA.

Oscars. "Robert Altman Receives an Honorary Award: 2006 Oscars." *YouTube* video, 8:01. https://www.youtube.com/watch?v=rcp8xjaFfb8.

———. "Sidney Poitier Remembers George Stevens." *YouTube* video, 4:19. December 10, 2014. https://www.youtube.com/watch?v=_5yPBdYmCdc.

Quentin Tarantino Fan Club. "Quentin Tarantino Reviews *Taxi Driver*." *YouTube* video, 8:06. November 7, 2017. https://www.youtube.com/watch?v=Bw6w8WyNdUQ.

Stamp, Shelley. "Audio Commentary." *The Blot*, DVD. Directed by Lois Weber. Milestone Films, 2006.

Syndicado Distribution. "Trespassing Bergman—Scorsese on Bergman." *YouTube* video, 1:34. December 7, 2019. https://www.youtube.com/watch?v=W8DM4li0o90.

Trailers from Hell. "Mark Pellington on *The Last Picture Show*." *YouTube* video, 3:10. July 3, 2013. https://www.youtube.com/watch?v=40c4VTdyjVU.

Turner Classic Movies. "Danny Glover on Oscar Micheaux's Silent Film *Body and Soul* ('25)." *YouTube* video, 20:21. May 15, 2020. https://www.youtube.com/watch?v=4XyXkNo_Kwl

WEBSITES

aficatalog.afi.com

cnn.com

dga.org

hollywoodreporter.com

imdb.com

indiefilmhustle.com

indiewire.com

lapl.org

latimes.com

mediahistory.org

newstatesman.com

newsweek.com

newyorker.com

npr.org

oscars.org

rottentomatoes.com

slantmagazine.com

tcm.com

time.com

vanityfair.com

variety.com

wikipedia.org

ACKNOWLEDGMENTS

Writing my longest and most ambitious book during a pandemic-induced lockdown, with limited access to library and research materials, presented a unique challenge. This is why I send a bigger-than-ever THANK YOU to all the usual suspects: my wonderful editor (and friend) Cindy Sipala, my fabulous photo magician (and friend) Manoah Bowman, and ever-helpful resources (and friends) Matt Tunia and David Wills.

Many thanks to essential director Peter Bogdanovich for providing kindness, inspiration, and his unique perspective. Many thanks also to Jacqueline Stewart for writing a brilliant foreword. Thanks to Joe Dante, a great director as well as a nice person.

Much appreciation for the assistance of Evan Macdonald, Claude Jarman, and Jeffrey Vance.

A round of applause for the team at Running Press, including Frances Soo Ping Chow, Fred Francis, Katie Hubbard, Kristin Kiser, Jennifer Kasius, and Seta Zink.

Double thanks to Turner Classic Movies for 1. existing, and 2. giving me the opportunity to write this book. I appreciate the input and assistance of Susana Zepeda, Charles Tabesh, John Malahy, Heather Margolis, Eileen Flanagan, Pola Changnon, and Genevieve McGillicuddy.

Thanks, as always, to Aaron Spiegeland at Parham Santana for the support.

Special thanks to the Los Angeles Public Library System. Long live the libraries of America.

INDEX

Page numbers in **bold** refer to illustrations or their captions.

CHECK OUT OTHER TITLES IN THE

 LIBRARY

TURNER **CLASSIC** MOVIES

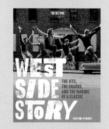

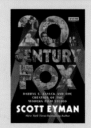

RUNNING
PRESS